W9-AVT-121

Contents

INTRODUCTION

This book is meant to be an aid in the design and building of functional, yet expressive doors. Whether you are building that one-of-a-kind front door you have always wanted, a quick closet door just to hide the mess, or a series of doors for a whole building, it is important that you pick the best door for the particular application. Perhaps you have an idea of the type of door you want, but are lacking specific details, or maybe you lack the expertise to break the door down into its components and build it from scratch. By following the detailed building instructions and patterns in this book, or by modifying them to suit your needs, you can easily overcome these common obstacles to the completion of a project.

You do not have to be a highly skilled craftsperson to benefit from the information set down here. This book can be used by anyone who has the urge to be creative with wood. House builders, remodellers, and home craftsmen, as well as professional millworkers and woodcrafters, will find both intriguing new ideas and a solid framework of basic information. Many of the doors presented can be built with very few power tools on either the job-site or in the home garage. And, even if you don't intend to build your own doors, you may find here valuable sources of information and inspiration for the design of your home or business.

The first chapter will prove helpful to those who are just learning or want to expand their understanding of design and installation techniques. Much of this information has been adapted from my previous book, *Make Your Own Handcrafted Doors & Windows*, which will be of interest to anyone who wants more general information about making handcrafted doors and windows. In this chapter, and in some of the following ones, I reveal those "secrets of the trade" that will help you give expression to your wildest creative fantasies.

Chapters 2–6 contain building instructions and patterns for a wide variety of batten, edge-joined, layered, and frame-and-panel doors. Some of the doors presented are ones that I have built myself, but the majority are those that I've come across in my travels and admire because they offer a unique solution to a design problem and are beautiful, long-lasting, and affordable. I have drawn the plans from photographs taken of the doors, and have tried to faithfully interpret and explain the techniques that were actually used in the construction of the particular door. Occasionally, I have taken the liberty of pointing out weaknesses or problems in a door's design, and show a better way to build it.

It was impossible for me to know what type of joinery was actually used to hold the rails and stiles together on the majority of the frame-and-panel doors included in this book. Most doors of this type made before approximately 1950 probably employed a through mortise and tenon at least at the corners, and often at the lock rail as well. Since then, this technique has been largely abandoned by production doormakers in favor of dowelling, which is far quicker but not nearly as reliable. Both of these methods have become outdated now that there are reliable high-powered plunge routers and mortising bits available (½-inch-wide bits which can cut up to 2½ inches deep make mortising, even on the end of a rail, nearly as easy as dowelling). I have, therefore, indicated a joint which I call a "spline tenon" for most of these doors. It is easy to make (there is no need for specialized equipment like a mortising machine), works well with cope-and-stick or butt-jointed frames, is vastly more reliable in exterior installations than dowels, and, when it is used, parts of the piece can still be moved at assembly time.

The doors in this book have been divided into three levels based on the type of equipment needed to build them and the complexity of the design and assembly. The doors that have a Level one designation can be built primarily with hand tools, although a few power tools like a table or radial arm saw, jointer, router, and perhaps a band saw would certainly make the work quicker and easier. Level two doors generally require the above-mentioned power tools, and might be quite a bit more complex in their designs, so you will need a well-organized work area, even if it is just a temporary area set up in a corner of a construction site. Level three doors consist of cope-and-stick doors and doors that employ other advanced techniques like template cutting, bent laminating, etc. (Many of these more complex doors, however, can be built using simplified techniques, and I have tried to indicate this in the construction directions whenever possible.) You will find that your doormaking will be much more enjoyable and profitable if you don't try to exceed the level you are comfortable with.

The last two chapters will be invaluable to those interested in mastering the intricacies of spindle shaper work and in learning how to finish, maintain and repair doors. The shaper is perhaps the doormaker's most important and versatile tool, and finishing and maintenance techniques are essential in ensuring that the door you have created will stand unscathed for years to come.

You do not have to invest large sums of money in machines or cutters to build beautiful and exciting doors. Some of the simple techniques like layering or making frame-and-panel doors with routers can produce wonderful results. So, let your imagination run wild, come up with a design that appeals to you, and don't be afraid to try something new. Your finished doors will stand for years as testimonials to your creative achievements.

Layered doors (above left) and frame-and-panel doors (above right) are just two of a wide variety of doors you will learn to build in the following pages.

1
DESIGNING AND INSTALLING A DOOR

Whether you are starting from scratch or replacing a door in an already existing home or building, you should first consider the many factors that can influence the design of a doorway. A doorway is a variable barrier. An entry door easily admits those who are welcome to enter, while providing protection from both the elements and unwanted visitors. Most buildings also have many interior doors which help to separate the functions of the various rooms within. Some merely provide a visual barrier, hiding from view the clutter in the closet, while others help keep living areas warm or provide for privacy and quiet.

A secondary function of the doorway is less obvious, but perhaps just as important. A doorway must work with the other elements of a building, both interior and exterior, to provide a pleasing aesthetic living environment. It should make a symbolic statement about the building, its inhabitants, and the surrounding environment. It provides the perfect opportunity for you to share your creative energy with the world.

Illus. 1–1 and 1–2. Aesthetically, an entry door is one of the most important elements in creating a harmonious design for any type of building.

In designing, there are many compromises that have to be made. If you are starting a completely new structure, you have a chance to make the choices that will serve you best all down the line. Still, you may have to choose between such desirable assets as energy efficiency or light, security or beauty, and elaborate design or affordability. After you have finished reading this section carefully, you may want to list, in order of importance, the design considerations that will shape your doors.

Design Factors
Technical Requirements

Standard manufactured doors are usually 6 feet, 8 inches high, and come in widths from 1 foot, 6 inches to 3 feet (Illus. 1–3). Exterior doors are available in 1½ or 1¾-inch thicknesses. Interior doors may be thinner. Often, doors can be purchased "pre-hung," meaning that they are already mounted in the jamb, on the hinges. Some will even have a lockset, or holes for the lockset, pre-cut for easy installation.

Building codes vary from one locality to another, and should be consulted by the custom builder so that he can make sure he is meeting the local requirements. Many areas now require the use of tempered glass in doors where the glass panes are over a certain size, and some require at least one 3-foot or wider door in any public building for wheelchairs. "Panic hardware" is also required for quick exit in case of fire in many public buildings.

For the custom builder, the sizes and thicknesses listed are mere guidelines. A call for a 7-foot or taller door is not uncommon for commercial buildings or even homes, and a 42- or 48-inch-wide entry door can add a touch of grandeur to a private entryway. Insulated doors up to 4 inches thick may be important energy savers for your part of the country, and you can obtain a feeling of stateliness by using extra-thick lumber for panel doors. However, building code requirements should be taken seriously as a question of liability could easily develop, especially in a commercial setting, that could involve you as the builder.

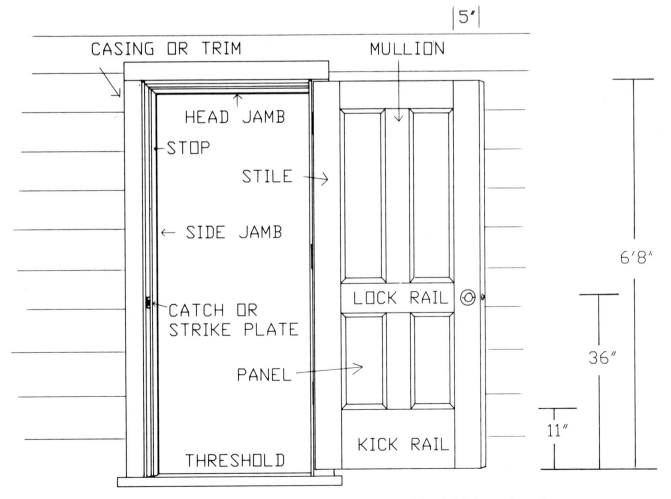

Illus. 1–3. Standard doors are usually 6 feet, 8 inches high and can vary in width from 18 to 48 inches. Custom door makers should only use these sizes as guidelines for creating unique and beautiful doors. Shown here are common terms used when referring to parts of doors and door frames.

Door Swing

The direction in which the door swings is generally determined by the layout of the room, the position of light switches, and whether or not it is an interior or exterior door. Inward-opening exterior doors are considered more secure by some because the pins on the hinges cannot be pulled out and the door removed. In places where outward-opening exterior doors may be

necessary, special screws are available that prevent a door from being removed in this way, but the lock bolt is still more vulnerable to tampering. Outward-opening exterior doors are easier to seal against the weather, and might be better to use in a place that is exposed to gusting winds and wind-blown rain. The bottom of the door is usually the problem area (Illus. 1–4). In difficult places, special thresholds and J-hook weather-stripping can be used.

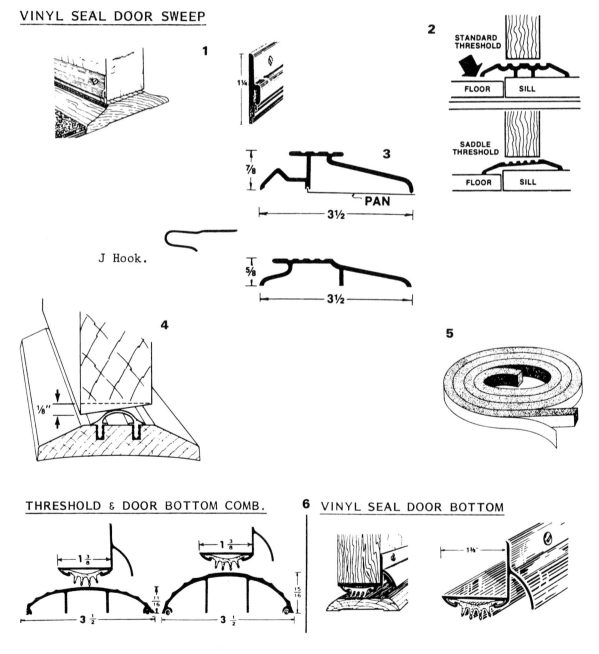

Illus. 1–4. Various systems are available for sealing the bottom of the door from outside air and wind-blown rain. As shown in the drawing, they are as follows: 1, a simple screw-on seal may work for outward-opening doors; 2, a saddle-type threshold is used where changes in floor levels occur; 3, a special extruded threshold with an interlocking J-hook extrusion on *the bottom of the door will stop wind-blown rain in difficult places; 4 and 6, flexible vinyl strips can be applied to either the threshold or the bottom of the door to stop air infiltration; and 5, various types of foam rubber or neoprene stripping with adhesive backing can be used to seal the edges and tops of doors.*

Security

One of the main functions of a good door is security. Security is more important to some people than to others. Thick lumber for both the door and the jamb, a small, high window, and a good double-lock-and-dead-bolt system will provide adequate security for most people. Side lights should be avoided if security is a concern and no alarm system is being used. Special locks may have to be ordered from the manufacturer for extra-thick doors such as insulated doors. Commercial installations will also require special security considerations in many cases.

Climate

One of the most important factors in determining the nature of any exterior doorway is the climate in which it will be used. Obviously, a cold-winter, hot-summer climate will dictate different entryway considerations than a more moderate or tropical climate. A solid-core wood door 1¾ inch thick has an R factor, or resistance to heat loss, of 2.90, just slightly better than a panel door of the same thickness at 2.79. A hollow-core door of the same thickness, which may look just like the solid-core door but weighs half as much, has an R factor of 2.18.

You can easily build a door with an insulated core that will provide an R factor of 10 (Illus. 1–5), but perhaps even more important than the R factor of the door are factors such as the direction it faces, the care with which it is hung and weather-stripped, and structures such as an overhanging roof, protective walls, or storm doors that help to shelter the doorway and prevent the influx of cold outside air.

Another factor to consider in your design is the room that the door enters into. If you have an alcove or "mud room" in the entryway that combined with another interior door to the living area forms a sort of air lock, it may be better to sacrifice some energy efficiency for more glass area (the R factor of insulated glass is 1.61 [a single layer of glass has an R factor of 1]), since the alcove will act as a buffer in maintaining the temperature of the living area.

In any climate, but especially in harsh northern climates or in areas that have distinct wet and dry seasons, the longevity of the door itself will depend greatly on the direction it faces and the amount of exposure it gets to sun and rain. Sunlight destroys finishes and discolors wood very quickly, and constant changes in temperature

THREE—LAYER INSULATED DOOR CONSTRUCTION

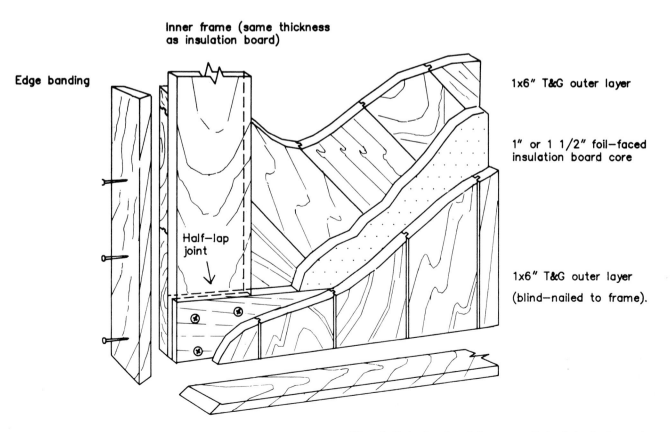

Inner frame (same thickness as insulation board)

Edge banding

1x6" T&G outer layer

1" or 1 1/2" foil-faced insulation board core

Half-lap joint

1x6" T&G outer layer (blind-nailed to frame).

Illus. 1–5. An insulated door, usually built in the layered, or assemblage, style will provide an R factor of up to 10.

Illus. 1–6. The bottom of this unprotected door has been bleached and cracked by ultraviolet radiation and moisture.

and moisture will cause rapid expansion and contraction of the wood that will loosen panels, delaminate even the best exterior grades of plywood, and force joints apart in short order (Illus. 1–6).

Paint or other sealers like stains or varnishes are the main defense against weather damage to doors, but the more you can physically protect your doors from the elements, the longer this finish will last. For your own comfort as well as the longevity of the door, always try to protect the entryway from exposure by sheltering it with a porch roof (Illus. 1–7) or a secondary storm-and-screen door combination. This is especially true if you want a varnished or oiled finish that will show the natural color and beauty of the wood. There are exterior-grade varnishes and stains available that provide some protection from ultraviolet light, the most harmful part of the spectrum, but even these finishes will have only a limited life in direct exposure.

You can also lessen the likelihood of major damage from the elements by keeping in mind that the wider a panel or frame member is, the more it is going to expand and contract. Even the best finishes pass some moisture. Plywoods and well-built laminated doors are cross-bonded to prevent expansion and contraction (Illus. 1–8), but solid wood will move with enough force to break even the best glue joints. Laminate doors often delaminate when the core is exposed to moisture because the thin outer veneers cannot hold the expansive force of the solid-wood core in check.

Limiting solid-wood panel and rail widths to about 12 inches and avoiding large expanses of edge-joined lumber will help prevent problems from expansion and contraction. It is possible to build a door simply by edge-joining enough 2 × 6's to span the width of the doorway. This might work well for an interior door, but should be used with care in exterior settings.

Illus. 1–7. The best protection for a varnished exterior door is an overhanging roof.

CROSS BONDING

| PLYWOOD LAMINATIONS | SOLID-CORE LAMINATE DOOR | TWO-LAYER (BATTEN) DOOR | THREE-LAYER (ASSEMBLAGE) DOOR |

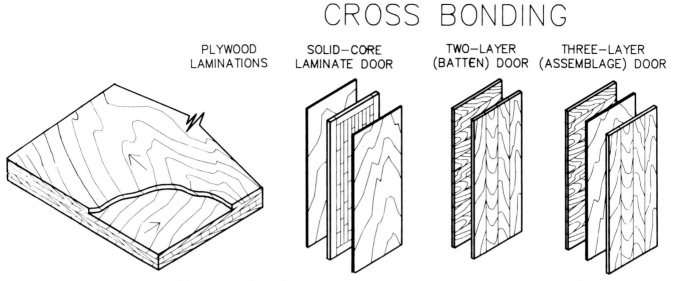

Illus. 1–8. The cross-bonding of thin layers of wood prevents expansion and contraction. Exterior-grade plywood should be used for all panels wider than 12 inches, and laminate doors should be carefully sealed to prevent delamination.

Materials

Your choice of materials will depend on the type of construction technique you plan to employ and the way in which you intend to finish the door, as well as the availability of different woods in your own locality. If you intend to paint your finished door, then the strength and workability of your wood will be more important than the beauty of the grain. Fir is a very strong and stable wood for paint-grade doors, but a bit difficult to work. Pine and redwood are easier to work, but are more easily damaged by bumps and scrapes because of their softness. If you are going to use plywood for panels or laminate doors, be sure that it is of a good enough grade for the situation, and of equal quality on both sides if both will show.

Your Abilities

Another major consideration if you are designing your own doorway is your own resources and abilities. A well-planned job that's within your capabilities is bound to be successful, but trying to do more than you are ready for will only cause you grief and frustration.

There are many ways to build solid, nice-looking doors. Some methods are simpler than others, especially if you are working with a limited amount of equipment. Even the simplest methods can be adapted to many different architectural styles. Consider carefully, and don't try to do more than you're capable of.

If you are replacing an existing door with something more to your liking, you will have to make a choice between working with the size and shape of the opening that already exists or making fairly major structural changes. The rough opening—the hole in the framing

and siding of the building—can be enlarged, but it will usually mean removing a considerable amount of siding, and reworking the structural support system around the doorway (Illus. 1–9).

Also of major importance are the flashing, trim, and sill, which serve to channel moisture outward and away from the interior of the house (Illus. 1–10). Note how these factors work on your existing doorway, and seek the advice of an experienced house carpenter during the design stage of your project if you are unsure of the consequences of the changes you intend to make.

Closing down, or decreasing the size of a rough opening is also possible. You may want to consider turning part of the doorway into sidelights or adding a wider, more elaborate trim detail to avoid having to re-side areas adjacent to the doorway that is being narrowed. This is easier than enlarging the opening, but still must be done with care to avoid leaks and to blend the change in, so that it doesn't stand out from the rest of the doorway.

Door Structure

Doorway

Aside from the door or doors themselves, a doorway is composed of several distinct parts. In new construction, a doorway begins its existence as an opening left in the wall framing. This opening, called the *rough opening*, is framed on either side by double studs which capture and support an upper beam called the *header*. The header must be strong enough to carry the load across its span, and will vary in size accordingly. If there are sidelights in the doorway, they may be framed as separate openings under a single header. Separate jambs are then installed in each opening. Careful consideration

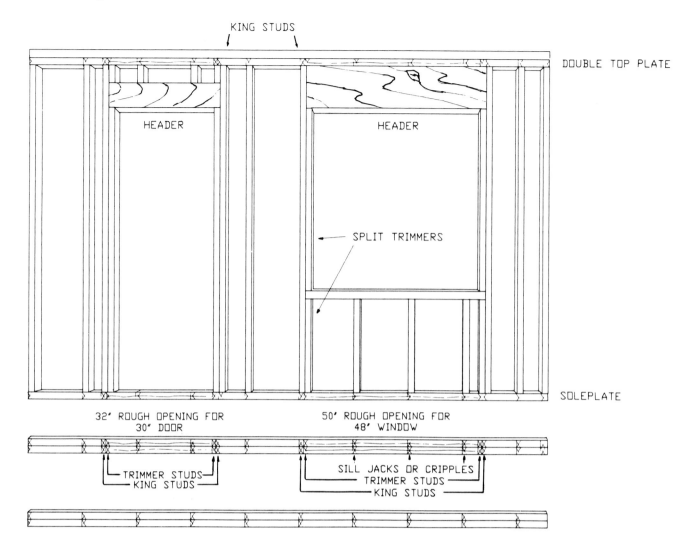

KING STUDS

DOUBLE TOP PLATE

HEADER   HEADER

SPLIT TRIMMERS

SOLEPLATE

32" ROUGH OPENING FOR   50" ROUGH OPENING FOR
30" DOOR   48" WINDOW

TRIMMER STUDS   SILL JACKS OR CRIPPLES
KING STUDS   TRIMMER STUDS
                            KING STUDS

Illus. 1–9 (above). In new construction, holes are left in the wall framing for doors and windows. These are called rough openings. A header spans the rough opening, or several rough openings at once if a series of doors or windows occurs, and the studs on either side of the header are usually doubled to help carry the load. Short studs below a window are called cripples or sill jacks. Enlarging an already existing rough opening will call for reworking of the framing, which may mean removing a considerable amount of siding. You can usually close up a rough opening by adding more framing and a wider trim detail. Illus. 1–10 (below). Flashing and trim help to prevent leaking around doors.

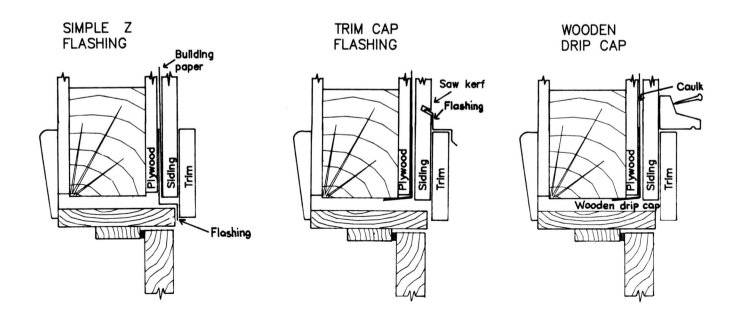

SIMPLE Z
FLASHING

Building paper

Plywood
Siding
Trim

Flashing

TRIM CAP
FLASHING

Saw kerf
Flashing

Plywood
Siding
Trim

WOODEN
DRIP CAP

Caulk

Plywood
Siding
Trim

Wooden drip cap

should be given to the trim details that will be used when windows and doors are made close together, or in rows.

When planning rough openings, remember that a door of any given width will require a rough opening of that width plus twice the thickness of the jambs plus 1 inch (to be divided into ½ inch on either side for shimming the jamb). For a 3-foot-wide door, this means that a rough opening of at least 38½ inches is necessary (assuming that the jambs are made from ¾-inch material). The height of the rough opening will depend somewhat on the thickness of the finished floor material. If a 80-inch door is to be used, the rough opening will have to be high enough to accommodate the door, the upper jamb piece, and a sill. The sill may vary in thickness and in type, depending on whether the door is interior or exterior and what the finished floor treatment will be. As with the width of the door, allow ½ inch at the top for shimming, and remember that it is easier to fill in too large an opening than it is to increase its size. Often, doors end up being cut down a bit at the bottom to accommodate the threshold and floor treatment, but this can easily weaken a door, and can be avoided with good planning.

Doorframe

The doorframe, or jamb as it is sometimes called, lines the rough opening and provides attachment for the door hinges themselves. These days, jambs are usually made from ¾-inch material, with thinner strips applied after the door is hung in place to provide stops for the door. (Decorative, plain, and hidden jamb details are shown in Illus. 1–11.) The stops literally stop the swing of the door, and provide a surface against which the door seals to prevent air infiltration. Weather stripping is often applied to the stops or the jamb.

The side jambs are rabbeted into the top or head jamb, and nailed through from above with three or four 6d nails (Illus. 1–12). The threshold is generally installed after the door jamb is in place and the door is hung, but before the stops have been installed. If it is a wooden threshold, it can also be attached to the jambs by nailing from the outside before the jamb is installed in the rough opening (Illus. 1–13).

The width of the jamb material will vary with the thickness and construction of the wall in which it is installed. Generally the jamb is as wide as the full thickness of the wall except where hidden jambs or special treatments like a brick or stone veneer or shingling are applied to all or part of one side of the wall (Illus. 1–14). The placement of the door in the jamb will depend on the direction of swing of the door. The door will usually be positioned so that it is flush, or nearly flush, with the surface of the wall on the side towards which it will open.

An alternative method for building jambs, called stop-

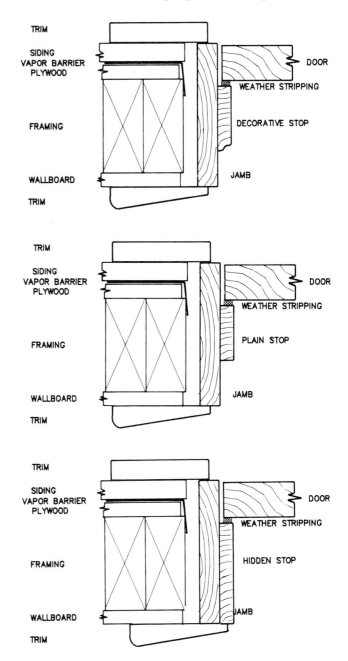

Illus. 1–11. Decorative, plain, and hidden jambs.

JAMB CONSTRUCTION DETAIL

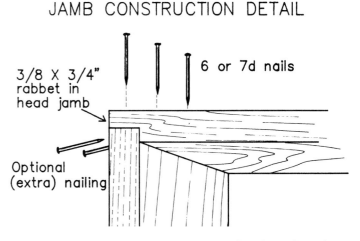

Illus. 1–12. Rabbet the head jamb to receive the side jamb, and then nail it from the top before installing the jamb in the rough opening.

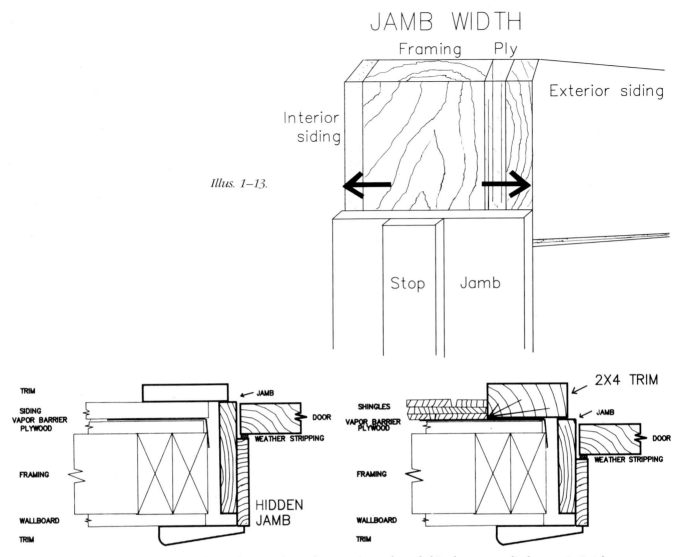

Illus. 1–13.

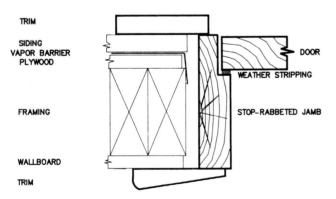

Illus 1–14. The jamb usually runs from the outside to the inside of the wall, unless hidden stops are used or you are working on shingled walls. Here, an extra-thick exterior trim

is used, and shingles are applied up to it. Brick or masonry can also be applied right up to the lower part of a jamb.

Illus. 1–15. Stop-rabbeted jambs are cut from one piece of 2-inch-thick lumber. It will be difficult to get a tight closure with this method if there is any warpage in the door or the side jambs.

rabbeted jambs, is more in line with old-fashioned door-framing methods (Illus. 1–15). For this method, begin with 1½-inch stock and cut a rabbet about ½ inch deep and wide enough for the thickness of the door. Attach the head and side jambs in the same manner as

with the previously described method, but make sure that the stops line up perfectly. At first glance, this would seem to be a more weather-tight method of construction, but if your door or the wall in which it is installed is not perfectly straight and true, it will be more difficult to get a tight closure. With applied stops, as in the first method, it is quite easy to adjust the run of the stops to the natural shape of the door, and as long as you use a bead of construction adhesive, as well as nails, every foot or so to attach the stops, there should be no problem with air infiltration between the stops and the jambs.

ARCHED HEAD JAMBS

The most common deviation from a rectangular shape for doors is some variety of arched or curved top. Making an arched-top door is relatively easy and there are many examples among the patterns in this book, but

VARIOUS HEAD JAMB SHAPES

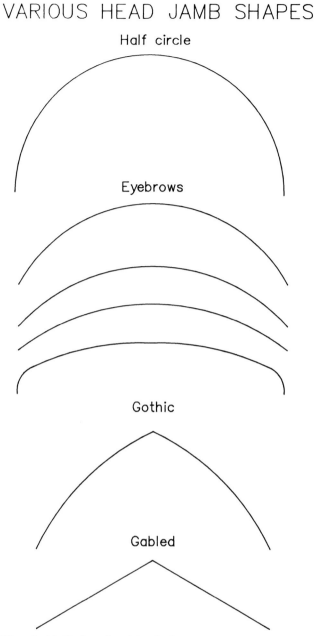

Half circle

Eyebrows

Gothic

Gabled

Illus. 1–16. Various head jamb shapes.

constructing a head jamb to match the arched top can be more difficult. There are several approaches which can be used depending on the situation.

The curves or arches or head jambs can be constant or varying, and can range from a full half circle to a very slightly arched segment often called an "eyebrow." These curves are made either by bending stock (usually by cutting it into thin strips and re-gluing them so that they hold their shapes), or by cutting the arch from either a solid piece or from a lamination.

Cutout Arches

In many cases, if the arch is not full it is possible to simply cut the curve into the lower side of a solid piece. This technique works especially well on the massive, exposed beams of post-and-beam construction. (See

Chapters 5 and 6 for several examples.) If, on the other hand, you prefer to keep the structural members hidden, you will most likely want to bend the wood to make the head jamb and stop for the top of the arched door. Before the advent of reliable glues and cheap electrical power for resawing, wood was often bent by steaming it to soften and loosen the grain; this method, however, has many problems, and is seldom used today.

MODERN BENDING METHODS

A more reliable method of bending is to resaw stock into pieces that are thin enough to take the desired bend naturally. Different species of wood vary in their abilities to take a bend, but nearly any species can withstand the most severe bend that would be necessary for a door top if it is cut thin enough and straight-grained, defect-free wood is used.

When building a curved top door, first build the jamb, since it is much easier to fit the curve of the door top to the curve of the head jamb than the other way around.

BUILT-IN FORMS

You can often make a bend for a short section of a curve with a large radius—called an eyebrow—by building up a hidden form out of framing material, and then veneering this frame with one or two layers of fairly thick bending material (Illus. 1–17).

AN INSIDE BEND FOR A JAMB HEAD

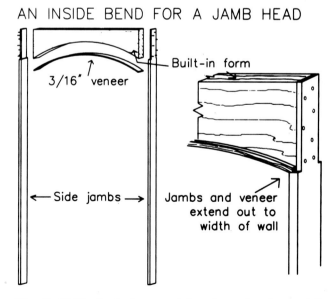

3/16" veneer

Built-in form

Side jambs

Jambs and veneer extend out to width of wall

Illus. 1–17. The 3/16-inch veneer is bent in against the partially assembled jamb and form, trimmed to the proper length, and then nailed and glued into place against the form as the end screws are tightened. Note that the rabbeted parts of the jambs and the form are the same thickness as the framing, while the jambs and the veneer must span the full thickness of the wall, including both layers of siding.

The built-in form can be cut from a solid piece, or built up from several layers of plywood, and should be the same thickness as the framing. It may be possible to make the form work as the structural header, or you may want to leave room below the actual header for the form.

Start by milling a piece of clear, vertical-grained wood of the proper width to a thickness of approximately ³⁄₁₆ inch. If you don't have the equipment to do the milling yourself, consider using ⅛-inch plywood material, called door skins, which is often available at lumberyards. This material bends easily, usually has a mahogany veneer surface, and is made with exterior-grade glue.

Determine the tightness of the curve by bending your veneer stock to test the amount of curvature it will take easily.

Since wood does not always bend evenly, make the actual cutting lines for your form from an easily made compass ruler rather than from a bent piece of stock. Once you have determined the radius of the curve, simply drive a nail through one end of a thin strip of wood, and make a notch in the other end at the radial distance from the nail. Lay out the form on a flat surface and project the midpoint of the arch down from the center of the form to the point where the center of the circle that the arch is a segment of would be. Now, swing the notched end of the stick across the form with a pencil tip held in the notch so that the circumference of the circle is drawn on the form. Cut the line with a band or jigsaw to make the form.

The ends of the form should be square, and cut to the same length as the inside of the jamb (the width of the door), plus twice the depth of the rabbet, which you will cut on the top of each side-jamb piece.

Make the rabbet cut on the side jambs so that it extends down from the top of each piece ³⁄₁₆ inch farther than the height of the form for the head piece. Then screw the side jambs to the ends of the form with their ends flush to the top of the form. Use screws on at least one end so that it can be loosened a bit later when you need to get the veneer into position.

Now bevel the veneer piece at one end with a hand plane so that it fits firmly against the end of the rabbet in the jamb. Bend the veneer tightly in against the form, using clamps where necessary to pull it in (See Illus. 1–18 for ways to apply the clamps.) When the veneer is snug against the form all the way along, except for the last little bit, cut it carefully in place (a little long) or mark it and remove it to cut it off. Try it against the jamb, and plane the end to fit as necessary.

When you are satisfied with the fit, glue and nail the veneer in place. Begin laying it in at the fixed end, with the screws out a little bit on the other end. When you pop in the loose end, loosen the C-clamps or short-bar clamps, as shown in Illus. 1–18, and tighten the screws (use bar clamps if necessary). When the jamb is tight against the end of the form, tighten the clamps again to press the veneer evenly against the form. If a little crack results between the form and the veneer, try to position it so that the curve is even from side to side, and then fill

CLAMPING AN INSIDE BEND

Drive screws partway in to prevent clamp slippage

Illus. 1–18. Screws can be temporarily driven partway into the top of the form to give purchase for clamps if they are needed to help bring the veneer in tight against the form.

the crack with an epoxy filler or panel adhesive after the glue has dried.

Now, with the jamb and form as integral parts of the door frame, install the jamb in the wall as a rectangular unit, lessening the need for special framing and trim work. The curved stop for the head jamb may consist of several laminations, and should be tightly attached to the veneer with glue and filler where necessary. Use nails or staples to help pull the stop laminations in tightly against the head jamb.

Inside Forms

Bending laminations around an inside form is a more common technique that is likely to give better results with fuller or tighter curves such as a half-circle. Once again, a good deal of thought and care should go into making the form, even though it will not be a part of the finished structure when you use an inside form. Depending on the type of clamps being used, you may want to cut out the inside of the form (so that it looks like the letter C) or leave it solid and attach battens around the edges on which you can put the clamps. If the clamps are short, use battens. You can make clamps like the one shown in Illus. 1–20 that will work nicely if you hollow out the form; however, it is important not to hollow out the form to the point that it becomes weak and will deform when the laminations are being bent.

When building the form, it is best to make it ¾ inch smaller than the desired circumference of the jamb so that you can make the stops first, and then use them as part of the form when you bend the jamb. This will ensure the best matchup between jamb and stop. It is also possible to cut the form down and bend the stops after the jambs, but whichever way you do it, make sure that the form is wide enough to support the entire width of the jamb, and is very sturdy. The ends of the form should also extend out tangentially a couple of inches from the halfway points of the circle so that the ends of the jamb head will be parallel for a couple of inches. This will give you some surface on which to rout or cut rabbets for a half-lap joint to attach the head to the side jambs.

As stated before, it is important that you are sure the laminations will take the desired bend. If you feel that you are forcing the wood, or if cracking occurs, then use thinner veneers. Drum or thickness sanders will give the best results when it comes to making veneers thinner than approximately ⅛ inch. You may be able to resaw thicker stock on either the table saw or a good band saw, and then plane it to thicknesses of ⅛ inch or more, but planers will often destroy such thin pieces.

AN EASY-TO-MAKE BENDING CLAMP

Angle iron

1/2" bolts

Illus. 1–20. Lots of clamps will be needed for bending around an inside form. You can make your own that will work on a hollow, or C-shaped, form from short sections of angle iron and ½-inch bolts.

The thickness sander will also produce a better surface for gluing. If you don't have a thickness sander, check local furniture makers or look through specialty catalogues for veneer makers.

Cut the veneers several inches longer than needed, and ¼ inch to ½ inch wider, as it will be difficult to align the edges perfectly when gluing. Remember that the outside veneer will have to be a couple of inches longer than the shortest veneer on the inside.

When you are ready to make the bend, take as many veneers as you can easily bend around the form (you can always do this in several stages if it is too difficult to get the thickness you want in one), and cover one side of each with an even coat of glue. It's easiest to work with the form by laying it down on the bench, though you could work with the form up on end if you made a stand to hold it up off the work surface. Line up the center point of the veneers with the top center of the form, and begin clamping here. Work from the center towards both edges, placing clamps every couple of inches as needed. Make sure that you have plenty of clamps on hand before starting; a typical 3-foot-diameter arch could use as many as 50 C-clamps. If you are using angle iron clamps, you will only need about 25, since they apply pressure all the way across. Use only a urea-resin-type glue and be sure to let it cure two to three times as long as normal for bent laminations.

With this type of bending, there may be some spring back if the veneers are thick, but it should be minimal. If the piece springs out a couple of inches after you take it off the form, just make a brace by nailing a piece of 1 × 4 across it that will hold it in its proper shape. Since the ends of this half circle are parallel to the side jambs where they meet, they can both be rabbeted to form a half-lap joint. The overlap of the joint should be at least one inch.

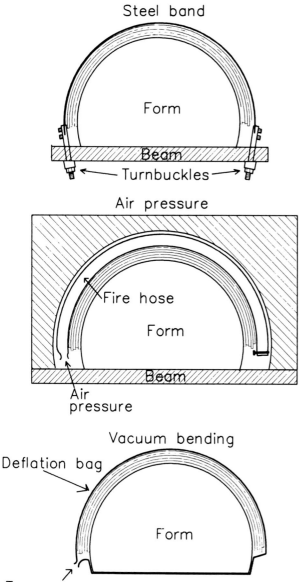

Steel band

Form

Beam

Turnbuckles

Air pressure

Fire hose

Form

Beam

Air pressure

Vacuum bending

Deflation bag

Form

To vacuum pump

Illus. 1–19. Several techniques for applying pressure to bent laminations include a metal band that is tightened with bolts, inside and outside forms with pressure applied through a hose, and deflation bags which use atmospheric pressure and vacuum to apply pressure.

Door Hardware

Door hardware generally includes locksets and hinges. Many other accessories are also available to beautify doors and improve security (Illus. 1–21). Butt hinges with removable pins are used for most doors, but other options do exist, including double-action butt hinges, pivot hinges, spring-loaded hinges, T-hinges, and strap hinges.

A double-action hinge, actually two hinges in one, allows the door to swing both ways. These hinges are often used on kitchen or bar doors. Pivot hinges are another form of double-action hinge that mount on the top and bottom of full-sized doors, and can be spring-loaded to always bring the door back to the closed position. Strap and T-hinges are often used for a more rustic look, or for a large swinging door such as a barn or garage door.

A large variety of locksets are available for doors, and it is important that you consider the use that the door will be put to when determining the proper lockset. For commercial or public installations, building codes often require "panic latches" that can be opened by pushing on a bar. Exterior doors in homes often have both a latch and a dead-bolt lock for security; these bolts are sometimes combined in entry sets. Interior doors can be fitted with passage latches that have no locking

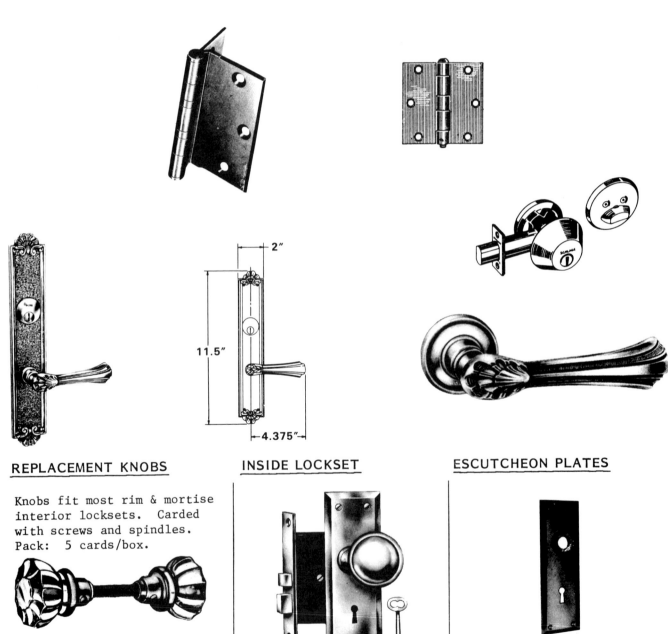

REPLACEMENT KNOBS

Knobs fit most rim & mortise interior locksets. Carded with screws and spindles. Pack: 5 cards/box.

Clear Glass Knobs: 2" dia. Polished brass finish.

INSIDE LOCKSET

ESCUTCHEON PLATES

Illus. 1–21. Door hardware includes locks, hinges, and various accessories.

mechanism, or privacy latches that can be locked from one side without the use of a key.

Though many types of locksets and variations exist, their methods of installation fall into three categories. The most common type of doorknob assembly is installed by boring two holes, a large one through the face of the stile, and a smaller one from the edge of the stile into the larger hole (Illus. 1–22). An expandable drill bit is handy for this type of work, because the sizes of the holes vary (Illus. 1–23). Mount the latch assembly into the smaller hole (Illus. 1–24); it is held in place by two screws in the faceplate that is mortised in flush to the edge of the door. Use a sharp ¾-inch chisel to cut the shallow mortise for the faceplate. Once you have done this, mount the knob assembly through the part of the latch that protrudes into the larger hole.

The distance from the edge of the door to the center of the knob is called the backset (Illus. 1–25); 2⅜ inches

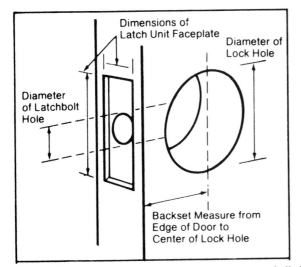

Illus. 1–22. A typical door-knob installation. First, drill the large hole, and then the smaller one. Finally, cut the faceplate mortise with a sharp chisel.

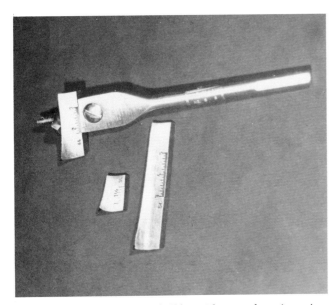

Illus. 1–23. An expansion drill bit with several cutting wings can cut holes of any diameter from under 1 inch to more than 5 inches.

Illus. 1–24. Mount the latch assembly into the smaller hole.

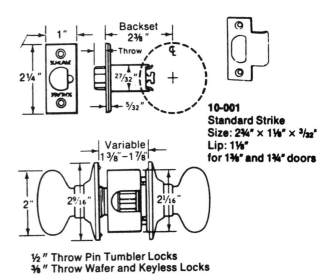

Illus. 1–25. The backset is the distance from the edge of the door to the center of the actuator knob.

is the most common backset for cylinder locks, but many can be ordered with a 2¾-inch backset as well, making the space between the doorknob and the jamb or stops a little larger.

When you have installed the lockset and it is working

STRIKE PLATE INSTALLATION

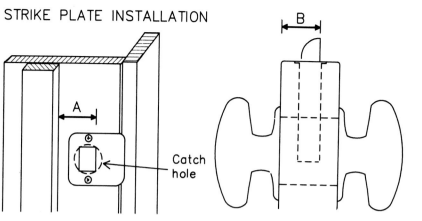

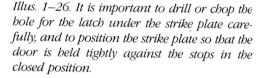

Illus. 1–26. It is important to drill or chop the hole for the latch under the strike plate carefully, and to position the strike plate so that the door is held tightly against the stops in the closed position.

properly, hold it against the doorjamb to mark the position for the strike plate. Also mortise the strike plate flush to the surface of the jamb, but first bore a hole into the jamb to accept the catch. Do not drill or chop the hole any larger than necessary (undermining the screws that hold the strike plate), and make sure that you position the strike plate so that it will hold the door tightly against the stop when it is closed (Illus. 1–26). Most locksets come with templates and instructions for installation.

LOCK MORTISE

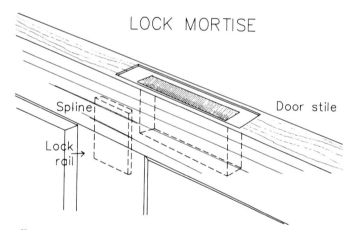

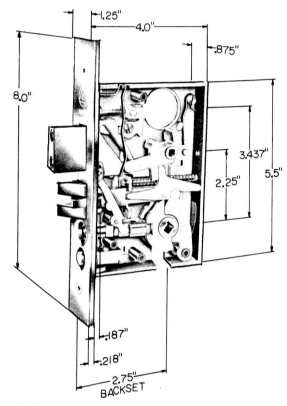

Illus. 1–28. Mortise locks have a very complex mechanism which combines a latch, a deadbolt, and sometimes a passage lock. This mechanism is housed in a flat metal box which must be mortised into the edge of the door.

Illus. 1–27. The mortises for mortise locks are very deep (4 inches or more). Make sure that you do not weaken the door by positioning the lock where it will undermine a key joint.

A second type of lock mechanism that is used for entryway combination locks can be installed by cutting a large mortise in the edge of the door where the lockset will go. These mortises are sometimes quite deep and as much as an inch wide (Illus. 1–27); you can start them with the plunge router and fence guide, but you will have to finish them with careful boring and chopping with a long mortising chisel. Use a template to mark the positions for various holes to be bored on either side of the door for the actuating levers. Then insert the mechanism itself in the mortise, and insert or mount the levers for the knobs, dead bolts, thumb latch, and handle on cover plates that you have screwed in place (Illus. 1–28).

These locksets must often be ordered left- or right-handed, depending on the side of the door they will be

mounted on, and are very complicated to install. If you have never installed one before, practice the procedure on a piece of scrap before attempting the actual installation on the door. A misplaced hole could literally ruin the whole door.

The third type of lockset is surface-mounted, and is generally the easiest to install, but it is not the most attractive or the most secure (Illus. 1–29). With this type, you have to screw-mount the box-shaped lock mechanism to the interior surface of the door, and mount a catch on the interior jamb. Drill a small hole through the door for the outside knob.

Other locking mechanisms include hook-and-eye catches, often used for screen doors, barrel bolts, and, the oldest of all, a stout bar of metal or wood held in place by sturdy brackets. For more complete informa-

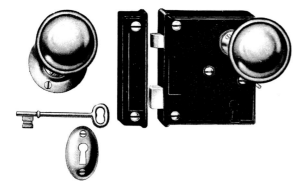

Illus. 1–29. Surface-mounted locks are easy to install but not very secure.

tion on the variety of specialty locksets and door hardware available, either ask to see the catalogues that your hardware dealer orders from or contact a locksmith who specializes in building locks.

Installing a Door

Whether you begin in the shop or on the job, the first thing to do once the door and jamb have been made is to mount the hinges on the door. Don't assemble the jamb until after the hinges have been mounted on it.

A piece of 4 × 4 with a slot like the one shown in Illus. 1–30 and 1–31 and a wedge will hold the door steadily on its edge. Remember that the pin on the hinge will be on the side (inside or outside) of the wall that you want the door to open to. The top hinge is usually set back 7 inches from the end of the door; and the bottom one 11 inches (Illus. 1–32). If a third and fourth hinge are used, space them evenly between the first two.

Doors can be mounted to swing in either direction, and to open either inward or outward. An inward-open-

ing door is considered more secure because the hinge pins are on the inside. Special screws are available that can prevent an outward opening door from being removed even if the pins are pulled out. Outward-opening doors are easier to seal against the weather. Building codes often require that doors on public buildings open outward.

Mounting Hinges

The width of the hinge mortise may vary depending on the size of the hinges used and the desired swing of the door. Several methods can be used to cut the mortises for the hinges. The simplest is to use a sharp chisel and a hammer. First, scribe around the hinge on the edge of the door with a sharp knife or pencil, and then chop straight in along the inside of the line as deep as the thickness of one hinge leaf. Be careful not to split the wood when chopping parallel to the grain. Now, pare and split the waste away from end to end or by working from the side. It's better to leave the mortise a little shallow than to cut it too deep.

Hinge-mortising jigs that can be used with routers are available, but they are expensive, bulky, and time-consuming to set up. They work best if you are hanging many doors at once (Illus. 1–33). A simpler method is to use a small router with a fence attachment set to the width of the mortise. Chop the ends of the cut as before with the chisel, set the router to the proper depth, and remove the waste by freehand cutting up to the end lines (Illus. 1–34 and 1–35). The fence will determine the width of the mortise. A couple of quick cuts with the chisel will remove any waste that the router couldn't get. You can also make a clamp-on template from ½-inch plywood, and use flush-cutting router bits to further simplify hinge mortising. Now set the hinges in the mortises and sink the screws to attach them to the door. Make sure that the heads of the pins are up. Once this is done, take the hinge jamb and mark the place where the bottom of the head jamb will meet it.

Illus. 1–30 and 1–31. A length of 4 × 4 with a slot cut in it and a wedge will hold the door securely on edge for hinge or lock mortising work.

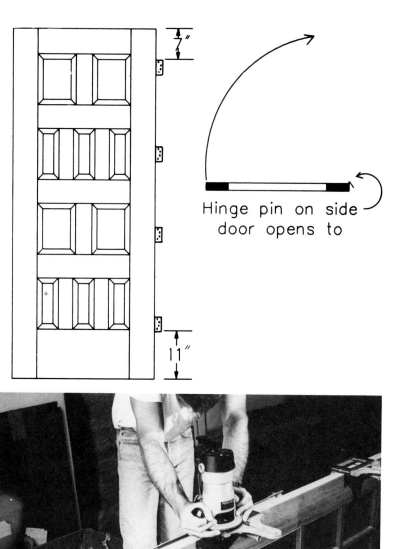

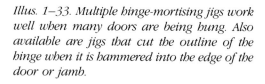

Hinge pin on side door opens to

Illus. 1–32. Place the top hinge 7 inches from the top of the door, the bottom hinge 11 inches from the bottom, and space additional hinges evenly between. Remember, the hinge pins are always on the side that the door opens to.

Illus. 1–33. Multiple hinge-mortising jigs work well when many doors are being hung. Also available are jigs that cut the outline of the hinge when it is hammered into the edge of the door or jamb.

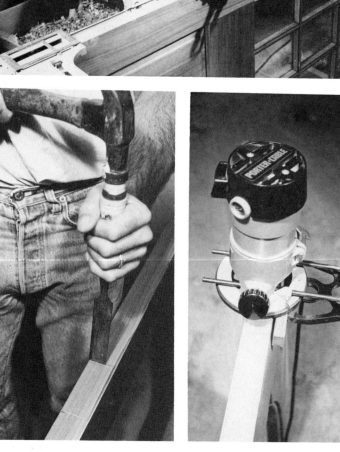

Illus. 1–34 and 1–35. A simpler method is to mark and chop the ends of the mortise with a sharp chisel, and then use a router with a fence to remove the waste.

Illus. 1–36. After you have mounted the hinges on the door, carefully mark their positions on the side jamb. Be sure that the top of the door is 3/32's of an inch below the place where the head jamb will be. In this photo, the side jamb is rabbeted to receive the head jamb.

When you have set the hinges, lay the door on the bench, hinge pins down, and lay the hinge jamb next to it. Put the other jamb under the door to hold it up so that the pins are ¾ inch above the surface of the bench. Now, slide the jamb under the leaves of the hinges, and line the place where the head of the jamb will begin 3/32 inch above the top of the door, and scribe around the hinges onto the jamb (Illus. 1–36).

Once again, chop the ends of the mortises and use the router to remove the waste. It will be necessary to change the setting on the fence slightly if you would like the door to sit slightly in from the edge of the jamb. When you have completed the mortises on the jamb, pop the pins on the top and bottom hinges and apply the loose hinge leaves to the jamb with the screws that are provided.

Now, assemble the jamb by nailing the head and side jambs together with 6 or 7d nails (Illus. 1–37), and place it in the rough opening. You can strengthen the hinges of heavy, solid wood doors by driving the hinge screws through the jamb and into the framing (if they are long enough). If you are hanging very heavy doors, use longer-than-normal screws. In any case, first nail the jamb and head together and place the unit in the rough opening. Plumb the hinge jamb first by shimming and/or nailing as needed (Illus. 1–38). Make sure that at least one edge of the jamb is lined up flush to the surface of the siding on the wall, and that the jamb is mounted so that it is square to the walls.

When you have plumbed and securely attached (but without sinking any of the nails) the hinge jamb, hang the door on the hinges by rejoining and pinning the separated hinges leaves. Now shim and nail the rest of the jamb into place so that the clearance is even all the way around the door. Leave slightly larger clearance along the latch side of the door when installing exterior doors, which swell and shrink more.

If the door tends to spring open, it probably means that the hinge jamb is twisted or that the hinges are mortised too deeply. Check the hinge jamb for squareness with the wall and move it with shims, if necessary. If the hinges are mortised too deeply, you can alleviate this problem by hand-planing along the hinge side of the door. You can also use a block plane to fine-tune the fit of the door to the latch jamb. On some single doors, and on most double doors it will be necessary to bevel the edge of the door, as shown in Illus. 1–39, so that it will close tightly without binding.

Once you have nailed the jamb with two 12d galvanized finish nails every 24 inches, apply a temporary stop to prevent the door from overswinging in the wrong direction and being damaged. At this point, install the threshold.

You can either make your own threshold or purchase a variety of wooden or extruded aluminum thresholds. For some interior doors, no threshold may be necessary, but for exterior doors a threshold is almost always needed to help drain water outward and to help obtain an airtight seal at the bottom of the door. The type of threshold that is best for a particular situation can vary widely.

Note that space must be left at the bottom of the jamb for the threshold, and that some types of weather stripping will require more than a ½ inch of space between the bottom of the door and the top of the threshold. Door bottoms can usually be cut off as much as an inch

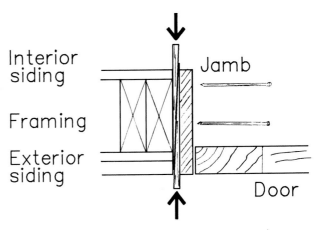

Interior siding
Framing
Exterior siding
Jamb
Door

Illus. 1–37. Shimming a door.

Illus. 1–38. Begin installing the jamb in the rough opening by shimming and nailing the hinge jamb. Once the hinge jamb is secured, reset the door on its hinges and make sure the head and lock jambs fit it before securing them.

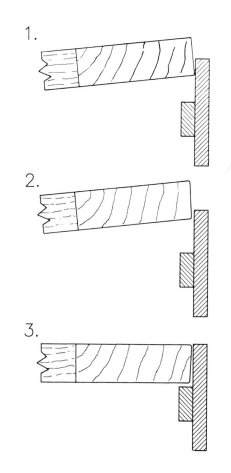

Illus. 1–39. Bevelling the edge of the door will help it close tightly without binding.

without weakening the door, but it is best to avoid this with thorough planning.

The threshold should be fitted as tightly as possible between the jambs, and should be sealed to the floor with caulk or construction adhesive. It is also important to seal wooden thresholds with a penetrating sealer before installing them.

Once the threshold is in place, install the lockset or latch (including the strike plate), and finally, apply the permanent stops and trim. Apply the stops to fit to the door in its closed position; this way, any slight twist or unevenness in the door can be compensated for, making for a tight closure all around.

Most cylinder locks can be installed easily with the door in place since only a couple of holes must be bored through the door. Combination locks requiring deep mortising should be done with the door on edge. The height of the lockset installation may depend somewhat on whether there is a step up to the door, but should usually be around 36 inches from the floor to the knob. Make sure that the strike plate is positioned so that the door closes tightly against the stops; the easiest way to ensure this is to install the lockset before applying the permanent stops. Use the temporary stop to help find the right distance from the edge of the jamb to

the strike catch, and then install the finish stop with the latch held lightly against the strike catch.

If you plan to use compression-type weather stripping, such as foam stripping, apply it to the stops before they are installed. For an exterior door, make the stop detail as wide as possible, at least ½ inch thick, and apply two beads of caulk to it all around so that you can glue it to the jamb. Apply small finish nails every foot. You can use a much lighter, smaller stop for interior doors.

Double doors will require an added piece called an astragal or T-moulding between the two doors to seal the closure between them. Usually one door is fixed in place with two barrel bolts, top and bottom, and the other door which closes against it has the lockset or latch.

Double doors are difficult to install because any twist or warping of the doors will show up dramatically where the doors meet. If one door is twisted, install the barrel bolts on the twisted door so that they will hold it straight when it is closed. Allow room for the astragal or overlapping rabbets when planning a double-door set. You can install the T-moulding so that it faces either in or out, and on either the opening door or the fixed door, depending on the situation.

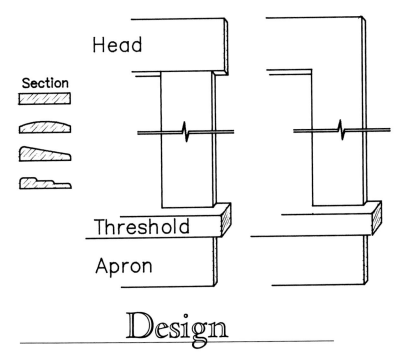

Head

Threshold

Apron

Illus. 1–40. Common door casing details.

Design

After giving thorough consideration to all the factors mentioned and the way they affect your particular situation, you will most likely want to draw out your ideas with pencil and paper. If you don't have a drafting table and the proper tools, use graph paper and a ruler as a straightedge. Use a large enough scale so that you can indicate details such as mouldings or inlays.

Remember that locksets are usually placed about 36 inches above the floor, but may be affected by a step up or down, or by the placement of a deadbolt. The drawing stage is the time to play with the visual effects and proportions of your design. Only when you are happy with your drawing are you ready to head for the shop.

2
BATTEN DOORS

Let's start simply and work our way up to the more complicated and challenging doors. A door is often intended to be used as just a means to hide the clutter in a closet or shed or to help define a space. Batten doors can be built quickly and easily with just a few hand tools, and though they sometimes aren't very weathertight, they will often serve perfectly well in sheds, garages, pantries, and similar areas. And, with a little more care batten doors can be made that are as weathertight and solid as any entry door.

Use good, dry tongue-and-grooved, splined, or ship-lapped lumber when building all batten doors with the exception of the most rustic ones. Do not edge glue the upright pieces to each other or glue the battens to the boards. The battens hold the upright boards together, but will not prevent them from swelling and shrinking

as the moisture levels in their surroundings change. If the upright boards have some form of interlocking edges, this swelling and shrinking can occur without the door warping or cracks opening up between the boards (Illus. 2–1).

On the other hand, if you edge glue the boards to prevent open cracks from forming or glue battens to just one side, you may end up with a very warped door. Battens applied to a wide expanse of edge-glued lumber will actually force the door to warp because the boards and the battens swell and contract at different rates (Illus. 2–2).

Because the upright boards must be allowed some movement in this type of door construction, it is also necessary in most cases to apply diagonal braces to the door between the battens to keep it from falling out of square. These diagonals can be used as a design feature, or, in many cases, they can be put on the least visible side of the door, making the visible side blend in better with its surroundings. As we will see, there are also ways to brace a batten door without applying diagonals.

A popular variation of the batten door is the framed batten door. In this type of construction, the horizontal battens are applied at the very top and bottom of the door, and vertical battens are also applied to form a frame around the layer of vertical boards. This makes a batten door look more like a frame-and-panel door, and it is still quite simple to build. Batten doors also tend to evolve into layered doors (see the following chapter), which are more weathertight and less likely to warp. Layered doors can be built with the same basic techniques, but can also have much more complex and intricate designs.

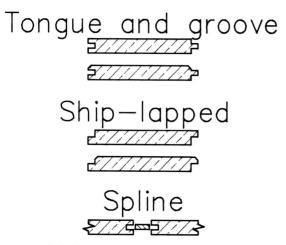

Illus. 2–1. If the boards have interlocking edges, cracks will not open up in batten doors.

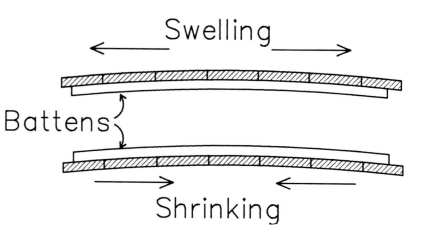

Illus. 2–2. Gluing the battens to the boards, or the boards to each other, can cause warping because the pieces will swell and shrink at different rates.

BATTEN DOOR VARIATIONS

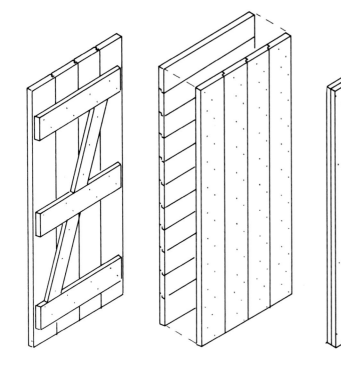

Illus. 2–3. Batten doors consist of a layer of vertical boards which are held together by horizontal battens and diagonal braces.

Building Techniques

When building a batten door, begin by cutting the boards that will form the vertical layer to length about one inch longer than the finished length of the door. The vertical pieces can later be trimmed to their finished lengths all at once, laid out side by side on the workbench. Check to be sure that they are all straight and will fit together tightly. Boards with warped edges can be straightened with a jointer and table saw, but then you will have to remill the tongue-and-grooved, ship-lapped, or splined slot if there is one.

You will more than likely have to make rip cuts on the two outer boards to square the edges and cut the door to width (Illus. 2–4). If possible, figure the placement of these cuts so that the two outer boards are of the same width. Avoid using a very narrow strip along one or both edges. If you don't have a table saw, make these two cuts with a circular saw or a good, sharp hand saw.

Bevelling the edges of the battens all around on the side that will be away from the door adds an attractive touch (Illus. 2–5). Do this before applying the battens because it's easier then and less likely to mar the door. For an especially large door, or for a decorative touch, notch the ends of the braces into the battens, thus seating them and further strengthening the door. If you do so, cut the notches and fit the braces before nailing the battens to the door (Illus. 2–6).

When you are ready to nail on the battens, check them for squareness to the door, and then tack each one in place with one or two small finish nails. Now, flip the door over, mark the nailing lines across the vertical boards, and nail through into the battens. A 6d or 7d galvanized nail is usually used with ¾-inch material so that the nails can project through both layers and be clinched to give them extra holding power (Illus. 2–7). You can also nail from the batten side if you don't mind the clinched nails showing on the flush side of the door.

Screws can also be used to apply battens, but they should be carefully counterbored, and be the exact length to hold the board without going through. If you are using nails, be sure to set the heads of the nails below the surface of the wood before flipping the door over again to clinch the nails. A large nailset can also be used to set the clinched parts of the nails below the surface of the battens. If the wood is hard or tends to split easily, you may want to predrill the nail holes with a bit that is slightly smaller than the nails.

Once the battens are permanently in place, carefully mark and cut the braces. If you have a long enough board, lay it the full diagonal length of the door between the upper and lower battens, and mark on both it and the battens to indicate where it is to be cut and its exact placement. Use a sharp block plane on the ends of the braces to adjust the fit, if necessary; bevel the edges as you did on the battens, and nail them on in the same manner.

Finally, check the dimensions of the door again, and trim the top and bottom as necessary for a perfect fit. Bevel or sand the edges to soften them; now the door is ready to hang.

Pages 31–39 include patterns, photographs, and building instructions for making both simple and framed batten doors. Remember, the wider and heavier these doors become, the more important the diagonal bracing and the fasteners used to hold the door together.

Illus. 2–4. The outer boards are ripped to the same width, and clamps are used to hold the boards together while the battens are applied.

Illus. 2–5. A nice touch is to bevel or round the edges of the battens and braces.

Illus. 2–6. If you are going to cut notches in the battens for the braces, do it before nailing the battens in place.

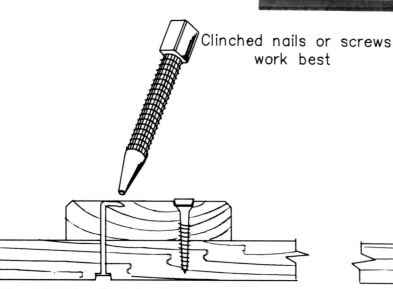

Clinched nails or screws work best

Blind nailing can be used with a full layer of t&g boards

Illus. 2–7. Either clinched nails or screws can be used to attach battens to the vertical boards. If you are using nails, first set their heads below the surface. Then clinch them and use the nailset to curl their tips down into the wood.

80 × 26″ Closet Door

Illus. 2–8 and 2–9. Pattern and photo for 80 × 26-inch closet door. See the following page for building instructions.

80 × 26″ Closet Door

description	no. of pieces	dimensions
a. vertical T & G boards	8	80 × 3¾ × ¾″
b. battens	2	24 × 3½ × ¾″
c. brace	1	60 × 3½ × ¾″
screws	22	#10 × 1¼″

The door shown in Illus. 2–8 and 2–9 is built with 1 × 4 tongued-and-grooved cedar panelling. Since it would be difficult to remill the tongues and grooves on the edges of warped boards, make sure that you purchase straight, defect-free lumber when building this type of door. Also, use only very dry material for interior applications.

First, cut the eight vertical boards so that they're 81 inches long, and then lay them out on a workbench or a pair of sawhorses to make sure that they fit tightly with each other. If they do, subtract the width of the doorway from the total width of the vertical boards, and divide the remainder by two. The figure you reach is the amount you will rip off each of the two edge boards. If you make these cuts by hand or with a circular saw, use a chalk line to snap the lines on the boards, and then cut to the outside of the lines. Use a hand or electric plane to straighten and trim these cuts.

Now, cut the battens to length and lay them in position on top of the vertical boards. The builder of this door had to cut two sections out of the stop on the hinge side of the door so that the batten could run all the way to the edge. This would be a good idea if a butt hinge were being used, but is not necessary with a strap hinge because the batten can be stopped about ¾ inch from the edge of the door.

Before attaching the battens to the vertical boards, lay out the diagonal brace, cut it to length, and mark and cut the notches in the battens. A square-ended batten and matching notch is stronger than an angled because the short section on the batten between the brace and the end can easily break off. Use a block plane or router to soften the edges of the battens and braces by chamfering or quarter-rounding them.

While assembling the door, work on sawhorses or lay two 2 × 4 sleepers on the bench to hold the vertical boards up off its top; this way, you can slide the clamps in under the boards, and make sure that the nails (if you are using them) aren't driven into the bench top. Now, use pipe clamps (two above and two below) to hold the vertical boards tightly together and C clamps to hold the battens in place, and begin boring and countersinking the holes for the screws. Apply the screws to the outer boards first, and work towards the middle. If you are using nails instead of screws, make sure that they are approximately ¼ inch longer than the combined thickness of the vertical boards and battens. Use two nails near opposite sides of the battens for each vertical board (Illus. 2–10).

Drive the nails through, set the heads below the surface with a nail set, and then clinch them (also with a nail set) by bending them over and setting the tips below the surface (Illus. 2–7). If you do not want to see the clinches on the flat side of the door, tack or clamp the battens in place, flip the door over, and make light nailing lines on the flat side with chalk or a pencil. Nail through, set the nail heads, and then flip the door and clinch the nails as before.

After nailing, remove the clamps and trim the top and bottom.

Batten nailing pattern

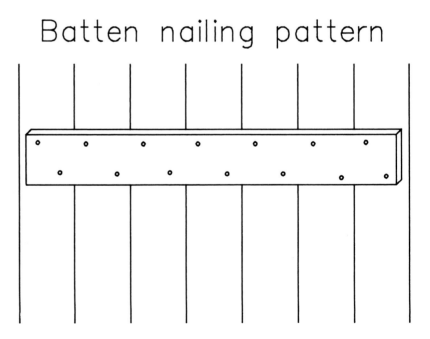

Illus. 2–10. Two nails per board near each edge of the batten will cause less splitting, and will hold it securely.

80 × 48″ Entry Door

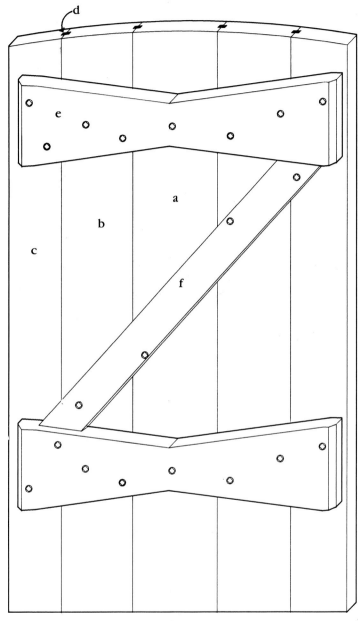

Illus. 2–11 and 2–12. Pattern and photo for 80 × 48-inch entry door. See the following page for building instructions.

80 × 48″ Entry Door

description	no. of pieces	dimensions
a. center board	1	80 × 12 × 1½″
b. vertical boards	2	79 × 10 × 1½″
c. vertical boards	2	78 × 8 × 1½″
d. spline strips	4	79 × 1 × ½″
e. battens	2	48 × 12 × 1½″
f. diagonal brace	1	50 × 5 × ¾″

The rustic-looking entry door shown in Illus. 2–11 and 2–12 was built with 1½-inch-thick vertical boards that were shaped with an adz or a slick (a large gouge) to give them a rough-hewn appearance. Slots were cut along the edges of the vertical boards, and plywood splines were inserted to ensure that the door would be airtight. Carriage bolts were used to secure the battens and the brace to the vertical boards, and large, wrought-iron strap hinges were applied on the inside of the door to support its weight to the 48-inch width of the door.

Another interesting feature of this door is the very slight curve on the top. The beam that forms the head jamb was probably cut with a chain saw, and then smoothed with a belt sander or large rasp. Trim two inches thick was applied to the inner face of the side jamb posts and the head jamb beam to form the pocket into which the door closes (Illus. 2–13).

To build this door, first cut the vertical boards to about 80 inches in length, and rip them to the widths shown in the cutting list. Next, cut ½ × ½-inch slots centered along the edges of all the inner boards, and rip plywood splines to fit them. The splines should be nailed or glued into one slot only on each board. This will prevent them from sliding downward, but will not prevent the boards from swelling and contracting naturally.

Now clamp the vertical boards together, and cut out, shape, and clamp the battens in place on top of them. Drill ⁵⁄₁₆-inch holes through the battens and the vertical boards and insert carriage bolts to secure the battens. When the battens are in place, cut and fit the diagonal brace into place the same way. Mark the curve on the top from the head jamb before assembling it, and then use it to make the trim piece that is applied to the inside of the jamb.

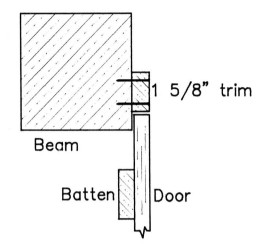

Illus. 2–13. An easy way to make the stop and trim for a curved-top door is to apply 2-inch-thick material, cut to match the curve of the top, to an exposed beam header.

84 × 36″ Entry Door

Level Two

The nicely crafted Dutch-style door shown in Illus. 2–14 and 2–15 does not need diagonal bracing because the battens are inlayed into the two-inch-thick vertical boards. The battens are screwed into the vertical boards and the screws covered with sturdy hardwood plugs. Since the battens are inlaid, the boards are locked in place, with no possibility of sagging.

To build this door, first cut vertical boards that are the full length of the door—84 inches. These boards have tongues and grooves milled on their edges, probably cut with a table saw or router after the lumber has been crosscut and ripped and then jointed so that the edges are straight. The edge of each board is rounded a bit also, to accentuate the vertical lines that separate the boards.

Once the vertical boards are ready, crosscut them in the middle where the door is divided into upper and lower sections. This door does not have a rabbet where the two sections meet, but if you are building a door that will be exposed to weather, add a rabbet, as shown in Illus. 2–16, to prevent leaking.

Now, clamp together the vertical boards for the lower section of the door, and use a circular saw or router to remove the wood from the areas where the battens will be applied. If you are using a circular saw, mark the area carefully; then set the saw for the proper depth (¾ inch) and make repeated cuts between the marks (Illus. 2–17). After making the cuts, use a chisel to remove the remaining waste and smooth the slot for the inlay. A router with a ½- or ¾-inch straight-cutting bit can be used in the same way to remove waste from the area where the batten will be inlaid. It is even possible to clamp guide boards to the vertical boards to guide the router or saw it when cutting the smooth, straight edge for the inlaid battens.

Remove the waste on the curved top batten with a router. The easiest method is to use a ½-inch straight cutting bit with an inboard-mounted bearing (Illus. 2–18). The bearing rides against a plywood template that is clamped to the vertical boards, and since it cuts perfectly flush to the bearing, there is no offset between the cut and the template. Guide bushings that mount to the router base are also available for this type of cutting, but the cut is usually offset from the template a little, making precise inlay work difficult.

When you have removed the areas for the inlays, carefully fit the battens into them and screw them into place, as shown in Illus. 2–19. To get a tight fit, first cut the battens slightly large, and then carefully plane them to a perfect fit.

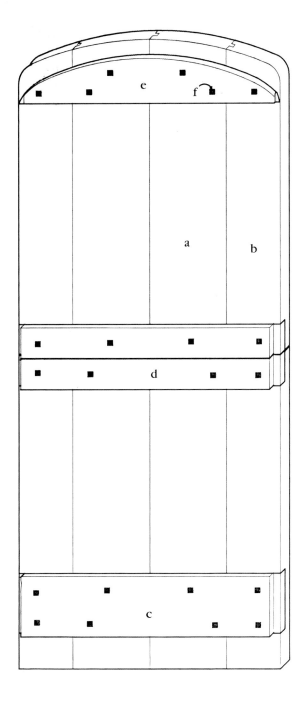

Illus. 2–14 and 2–15. Pattern and photo for the 84 × 36-inch entry door.

84 × 36″ Entry Door

description	no. of pieces	dimensions
a. middle vertical boards	2	84 × 11 × 2″
b. outer vertical boards	2	82 × 8 × 2″
c. lower batten	1	36 × 8 × 1½″
d. middle battens	2	36 × 4 × 1½″
e. top batten	1	36 × 6 × 1½″
f. screw plugs	22	¾ × ¾ × ⅜″
screws	22	#10 × 3″

Countersink the screws about ¼-inch, chop out square holes around them, and inlay square plugs,

¾ × ¾ × ⅜ inch thick, to cover the screws. The edges of the plugs can be chamfered with a sander or plane to give them a facetted look. Note that the battens on this door were cut down flush to the vertical boards on both sides about 1 inch from the edge. The builder must have planned to have the door mounted inside-out. The hand-carved hardwood latch and handle on this door are quite easy to build and makes a beautiful addition to this piece. (See pages 00–00 for more information on handles and latches.)

A special jamb and stop detail is also used so that the plaster extends smoothly from the surface of the wall into the doorway. This same detail can also be used on the exterior of stuccoed buildings (Illus. 2–20).

DUTCH DOOR

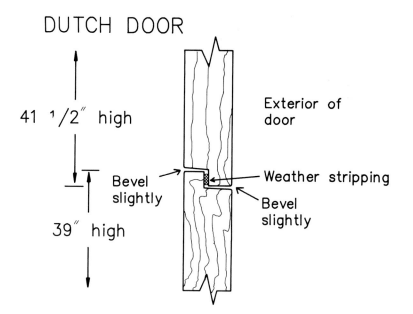

41 ¹/2″ high

Bevel
slightly

39″ high

Exterior of
door

Weather stripping

Bevel
slightly

Illus. 2–16. Interlocking rabbets are usually cut where the two parts of a Dutch door come together.

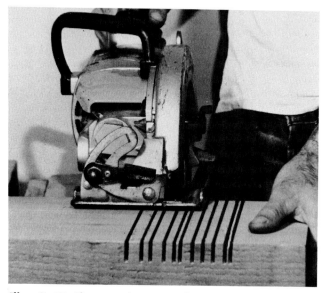

Illus. 2–17. If you make repeated cuts with a circular saw, you will be able to remove the waste more easily with a chisel when cutting a slot across the grain for inlaying the battens.

Illus. 2–18. A ¹/2-inch straight-cutting bit with an inboard-mounted guide bushing is great for waste removal when you are working with a template.

Section

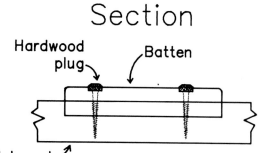

Hardwood plug

Batten

Vertical board

Illus. 2–19. The squared-out plugs that cover the screws are a nice touch.

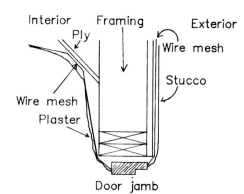

Interior   Framing   Exterior

Ply

Wire mesh

Wire mesh

Stucco

Plaster

Door jamb

Illus. 2–20. Plaster or stucco can be wrapped into a jamb that is set off from the framing edges.

96 × 58″ Framed Batten Barn Door

Level Two

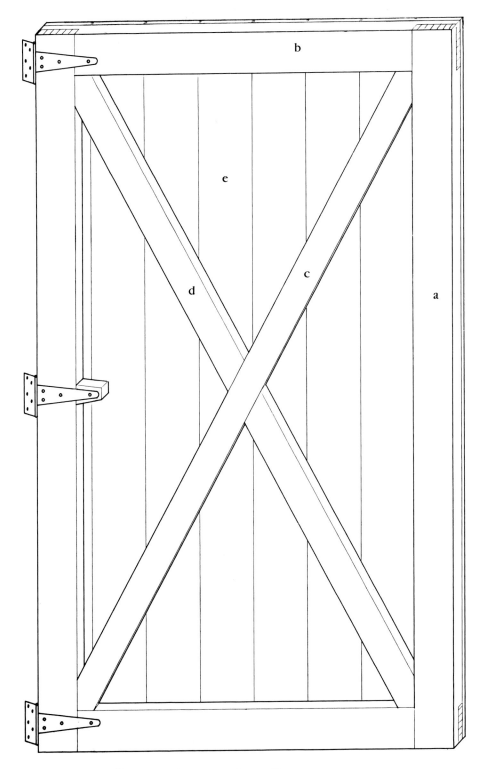

Illus. 2–21. Pattern for the 96 × 58-inch framed batten barn door. See the following page for a photo and building instructions.

96 × 58″ Framed Batten Barn Door

description	no. of pieces	dimensions
a. frame stiles	2	96 × 5½ × 1½″
b. frame rails	2	58 × 5½ × 1½″
c. brace	1	97¼ × 4 × 1″
d. braces	2	48 × 4 × 1″
e. vertical boards	8	96 × 7½ × ¾″

Illus. 2–22.

A common approach to building a larger batten-type door, as shown in Illus. 2–21 and 2–22, is to connect the horizontal battens with vertical pieces to form a frame around the entire door. The layer of vertical boards can then be nailed or screwed to the frame, making construction much easier. The X-shaped braces are then added to reinforce the frame.

To build this door, first cut the vertical and horizontal frame pieces to the full length and width of the door. Then use either a hand saw, circular saw, or radial arm saw to cut half-lap joints at the ends of all these pieces (Illus. 2–23). When this is done, lay the frame pieces out on a flat surface, apply construction adhesive to the meeting surfaces of all the half lap joints, and assemble the frame, being careful that it is kept square. Drive several nails or screws through each half-lap joint to secure it.

Before attaching any of the vertical boards to the frame, lay them all out on the frame, and move them to one side or the other as necessary so that the two outer boards end up being of equal width. After ripping the two outer boards to width, begin at one edge and nail or screw the 1 × 8 tongue-and-groove vertical boards to the frame, applying construction adhesive where the

Half–lapped corner joint

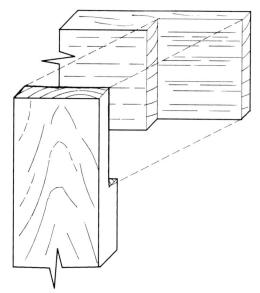

Illus. 2–23. Half-lapped corner joints greatly strengthened the frame of this batten door.

boards meet the frame as you go. Glue can be used here because the frame is two inches thick and the vertical boards are edged-glued. Two-inch #10 screws will work very nicely, and won't cause any splitting in the vertical boards if you drill and countersink them as you go.

When all the vertical boards have been applied, flip the door over, and lay the first brace (the continuous one [C in Illus. 2–21]) on top of the frame to mark it for cutting. A nice touch would be to plane the boards for the braces on these doors so that they are about ½ inch thinner than the frame pieces. Apply construction adhesive to the inside of the brace, tack this brace in place with two finish nails, cut the two shorter pieces for the other brace, and glue and tack them in place, too. Now, carefully turn the door over again, and draw lines that show where to screw through the vertical boards to hold the braces.

The strap hinges used on this door will also help reinforce it, making a very strong, solid door that is not very heavy for its size.

3
LAYERED DOORS

Layering is an exciting method of door building that is really just a logical extension of the batten door method. A batten door can be thought of as a two-layer door; one vertical layer and one horizontal layer create a cross-bonded unit that can be quite strong and rigid if the materials involved are used carefully.

Layered doors usually incorporate a third layer or core which helps give stability and rigidity to the two outer layers (Illus. 3–1). The building techniques used for most layered doors require little more in the way of tools and machinery than batten doors do, but the design possibilities become much more exciting because these doors are not dependent on visible battens and braces for their strength.

I have also included in this section some doors such as the greenhouse door on pages 47 and 48 that are not actually supported by their center layer, but gain strength by overlapping the frame pieces of the two outer layers in such a way that all the joints are offset (Illus. 3–2). The two outer layers are glued and nailed to each other, and the center layer (usually a thin translu-cent plastic material) is sandwiched between them. This is a very effective way to make a beautiful lightweight door for any area where insulation is not a consideration.

Solid layered doors, on the other hand, tend to be thick and heavy. Three layers of ¾-inch-thick material will make a door that is 2¼ inches thick, quite a bit thicker than most standard doors, which range from 1½ to 1¾ inches thick. This is often desirable for an entry door, but could be a problem when some types of lock-sets are being used; locksets are usually designed for a maximum door thickness of 2 inches. This problem can be avoided if you use thinner material such as ¼-inch plywood for the core or select thinner material for one or both of the outer layers.

Layered doors up to 4 inches thick are sometimes constructed when a variation of this technique is used to create a highly insulated door needed in regions with extremely cold winters, or for saunas. In this type of door, a core of 1½-inch-thick insulation board, surrounded by a frame of solid wood, is covered by inner

LAYERED DOORS

1 x 6 core

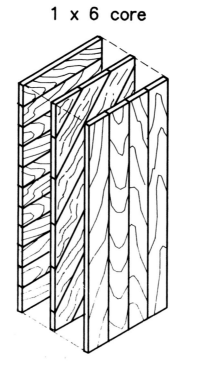

Plywood core

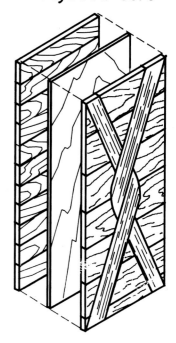

Illus. 3–1. Layered doors can have either a plywood or solid-wood core.

OFFSETTING JOINTS

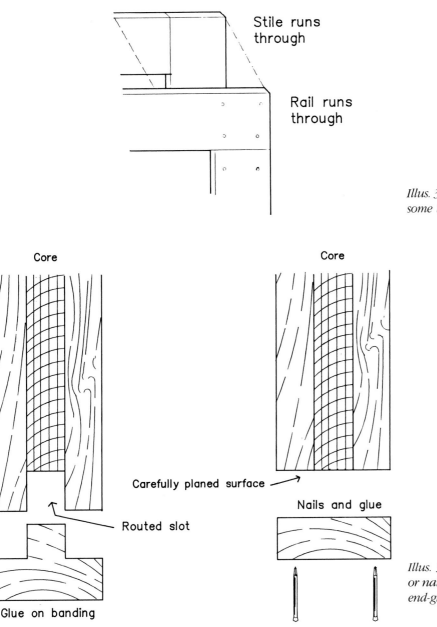

Stile runs
through

Rail runs
through

Illus. 3—2. Offset joints will also help strengthen some types of layered doors.

Core

Core

Carefully planed surface →

Routed slot

Nails and glue

Glue on banding

Illus. 3—3. Edge bandings can either be glued or nailed to layered doors to cover plywood or end-grain core material.

and outer layers of panelling or plywood. An R factor (resistance to heat loss) of up to 10 can be obtained with this type of construction.

One advantage of layered doors is the freedom of design they allow the creative designer-builder. Since the hidden inner layer is providing most of the support and rigidity for the door, the outer layers can be arranged in almost any design. Use a piece of graph paper to create the design for the outer layer or layers if the design is a complicated one, and then enlarge it to full size by drawing a grid on paper or thin plywood that corresponds to the grid on the graph paper. For example, if the graph paper has 4 squares to the inch, make your full-sized grid at 4 squares to the foot. An original sketch at a scale of 1″ = 1′ can then be transferred to the full-sized grid, and the pieces can be cut to form a pattern.

Before moving on to the patterns and ideas for layered doors, let's explore some techniques for hiding the inner layer or core so that it doesn't show along the edge of the door. It is possible to construct a layered door with two vertical layers arranged so that the edges of the boards overlap. A third, outer layer that doesn't need overlapping joints for strength can then be applied in any type of design. With this method, the core will be visible along the edge, but no end grain or plywood will show. If plywood, or a layer of horizontal or diagonal boards is to be used for the core, an edge banding of 1-inch material can be joined to just the core piece before assembly. Another option is to band the entire edge (Illus. 3–3). A routed slot can even be cut in the edge of the door to receive a tongue on the edge-banding, making a joint that is strong enough so that it does not need nails.

80 × 36" Utility Door

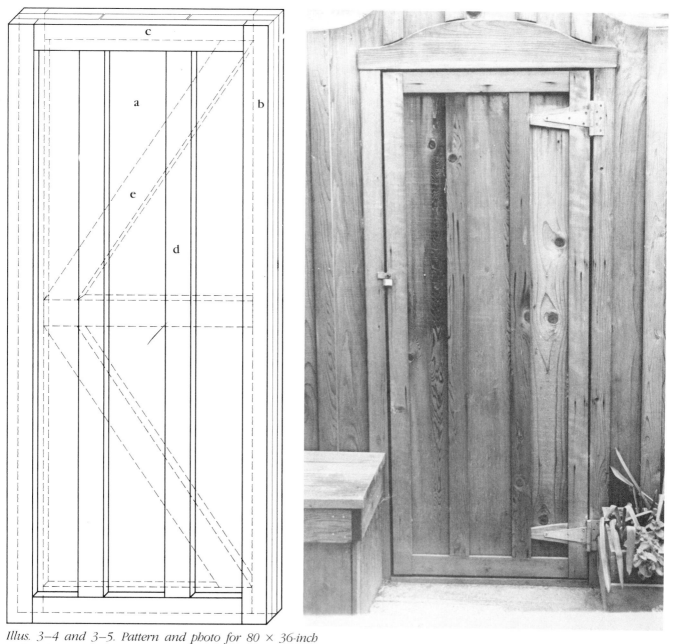

Illus. 3–4 and 3–5. Pattern and photo for 80 × 36-inch utility door.

80 × 36" Utility Door

description	no. of pieces	dimensions
a. middle layer boards	3	80 × 12 × 1"
b. frame stiles	4	80 × 3½ × 1"
c. frame rails	5	29 × 3½ × 1"
d. vertical battens	2	73 × 3½ × 1"
e. braces	2	43 × 3½ × 1"

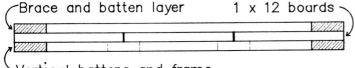

Brace and batten layer   1 x 12 boards

Vertical battens and frame

Illus. 3–6. Top view of layered utility door.

The door shown in Illus. 3–4 and 3–5 is built with layer and batten door construction techniques. A center layer of three 1 × 12-inch boards is sandwiched between two frames, one of which has diagonal braces. The outer layer consists of a frame with two extra vertical battens; this frame covers the cracks between the 1 × 12's, and helps the door blend in with the siding treatment of the wall into which it is mounted (Illus. 3–6).

To build this door, first cut the three 1 × 12's to exactly 80 inches in length. Next, rip enough stock to make all the frames, braces, and battens. Cut the four frame stiles (b in Illus. 3–4) to length, and attach them to both sides of the outer two boards. Now, lay out the core boards, with the frame stiles attached, on the table with about ⅛ inch of space between them. Place two scraps under the center board to hold it up at the same level as the outer ones. Make sure that there is at least ⅛ inch of

space between the boards; this way, swelling won't force the frame joints apart later.

Cut the frame rails (c) to length so that they will fit tightly between the frame stiles, and lay the top and bottom ones for the inner layer in position under the vertical boards. Use bar clamps to hold the frame stiles tightly against the ends of the frame rails while driving nails or screws through the vertical boards and into the frame rails. Now, cut and nail the top and bottom frame stiles for the outer layer into place on the top side of the door.

The door will hold together as a unit now, and the remaining pieces of both layers can be cut and fit into place. This rather heavy door would probably sag without the diagonal braces on the inner side, and would not be nearly as nice looking without the outer layer.

78 × 42″ Entry Door

Level One

As shown in Illus. 3–7 and 3–8, layering and board-and-batten techniques can be used used to create a unique door that is very simple to build. The battens are used more to give the door a rustic look than to hold it together, although they do that as well. The two layers of vertical boards are what make the door weathertight and strong, and keep it from sagging even without a brace.

To build this door, first lay out the inner layer of 1 × 6 boards on your workbench. Make sure that all the edges are straight and meet tightly. If there are any warped boards, joint them straight or discard them. Don't worry about the lengths of the top ends of the boards for now; you can trim them after assembling the door. The material used for the two vertical layers of the door shown in Illus. 3–7 and 3–8 was not tongue-and-grooved, but you can use tongue-and-grooved or ship-lapped material, especially for the inner layer, if it is available. Also, make sure that the two outer edge boards are the same widths and not too narrow. You may have to rip them to get the proper spacing that corresponds to the width of the door.

Use wider boards, in this case 1 × 10's, for the outer layer so that the cracks between boards on either layer will be offset and covered by the other layer. You could use the same width board for both the inner and outer layers of vertical boards, but it would mean having edge boards of different widths on the outside of at least one

of the layers. Liberal use of a panel adhesive glue between layers will also help ensure that this type of door stays solid and airtight.

Lay the outer layer over the inner layer, applying glue between them as you work, and clamp both layers on their edges with bar clamps to hold the boards in place while you are applying the battens. Cut the battens for this door from a single wide piece of material to match the slightly gabled head jamb. This can be done with a circular saw or hand saw. After cutting, shave them along their edges with a drawknife to give them a more rustic look. Don't forget to cut the ends of the battens back far enough so that they don't interfere with the stops if they are on the same side of the door.

Either attach small nails under the battens to help hold the layers together, or drive finish nails through from the inside into the battens, and then set them and add putty so they don't show. If tongue-and-groove material is used on the inner layer, it can be blind-nailed through the middle layer and into the battens. Carriage bolts hold the door together, but you might have to use a lot of them if the inner layer is not tongue-and-grooved. Once you have attached the battens, trim the top of the door to match the head jamb.

The head jamb for the door shown in Illus. 3–7 and 3–8 was cut with a chain saw from a very large timber. If such large lumber is not available, build a form into the framing of the structure (Illus. 3–9), and then line it

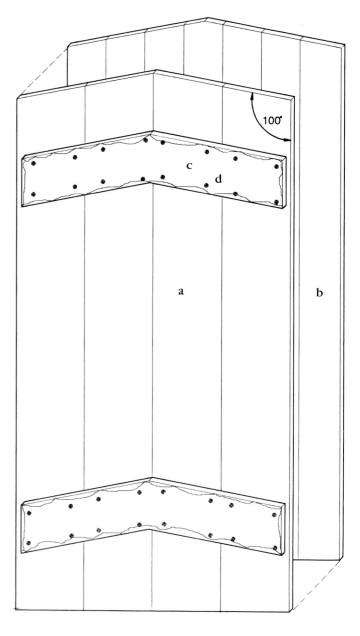

Illus 3–7 and 3–8. Photo and pattern for 78 × 42-inch entry door.

78 × 42″ Entry Door

description	no. of pieces	dimensions
a. outer layer	4	76 (longest) × 10 × ¾″
b. inner layer	7	76 (longest) × 6 × ¾″
c. battens	2	38½ × 11 × 1″
d. carriage bolts	32	2½ × ¼″

with pieces of ¾-inch-thick material. It would be helpful if you built the jamb first, so that you can match the battens and the shape of the top of the door to it exactly.

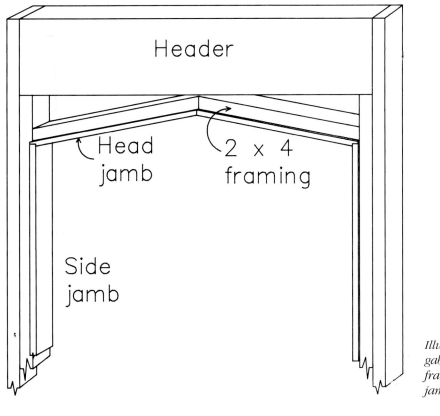

Header

Head jamb

2 x 4 framing

Side jamb

Illus. 3–9. In regular stud wall framing, the gabled head jamb of this door would be framed in under a concealed header, and the jamb would be nailed directly to the framing.

80 × 36″ Entry Door

Level Two

The beautiful door shown in Illus. 3–10 and 3–11 appears at first glance to be a frame-and-panel door. However, two indications that this is a layered door are the flush panels and the fact that when the door is opened and the edge examined, the middle layer can be seen. The middle layer in this door was made with kiln-dried 1 × 6 stock, laid horizontally, and the inner layer with boards of the same stock laid vertically for cross bonding. Generally, a plywood core is better, but if the wood is very stable and the door is not exposed to severe weather conditions, solid wood will work.

To build this door, first cut the boards for the inner layer to length. This layer can be seen from the inside of the house, so make sure that the edges fit tightly together and that the two edge boards are about the same width and not too narrow. Tongue-and-groove panelling will also work well for this layer. Lay the boards out on a pair of sawhorses and clamp them lightly together, with the clamps underneath the boards. Apply an even amount of a thick, viscous panel-adhesive glue to the top of the boards with either a toothed trowel or a caulking gun.

Now, nail the boards for the middle layer in place one at a time. Use very small finish nails, no longer than the combined thickness of the two layers. Driving them in at angles will make them grip better. Start at one end, and move the door on the sawhorses as you work, so that you have something solid to nail against. Carefully trim the edges after you have completed the nailing.

Remove the clamps and place the door on the assembly table. Begin cutting the pieces for the outer layer and the outer "frame" pieces. Lightly clamp these pieces in place on the two inner layers; then cut the upright and cross pieces (f, g, and h in Illus. 3–10) so that they butt together in the center for now, as if the center piece and center circle (j & k) were not there. Line these pieces up carefully where they will go, and then cut out the center piece and center circle so that they fit tightly together (use a coping saw or scroll saw to cut the hole out of j); then lay them in place over the cross pieces. Carefully position and mark the center pieces on the cross pieces; then cut these marks so that j and k can be inlaid into the center of the cross pieces.

Before gluing, sand the outer edges of all the pieces slightly round. This makes each piece distinct and adds a certain ambience to the door. Now, glue and nail in place all the pieces. Apply the panel adhesive to the backs of the pieces as you work. Start with the outer frame, which can be clamped down tightly with C clamps. Once this is done, apply glue to f, g, h, j, and k

Middle and inner layer
1 x 6"

Illus. 3–10 and 3–11. Pattern and photo for 80 × 36-inch entry door.

80 × 36″ Entry Door

description	no. of pieces	dimensions
a. back layer	7	80 × 6 × 1″ T & G
b. middle layer	15	36 × 6 × 1″ T & G
c. stiles	2	80 × 5⅛ × ¾″
d. top rail	1	26 × 4 × ¾″
e. bottom rail	1	26 × 5 × ¾″
f. lower upright	1	33 × 4 × ¾″
g. upper upright	1	34 × 4 × ¾″
h. center rail pieces	2	11⅛ × 4 × ¾″
i. panel material	30′	5¼ × ¾″
j. center piece	1	7 × 7 × ¾″
k. center circle	1	5¼″ diameter × ¾″

and place them in position. Use small finish nails, but instead of surface nailing, toenail them along the edges

(Illus. 3–12). Short sections of spline can also be routed into the edges where you can't put nails to lock the pieces together.

Now, cut the diagonal "panel" pieces and fit them into the remaining spaces. Work from the center towards the edges. These pieces could be made from straight 1 × 6 stock, but a stronger panel will result if you use tongue-and-grooved or ship-lapped stock because the edges that you are not able to blind-nail will still be held in place because they interlock with the previous board. Again, apply panel adhesive as you work. You may need to use a surface nail or two as you complete each panel. Just sink it and add putty and it will almost be unnoticeable. Specially chosen knotty redwood was used for the door shown in Illus. 3–10 and 3–11 to add a certain decor, but other contrasting wood colors or grains will work just as well.

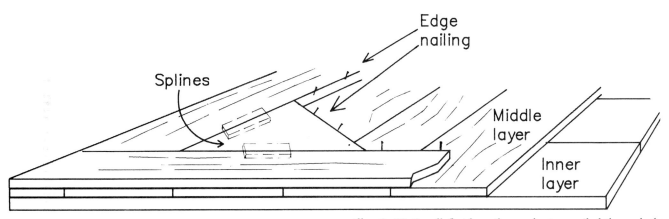

Illus 3–12. Small finish nails can be toe-nailed through the exposed edges of the pieces on the outer layer, or they can be locked into each other with short splines placed as needed.

80 × 36″ Greenhouse Door

Level One

The unique layered door shown in Illus. 3–13 and 3–14 relies more on the outer framework than the middle layer for its strength and rigidity. The middle layer (g in Illus. 3–13) is a sheet of translucent fibreglass material of the type that is often used for greenhouse roofs. It is sometimes called oronyte, lascolite, or flat fibreglass, and can be purchased in 4 × 8-foot sheets, as well as in 50-foot-long rolls. This material cuts easily with a fine-toothed saw, or it can be scored with a knife and broken. Nails can be driven through it without cracking or breaking it so you can make it the full size of the door if you want. It is also alleged to have very good resistance to ultraviolet radiation, and won't turn brown or yellow with age.

To build this door, it is probably easiest to first build the inner frame and clamp the pieces lightly together on the workbench. Also cut the inner brace (f in Illus. 3–13), and toenail it in place with small nails. The inner brace, like the outer brace, has the two decorative cuts on its edge. Mark these cuts carefully on the board with a pencil (make a paper pattern if necessary), and make them with either a narrow band-saw blade or a jig or scroll saw. Once one brace has been cut out, it can be used as a pattern for the other one.

Now, cut the outer layer. Note that the rails for the outer layer run the full width of the door; and that the stiles run the full length on the inner layer. The diagonal brace on the outer layer is also notched into the stiles on both sides. When you have cut all the pieces for both layers, lay them on top of each other to mark the positions of the notches in the stiles for the diagonal brace in the outer layer.

Now, cut the sheet of flat fibreglass to size, and apply a bead of construction adhesive to the upper side of the inner frame all the way around, including the diagonal brace. Position the sheet of fibreglass on top of the inner layer, and apply more construction adhesive to the top of the layer of fibreglass. Now lay the outer layer of wooden pieces in place on top. Use clamps to hold the pieces in place if necessary. Nail the joints together with nails that will project all the way through and protrude about ¼ inch, but don't drive the nails all the way through until most of them are in place.

When you have enough nails in the door to hold all the joints together, remove the clamps, slide one end or edge off the workbench, and drive all the nails in that area through. Then set and clinch them, and slide another part of the door off the edge so that you can nail it. If you have nailed the pieces together adequately, and have used construction adhesive, the door will be very strong.

The pieces of bamboo on the door shown in Illus. 3–13 and 3–14 are purely decorative, and are simply cut to fit between the rails and braces, and then drilled and toenailed into place (Illus. 3–15).

Illus 3–13 and 3–14. Photo and pattern for 80 × 36-inch greenhouse door.

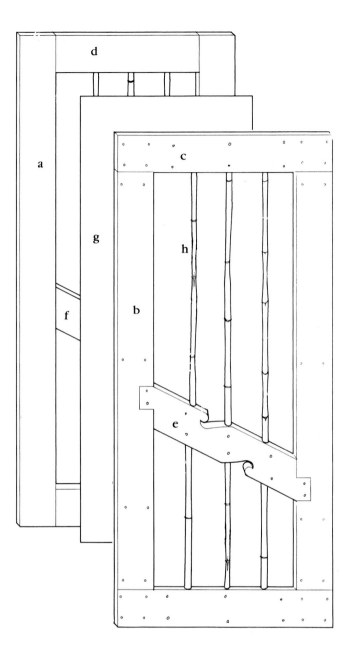

80 × 36″ Greenhouse Door

description	no. of pieces	dimensions
a. stiles	2	80 × 6 × ¾″
b. stiles	2	68 × 6 × ¾″
c. rails	2	36 × 6 × ¾″
d. rails	2	24 × 6 × ¾″
e. diagonal brace	1	34 × 6 × ¾″
f. diagonal brace	1	27 × 6 × ¾″
g. sheet of flat fibreglass	1	72½ × 29″
h. lengths of bamboo	6	72 × ¾–1″

Illus 3–15. The bamboo pieces used on this door are carefully cut to length, and then drilled and toe-nailed to the edge of the 1-inch-thick rail pieces.

76 × 24″ Insulated Sauna Door

Level Two

Though the sauna door shown in Illus. 3–16 and 3–17 is built with the same techniques used for insulated doors, it also incorporates unique and interesting features that might work well on other doors, too. The grooved handle that is applied to the left side of this door works not only as a handle, it also creates a step or rabbet along the side of the door that acts as an extra stop to seal the door more tightly when it is closed (Illus. 3–19). A "ball" or "bullet" catch is used on this door so that people entering and leaving the sauna need only push or pull the door to open and close it (Illus. 3–18).

The method used to incorporate the window in the upper part of this door is a good one to use for windows in any layered door. The window is cut in, and then installed with a jamb and sill just as though it were being installed in a wall. The sill, which projects out from the surface of the door, will help prevent moisture from seeping into the door if the door is located in an exposed setting.

To build this door, first make a frame of 1½ × 1½-inch material that is 1½ inches smaller in both width and height than the finished door will be. Extra rails can be added for strength, if necessary (place them under the horizontal piece of trim in the lower part of the door). The corners of the frame can be nailed (drill to avoid splitting) or screwed together.

Next, apply plywood or other siding material to the side of the frame that is up. Use small nails and construction adhesive to secure this piece to the frame. You may want to cut out the window hole before applying the siding layer to the frame, but it is not absolutely necessary. It can be cut out later with a circular or reciprocating saw.

Now, turn the assembly over and fill the area inside the frame with insulation board—the rigid foam-type will work best. Apply the inner layer of panelling—in this case, 1 × 6 ship-lapped boards—to the frame. Do not use construction adhesive here since panelling in a sauna will shrink and swell a lot, and construction adhesive will prevent it from doing so.

Now, construct the window frame as a separate unit and insert it into the hole. Rabbet the head jamb of the window and the bottom of the side jambs as shown in Illus. 3–20 and nail the pieces together with 4–6d nails. You can make the sill in two pieces; the outside one should run from the inside face of the door to 1 inch past the outside face, with ears that extend out over the outside face. Tack on the inner part when the window is in place. Apply one set of stops to the jamb with small nails and glue, lay the glass in place, and apply the outer stops with nails only.

Before installing the glass, complete the construction of the door. Either mitre the ends of the side and top pieces (a and b in Illus. 3–16) or run the side pieces past the top pieces so that the end grain on the top pieces doesn't show on the sides of the door. Attach these pieces with 6–8d finish nails and construction adhesive. Next, apply the ¼ × 2½-inch trim on both sides of the door with small finish nails, and finally, install the glass. Cut the handle from a piece of 2 × 6-inch material, make a 1 × ½-inch-deep cove cut on both sides with a router that will serve as a fingergrip.

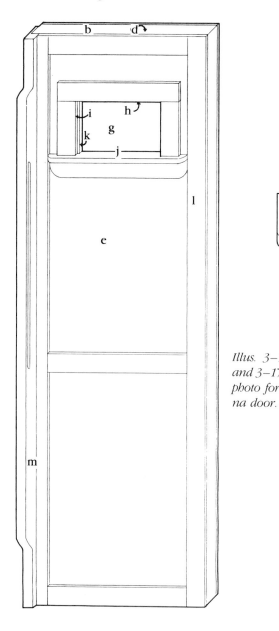

Section

a. Side piece
c. Internal frame stile
f. 1 x 6 t&g siding
Face trim

Insulation
Handle

Stops
Double glazing
Window sill

Illus. 3–16 (left and above) and 3–17 (right). Pattern and photo for 76 × 24-inch sauna door.

76 × 24″ Insulated Sauna Door

description	no. of pieces	dimensions
a. side pieces	2	76 × 3 × ¾″
b. top pieces	2	24 × 3 × ¾″
c. internal frame stiles	2	74½ × 1½ × 1½″
d. internal frame rails	2	19½ × 1½ × 1½″
e. plywood face piece	1	74½ × 22½ × ¾″
f. t&g panelling	13	22½ × 5½ × ¾″
g. insulated glass	1	11 × 7 × ½″
h. head jamb	1	12½ × 3 × ¾″
i. side jambs	2	8¼ × 3 × ¾″
j. window sills	2	19 × 3 × ¾″
k. window stops	60″	1 × ½″
l. trim	32′	2½ × ¼″
m. handle	1	76 × 6 × 1½″

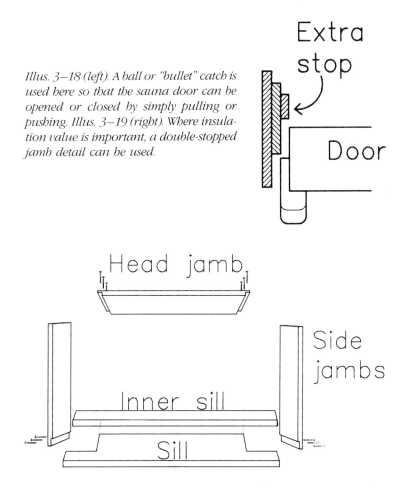

Illus. 3–18 (left). A ball or "bullet" catch is used here so that the sauna door can be opened or closed by simply pulling or pushing. Illus. 3–19 (right). Where insulation value is important, a double-stopped jamb detail can be used.

Illus. 3–20. A simple five-piece window jamb like the one used in this sauna door can be installed in many types of doors.

80 × 36″ Layered Entry Door

Level Two

The cores for the layered door shown in 3–21 and 3–22 were made in an ideal way. Cut a piece of ½ inch-thick exterior-grade plywood (b in Illus. 3–21) so that it's about 2 inches smaller in both height and width than the finished size of the door. Cut pieces of the same type of solid wood (the door illustrated here is made of redwood) as will be used on the outer layers of the door (d); glue these pieces with a waterproof urea resin glue to both the tops and sides of the edges of the plywood. Run the side pieces past the side and bottom pieces of the outer layer so that no end grain shows on the edges of the door. When the glue is dry, plane the joints between the plywood and the redwood so that they are perfectly flush.

Now apply the inner and outer layers to the core, and plane the edges and ends flush. If you glue and clamp the edge boards of the inner and outer layers tightly to the core, you will not have to band the edges afterwards. Most of the exposed end grain will be at the top and bottom on the inner layer, where it won't be visible.

Use tongue-and-groove panelling or straight-edge joined boards for the inner layer, and blind nail and glue it (with construction adhesive) to the core. If the nails project through the core clinch and set them. Use C clamps along the edges to get tight contact between the inner layer and the core. Make sure that you arrange the boards so that the two edge boards are approximately the same width.

Make the outer layer from kiln-dried 1 × 6 boards that do not have tongue-and-grooves on their edges. If necessary, plane the stock down to a ½- or ⅝-inch thickness to ensure that the door is not too thick. You may find it helpful to draw a full-sized pattern of the design or to draw the design on the core of the door to help you position the boards.

First, cut the four boards to form the X in the center of the door. You do not have to trim their ends now. Lay the two with the curved ends out first; then mark the angle for the end cut on the other two parts of the X, and plane or recut the ends of these boards until they meet the edges of the first two boards perfectly.

Clamp the boards that form the X in place, but don't apply any glue yet. Now, start working from the outside, towards the center, cutting and laying out the boards

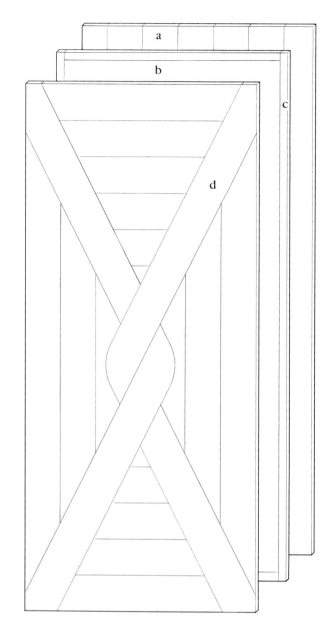

Illus. 3–21 and 3–22. Photo and pattern for 80 × 36-inch layered entry door.

80 × 36" Layered Entry Door

description	no. of pieces	dimensions
a. vertical boards	7	80 × 5½ × ¾"
b. piece of plywood	1	78 × 34 × ½"
c. edge banding	20'	1 × ½"
d. outer layer boards	52 linear feet	5½ × ¾"

that form the field around the X. You may want to make a template out of poster board or thin plywood for the two boards on either side of the center of the X to ensure that you make the cuts precisely. If necessary, you can also plane a little off the edge of the next board to help ensure the precise fit.

When you have fit all the boards together precisely, take each individual board out of the design and sand the outer edges round so that each board appears distinct (Illus. 3–23). Now, remove all the pieces and, beginning with the X again, apply construction adhesive to the inner face and edge-nail the pieces in place. Make sure that you do not apply too much glue and that you push each piece down tightly against the core. Next, glue and nail the "field" pieces in place, working this time from the center towards the edges. Seal the end grain of each piece with varnish before putting it in place. Again, use C clamps around the edges to ensure that they fit tightly against the core. You may have to either drive a few finish nails through the surface and then set and putty them or route short splines into the edges.

Illus. 3–23. Sand the outer edges of all the pieces slightly round to bring out the design.

4
EDGE-JOINED DOORS

Edge joining boards without battens or layering is another way to make a sturdy, solid door. One would think that a method this simple would be used more frequently, but it does have it's limitations. The danger here is not that the door will warp, as with batten doors, but that it will swell or shrink excessively. The boards are glued edge to edge all the way across (most of the swelling will be across the grain, not with it), so there is no built-in mechanism for absorbing their expansion and contraction as in frame-and-panel doors, and no stabilizing core as with layered doors. A 36-inch-wide edge-joined door used in a setting that is exposed to weather can swell and contract as much as ½-inch (Illus. 4–1).

But, if the door is well protected from harsh climatic changes—that is, it is protected by an overhang, is carefully finished, or is situated in a dry climate or in the interior of a building—then there is no reason to shun this method of construction. Splines or tongue-and-groove lumber can be used to strengthen the edge joints, and interesting hardware, small windows, etc., can be included to accent an otherwise understated design. Appliqués and inlays can also be incorporated into edge-joined doors, but anything that runs across a wide expanse of the grain could cause problems.

Use a weatherproof glue when joining wood for exterior doors. Urea-resin-based glues (a powder that is mixed with water) work the best and can be easily cleaned up with a wet rag. Since this type of glue is stronger and has a longer working time than other glues, use it even if you are building interior doors. Yellow and white glues set so quickly that you may not have enough time to complete complicated assemblies before the glue hardens. Also, be sure to apply clamps to both sides of a door when edge joining, and to check the door for flatness with a straight edge (Illus. 4–2). Too much clamp pressure on one side can cause a permanent warp.

Following are some interesting ideas for making edge-joined doors.

CROSS GRAIN SWELLING

Illus 4–1. Cross-grain expansion and contraction can be a problem in edge-joined doors.

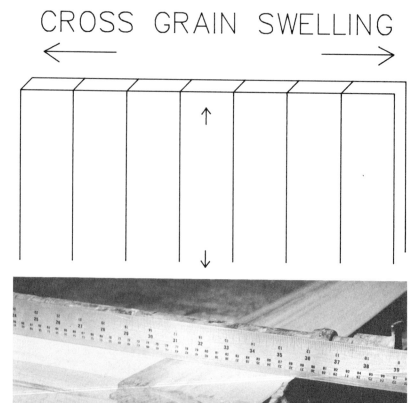

Illus. 4–2. Always put clamps on opposite sides of a door when gluing, and check with a straightedge to be sure the assembly is flat.

80 × 30″ Entry Door

Level Two

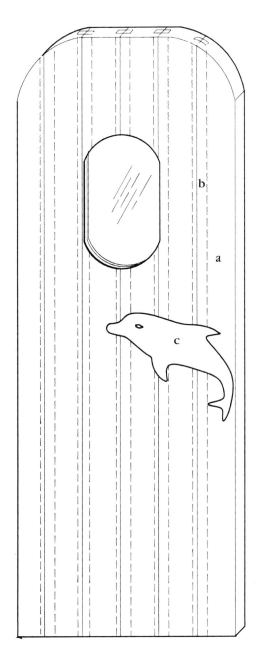

Illus. 4–3 and 4–4. Pattern and photo for 80 × 30-inch entry door. See the following page for building instructions.

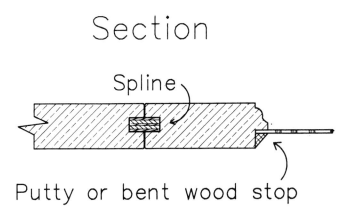

Section

Spline

Putty or bent wood stop

80 × 30″ Entry Door

description	no. of pieces	dimensions
a. upright pieces	6	80 × 5½ × 1½″
b. plywood splines	5	80 × 2 × ½″
c. sheet metal appliqué	1	16 gauge × 16 × 10″

To make a door like the one shown in Illus. 4–3 and 4–4, first joint the edges of the lumber you will use to ensure that the pieces will meet tightly. Then line up the boards to the width needed; plan the layout so that the two edge boards will be about the same width and not too thin. Next, use a dado head on a table saw or a slotting cutter on a heavy-duty router to cut a ½ by ½-inch slot along the edges of each board (except the outer edges). To ensure that the slots will be aligned properly, keep the same faces of the boards up all the time as you lay out and cut. You can either sand or rout a slight roundness or chamfer along the edges of each board to make them more distinct or leave the corners alone for a flat uniform look.

Plywood ½-inch thick will work best for splines because it is already a uniform thickness (careful, it may not be exactly ½-inch thick) and won't split like long strips of solid wood can. You might want to bevel the edges of the plywood strips with a hand plane to make them easier to insert into the slots (Illus. 4–5). Apply a waterproof glue to all the meeting surfaces of the joints and splines, and use bar clamps on alternate sides of the door, about one foot apart, to clamp it together.

When you have clamped the door together, lay a straight edge across it in several places to ensure that it is flat. Be sure to clean up any squeezed-out glue before it sets.

Once the glue has dried, cut the curved top edge and window hole with a jig saw, and clean the cuts with a long flush trimming router bit and template (Illus. 4–6) or, in the case of the outer edges, with just a block plane. Then use a router cutter with ball bearing guides to make the bead and rabbet for the window. An inserted window jamb and sill is not necessary for this type of door, because the wood is edge joined to work as a solid unit. Simply glue the glass in place in the rabbet with clear silicone caulk and putty, or bend and nail in place thin strips of wood as stops.

The dolphin appliqué on this door is cut from sheet metal and painted black. You can make the head jamb for a curved-top door like this from a solid piece of heavy lumber by bending material into a form in the framing, or by bend-laminating strips before installing the jamb.

Illus. 4–5. Bevel the edges of the splines slightly with a hand plane to make them easier to insert in the slots.

Illus. 4–6. A flush trimming bit like the one shown here can be used with a template to clean up the edge of the window cut in this door.

80 × 34″ Rustic Entry Door

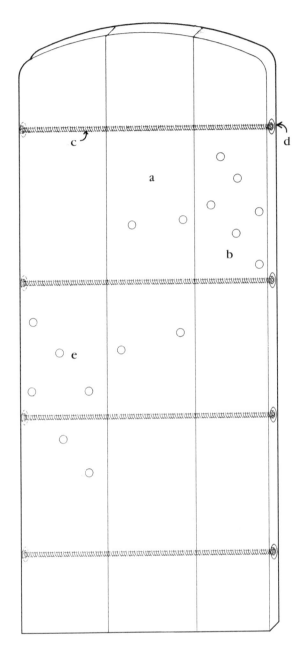

Illus. 4–7 and 4–8. Pattern and photo for 80 × 34-inch rustic entry door. See the following page for building instructions.

80 × 34″ Rustic Entry Door

description	no. of pieces	dimensions
a. vertical boards	2	80 × 12 × 3″
b. vertical board	1	80 × 10 × 3″
c. threaded rods	4	34 × ½″
d. nuts and washers	8	
e. glass marbles	16	1″ dia.

The door shown in Illus. 4–7 and 4–8 was built from recycled 3-inch-thick lumber, and is held together by four pieces of threaded rod that run through the door from edge to edge. Large glass marbles have been glued into bolt holes in the lumber that were there from its previous use.

To build this door, first cut the vertical lumber to a length of about 80 inches, and straighten their meeting edges with a combination of hand planing and electric hand planing. Do not cut these pieces on the jointer; they are too large, and there is the possibility that hidden nails will ruin the jointer blades. Once the edges fit tightly together, lay the boards out with their bottom ends aligned, and mark the positions of the bolts across one face.

Drill a 1½-inch-diameter hole about ¾ inch deep on the outer edges of the edge boards where each bolt will go (Illus. 4–9). This will be the countersink hole for the nuts and washers that go on the ends of each threaded rod. Use a ¾-inch spade bit in an extension shank to drill the holes for the threaded rod; drill through each board separately. If the holes aren't exactly on the mark, make adjustments for where you will start the hole in the next board. The ½-inch rod in the ¾-inch holes should make it possible for you to adjust the bit so that it doesn't wander from the center of the board.

After you have drilled the holes through, cut the pieces of rod to length about ⅜ inch shorter than the width of the door, clean up the threads on the cut ends with a file or thread straightener so that they will accept the nuts, and prepare to insert the rods into the holes. Before bolting the vertical boards together, apply a thin coat of urea resin glue to the meeting edges of the vertical boards. Insert the rods. Place the nuts on the threaded rods. Tighten the nuts with a pair of socket wrenches.

Now trim the "eyebrow" top and bottom of the door and glue the marbles in the holes with a clear silicone caulk. Cut the curved top with a reciprocating saw, and then plane or belt sand it.

The head jamb of this door appears to have been cut from a solid piece of lumber, but a simpler approach would be to apply a piece the thickness of the door to the lumber to form the curved pocket for the door (see Illus. 2–13).

Illus 4–9. First drill a 1½-inch-diameter hole, about ¾-inch deep, to house the nut and washer.

80 × 36″ Modern Entry Door

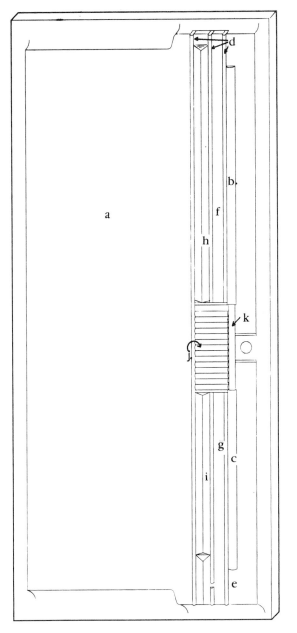

Illus. 4–10 and 4–11. Pattern and photo for 80 × 36-inch entry door. See the following page for building instructions.

80 × 36″ Modern Entry Door

description	no. of pieces	dimensions
a. door body strips	18	80 × 2 × 2¼″
b. half round strip	1	32 × 1¼ × ⅝″
c. half round strip	1	25 × 1¼ × ⅝″
d. flat strips	3	35 × ½ × ½″
e. flat strips	3	28 × ½ × ½″
f. flat strips	1	35 × 2 × ½″

description	no. of pieces	dimensions
g. flat strips	1	28 × 2 × ½″
h. triangular strip	1	35 × 2 × 1¼″
i. triangular strip	1	28 × 2 × 1¼″
j. half sections of brass tubing	15	4¾ × ¾ × ⅜″
k. half sections of brass tubing	1	12 × ¾ × ½″

CROSS SECTION

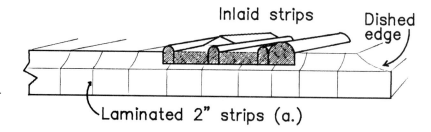

Inlaid strips

Dished edge

Laminated 2" strips (a.)

Illus. 4–12. This cross section shows the ends of the inlaid strips of darker wood.

The beautiful door shown in Illus. 4–10 and 4–11 has a modern feel to it; it is built by laminating and appliquéing strips of various types of wood and pieces of brass tubing in an interesting and eye-pleasing design. The body of the door consists of narrow strips of mahogany, running vertically, that have been edge-glued to the full width of the door. If you are relying solely on flat glue joints to hold the door together, as in this case, then cut strips no wider than a couple of inches (Illus. 4–12). This way, they will be less likely to warp and separate from the next piece.

The thickest part of the door, the whole center area, is 2¼ inches thick, but the outer surface is routed down around the edges with a large cove or raised panel cutter, giving the door the look of one large raised panel.

To build this door, first edge-join strips of mahogany or another light, stable wood to the full width of the door. This can be done in stages; start by gluing the strips into 12-inch-wide sections. Next, run each of these sections through the thickness planer to flatten and smooth them, and then assemble them to the door's full width.

After assembling the sections, flatten and smooth the surface with a plane. Then use a router with a large panel raising bit, with guide boards clamped to the door, to cut the profile around the outer edge. Next, rout the slot, about 6 inches wide and ½ inch deep, from top to bottom along the entire right side of the outer surface of the door with a ¾-inch straight-cutting bit; the pieces of contrasting woods and metal will be applied to this outer surface for decoration.

Now assemble strips of wood, metal, or other material to fill the slot that was just routed. For the door shown in Illus. 4–10 and 4–11, a darker rosewood with striking grain patterns and highly polished surfaces was cut in various ways; the bevels and crosscuts made on it create an interesting ambience. The horizontal pieces of brass tubing were cut in half, probably with a metal-cutting band-saw blade, glued to a halved piece of wooden dowel with an epoxy glue, and then glued into place in the slot (Illus. 4–13). The thin strips of rosewood on either side of the tubing (shown as d in Illus. 4–10) cover the ends of the tubing.

Note also that the rounded piece of rosewood (b) is not set into the slot, but mounted on the raised surface of the door and undercut slightly so that it can be used as a handle when the door is opened. The inner side of this piece is flattened; screws that come through from the other side hold it tightly to the door.

Illus. 4–13. Half pieces of brass tubing, epoxied to dowels and then glued into the door, add a striking contrast to the darker wood.

After studying the techniques explored here, use your artistic talents to create similar designs with just about any material available. Remember, however, that appliqués that run across the grain of edge-joined doors should not be glued in place because they will expand and contract at different rates than the body of the door and could either cause warping or separate from the door.

5
FRAME-AND-PANEL DOORS

The techniques for frame-and-panel door construction have evolved during literally centuries of trial and error. There is evidence that the ancient Egyptians used frame-and-panel construction, and, in essence, the principles of this method are still unchanged. Today, free-floating panels (of either wood or glass) are housed in a slot or between pieces of moulding and suspended in a rigid frame of boards that consists of stiles (vertical side pieces) and rails (horizontal frame pieces). Smaller frame pieces are often called mullions or muntins. These two terms are often used interchangeably, but for the sake of clarity, I will refer to the horizontal pieces as muntins and the vertical pieces as mullions.

Frame-and-panel construction may have developed originally as a more efficient way to use materials or as a way to build doors without the use of either glue or nails. But, more important to today's builder, this technique has the added advantage of allowing the wood to move through it's natural cycles of expansion and contraction without excessive swelling, warping, or cracking. Frame-and-panel doors will still swell and shrink slightly as the seasons change, but if the wood is carefully sealed with paint, varnish, or oil, the door will usually stabilize in a very short time.

Frame-and-panel door construction was once considered a rather specialized craft, limited to the professional jointer. Today, with routers and other power tools and plenty of dimensioned lumber of all kinds available, anyone can build one. Powerful "plunging" routers have revolutionized the building of frame-and-panel doors because they can be used to quickly and easily cut mortises for mortise-and-tenon or spline-tenon joints—the best and most common method of joining rails and stiles.

There are other ways to make these joints, and certainly not everyone owns or even wants to own a plunge router, so before looking into various decorative techniques let's explore various methods of joinery.

Mortise-and-Tenon Joint

The tenon is an extension of the rail or mullion (Illus. 5–1). It is usually about a third of the overall thickness of the frame stock, and fits into a matching slot or hole called the mortise. Doors built 50–100 years ago often have a tenon that runs all the way through the stiles at all four corner joints. This "through" mortise-and-tenon joint was standard then because there were no glues that could be expected to hold the joint together through years of weathering. The through mortise and tenon could be locked in place mechanically either with wedges driven in from the outer edge or with pegs driven into holes bored through the joint (Illus. 5–2 and 5–3).

Making a Mortise and Tenon by Hand

No matter how you cut the joint, it is usually best to first make the mortise, and then cut the tenon to fit it. It is much easier to fine-tune the tenon so that it will fit than to have to work on the mortise.

Mark out the sides of the mortise on both the inner and outer edges of the stile with either a single- or double-toothed marking gauge. If you are using a double-toothed gauge, always work from one side of all the pieces. With a single-toothed gauge, you can be assured that the mortises and tenons will be in the exact center of all the pieces if you mark from both sides.

The top to bottom placement of the mortises on the stiles will depend on the width and placement of the rails. I usually stop the tenons (and mortises) at least

TENON

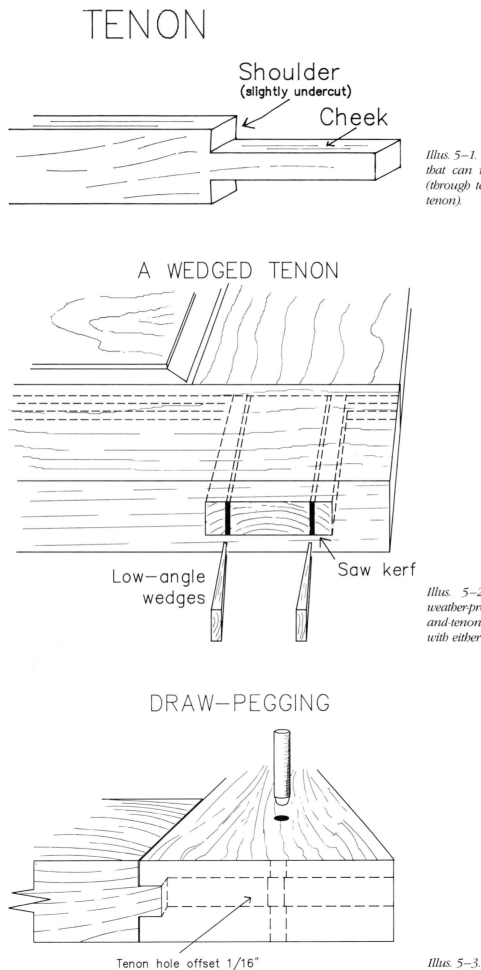

Shoulder
(slightly undercut)

Cheek

Illus. 5–1. The tenon is an extension of the rail that can run all the way through the stile (through tenon) or stop in the middle (blind tenon).

A WEDGED TENON

Saw kerf

Low—angle wedges

Illus. 5–2 and 5–3. Before long-lasting, weather-proof glues were invented, mortise-and-tenon joints were locked mechanically with either wedges (left) or pegs (below).

DRAW—PEGGING

Tenon hole offset 1/16"

Illus. 5–3.

one inch from the top of the door, and two inches from the bottom in case the door has to be trimmed.

To cut the mortise, first bore a series of holes as close together as possible in from both edges until they meet in the center (Illus. 5–4). Don't bore all the way through, as the wood will probably break out when the bit emerges, and the bit may not come out exactly where you planned. After boring, use a mortising chisel of the same width as the mortise (usually ½ inch) to remove the remainder of the waste. A swan's-neck chisel is also handy for mortising, especially if the mortises don't go all the way through (Illus. 5–5).

To make a through tenon, first cut the rail to the full width of the door, and then mark the shoulder cut the width of the stile back from each end. A blind tenon would probably stop an inch or two from each edge of the door, making the rail that much shorter to start with. Use a sharp knife guided by a square to make a "score" cut across the grain of the rail where the shoulder will

be made (Illus. 5–6). Then make a shallow paring cut with a chisel on the tenon side of the score (Illus. 5–7). This will result in a shallow groove in which a sharp back saw can be started.

Before cutting, also mark the shoulder cuts on the edges of the rail to help ensure that the saw cuts squarely. Now, mark the cheek cuts of the tenon along the edges and the ends of the rail using the same marking gauge setting that you used on the mortises.

Cut the shoulder first; keep the saw flat in the groove of the score cut and undercut slightly, if anything, so that the outside of the joint will close tightly. Now remove the waste from the cheeks of the cut either by splitting it if the wood is straight grained and splits easily or by sawing. In either case, cut or split to the outside of the line; then use a rabbet plane to flatten the cheeks of the tenon and get it the proper thickness. Work the cheeks of the tenon carefully until it slides completely through the mortise. The shoulders should both fit tightly against the edges of the stile (Illus. 5–8).

A "haunch" was traditionally left on the top of the tenon of the upper rail and the bottom of the lower rail (also sometimes between two separate tenons on a wide kick rail) to fill the part of the panel slot above and below the tenons (Illus. 5–9). If making one, mark it to

Illus. 5–4. The first step in cutting a mortise by hand is to bore a series of holes to remove as much waste as possible. Never bore all the way through; and, when making through mortises, always bore in from both sides to the middle.

Illus. 5–6. When hand-cutting tenons, first use a sharp knife to score the line where the shoulder will be cut.

Illus. 5–5. A "swan's-neck" chisel can be used for removing the waste from the bottom of blind mortises.

Illus. 5–7. Then pare back from the end of the piece towards the score cut with a chisel, to form a shallow groove in which the hand saw can be started.

(Above) Stylized flowers against a darkly stained background adorn the panels of this weathered door. (Upper right) An unusually wide sun door, made with glass panels set into redwood frames. (Right) Router bits were used to shape the beads and rabbets around the glass and the wooden panels of this door.

(Upper left) This door, made with a solid wood frame and plywood appliqués, is painted in muted colors to match the surrounding elements. (Left) A natural-wood Victorian door with stained glass. (Above) Contrasting woods and interesting lines enliven this custom-made door.

(Above) This elegant entry door was made with a table saw, a router, and a few hand tools. (Upper right) Router cutters with ball-bearing guides and templates can be used to make panels with curves that follow the lines of the frame pieces. (Right) Several layers of 1-inch material can be nailed and glued together to make a very solid door.

(Right) These doors were made with 1-inch material that was blind-nailed over a core. (Below) Custom doors are often designed to work as the focal point of unusual entryways.

Assemblage or layered doors offer a wide variety of design possibilities. The upper door is a three-layered redwood door. The lower door is made from two layers of redwood with a layer of translucent material sandwiched between.

E

(Upper left) The glass panels in this door and the sidelights were made with 6 × 9-inch pieces of bevelled glass. (Upper right) An interesting frame-and-panel door made with mouldings. (Right) Carved and painted appliqués can be used to create intricate visual displays.

(Above) An adze was used to texture the surface of this door. (Upper right) Shoji (screen-like) doors made with paper- or plastic-panel materials in a light wooden frame. (Right) An intricately carved and stained pair of entry doors.

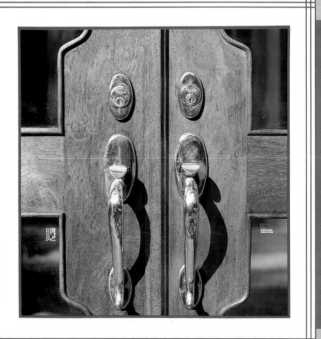

(Upper left) A simple but elegant batten door with a hand-carved wooden handle. (Upper right) A complex pattern and bright colors add interest to this screen door. (Right) Brass hardware, fine hardwoods, and an interesting design.

Illus. 5–8. Make the shoulder cut with a fine-toothed back saw, undercutting slightly so that the outsides of the joint fit tightly.

Illus. 5–9. After cutting the shoulders and the cheeks, cut a "haunch."

the depth of the panel groove and cut it with the back-saw. On the inner side of the tenons, the shoulder cuts will continue around the edge so that the tenon stops about 1 inch in from the edge.

Modern Mortise-and-Tenon Methods

There are several more modern approaches to cutting mortise-and-tenon or spline-tenon joints. Through mortise-and-tenon joints are rarely used today. A blind tenon that is 2½–3 inches long is adequate for most doors less than 42 inches wide, and much quicker to make. Through mortises can be made with these methods, too; simply cut in from both edges until the mortises meet in the middle.

Whenever possible, position the mortises in the exact center of the edge of the stiles. Even if the panel slot is offset for one reason or another, the mortise should be centered. This will save time and effort in the cutting of the tenons, because once the table saw is set, the pieces can simple be run through twice—once on each side—to make a perfectly centered tenon.

The best method for centering the mortises is to use a machinist's calipers to carefully check the thickness of the cheeks on either side of a test piece that is exactly

the same thickness as the frame stock you are using (Illus. 5–10). Set the guide fence on the drill press or router as close to centered as you can get it by lining up the cutter on the marks you have made with your marking gauge; then make a test cut, and check it with the calipers. When the cheeks are exactly the same thickness, the mortises are centered. Keep the calipers handy while you are cutting the mortises, and check every couple of cuts to make sure that the mortises stay accurate.

Using the Drill Press or Mortise Machine

Until very recently, the most common method of machine-cutting mortises was with a drill press or mortising machine and a square chisel-boring attachment (Illus. 5–11). These attachments come in sizes from ¼- to ½-inch thick and will usually cut no deeper than 3 inches in one cut. The twist bit inside the hollow chisel bores the middle of the hole and removes the waste; the square chisel is advanced by downward pressure, and squares out the hole. Do not overheat these chisels; this will ruin the temper of the steel. The bits and chisels can be purchased separately, and are quite expensive. A special quill attachment is also necessary for this type of mortising, as well as a fence and hold-down attachment that is bolted to the drill-press table.

Illus. 5–10. Use a machinist's calipers to check the thickness of the cheeks of the mortise to be sure that it is centered.

Illus. 5–11. A square chisel-boring attachment can be used on either a drill press or mortising machine to cut mortises.

If you plan to mortise this way, go ahead and mark out the positions of the mortises in the same manner as that described on page 62 of this section. If you are making several doors with the same configuration, mark out the positions of the mortises on only one of them; then lay them out side by side with the inside edges up, and use a square to transfer the position markings from one to the other (Illus. 5–12). You won't have to use the marking gauge to mark the sides of the mortises because they will be automatically positioned by the fence once it is set up.

When you are using this method, an outfeed roller or table extension of some kind will be necessary to support one end of the stile while you are working on the other end. If you have carefully centered the mortise on the edge of the piece, you will be able to work from either side, which will eliminate having to move the support roller from one end to the other.

When everything is properly lined up, cut one hole at the end of the mortise; then move down and make the next cut about ¼ inch away from the first one. Continue in this manner until you have covered the entire length of the mortise. Leaving this space between your cuts will prevent the chisel from deflecting towards the hole you have just cut, which can cause damage to the cutters. Now, go back and center your cutter on the areas between the holes, and remove the remaining waste.

Mortising with the Plunge Router

In the last few years, the plunge router has become a popular tool for cutting mortises. For this method, you need a ½-inch-collet plunge router with a rating of at

Illus. 5–12. You can use a square to mark the ends of several mortises at once.

least 1½ horsepower and a fence attachment. A spiral-fluted ½-inch by 2½-inch carbide cutter will give the best results and last the longest in both hard and soft woods (Illus. 5–13).

Illus. 5–13. Either a straight or spiral-fluted router cutter will work well when you are plunge-routing mortises. One-half inch shank bits are available that will cut up to 3 inches deep.

Mark the positions of the mortises on the edges of the stiles as already described; then put a trial piece that's the same thickness as your frame stock in the bench vise, and carefully set the fence on the router base so that it cuts a slot that is perfectly centered on the edge of the piece. Make as many test cuts on the trial piece as you need to be sure that it is right. Plunge the bit into the wood and move it slowly along the work until you find the depth of cut that works well without overloading the router or causing the bit to chatter. You will note during these test cuts that when you cut in one direction, the rotating bit holds the fence tightly against the work, while in the other direction it tends to "wander." Make all your cuts in the direction that holds the fence to the work.

Once you have the fence set right, tighten the setscrews as tightly as possible by hand. A pair of pliers can be used to get them a little tighter, but be careful not to crack the castings of the router base. Now, take your marking gauge and set it for the exact center of the edge of the workpiece. Mark the center of the edge at the end of the mortise where you will be starting all your cutting passes, and bore a half-inch hole here to the depth that the mortise will be cut (Illus. 5–14). This is to ease the entry of the router bit into the wood. Most straight-

Illus. 5–14. If you prebore a ½-inch or smaller hole at the starting end of the mortise before routing, you will make it easier to enter the bit and will prevent overheating.

cutting router bits do not bore well (though they will if enough pressure is applied), and will last considerably longer if you bore the starter hole separately.

Once you have bored all the starter holes, begin cutting the mortises. Drop the bit into approximately the right depth, lock the plunge mechanism, and draw the router slowly along the work until you reach the other end. When you reach the other end of the mortise, release the plunge lock, and pull the bit all the way out of the mortise before moving it back to the starting hole. A 3-inch-deep mortise can be made with 4 to 10 passes, depending on the hardness of the wood.

You can make through mortises in stiles up to 6 inches wide simply by marking carefully on both edges and cutting in from both edges to the middle. Deeper mortises can be routed, and then bored, and finally chiselled with a mortising chisel of the proper width.

Generally, a board 1½-inches thick, or thicker, will provide a wide enough surface to stabilize the router while doing this type of mortising, but for narrower stock, a mortising jig like the one shown in Illus. 5–15 can be made. The jig holds the stiles or rails firmly and triples the width of the surface that the router base rides on. Adjustable end stops can also be incorporated in the jig.

It is possible to make your own horizontal mortiser using a plunge router and a sliding table mechanism that is sold as an accessory for Inca table saws (Illus. 5–15). Once again, an outboard roller will be necessary to support one end of a stile while you mortise the other.

A SHOP—MADE MORTISING MACHINE

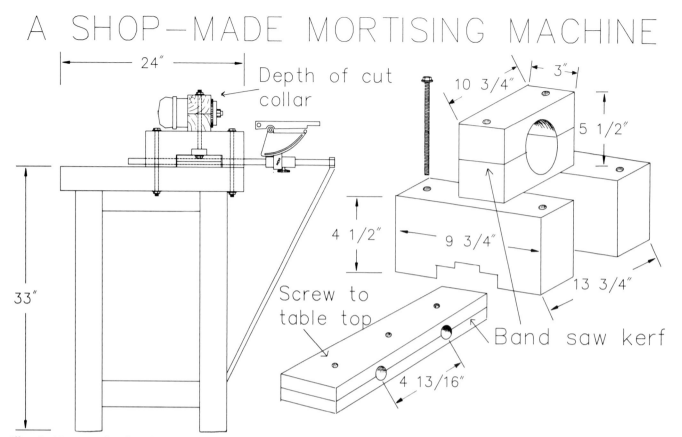

Illus 5–15. For a few hundred dollars, you can make your own horizontal mortiser which uses a heavy-duty router motor and a sliding table (which moves from side to side and in and out) that's available as an accessory for Inca table saws.

Making Tenons

The other half of the mortise-and-tenon joint, the tenon, must be cut with equal care (if you elect to use this method) so that the joint will be as strong as possible and close tightly on both sides.

The shoulder cut is the most critical part of the cutting sequence for the tenon. It must be perfectly square both across the rail and when viewed from the edge. It may help to set your saw blade so that it actually undercuts the shoulder a bit, ensuring that the outer edges of the joint will close tightly. The most accurate way to do this is with a table saw and a clamp-on fence that is square and parallel to the blade. If you are cutting a through tenon, you can use the stile to get your fence set at the right distance and parallel to the blade, as shown in Illus. 5–16.

Use a scrap piece of wood the same thickness as the frame stock to test the height of the cut until it leaves a tenon that is just right for the mortise. As you make the cuts, keep the end of the workpiece tight against the fence and be careful not to cock it one way or the other. This method is safe as long as the end of the piece is at least 4 inches wide. For narrower pieces, use a sliding cutoff table with a clamp-on stop.

Now you can remove the waste from the cheeks of the tenon by any of several methods. If the tenon is fairly short, you may be able to remove the waste with two more cuts with the table saw by raising the blade as high as the length of the tenon, and resetting the fence closer to the blade. Now stand the rail on end and run it against the fence so that it will remove the waste from each side in one cut.

Other options for longer tenons that can't be cut with the table saw include repeated cuts across the length of the cheeks, splitting, and planing the tenon to the desired thickness; and band-sawing carefully along lines drawn with a marking gauge. If you band-saw, be sure to stay outside the lines (Illus. 5–18) and use a plane to get the tenon to its final thickness.

Spline-Tenon Joint

The spline-tenon joint is a variation on the mortise-and-tenon joint in which mortises are cut both on the edges of the stiles and the ends of the rails, and a long spline is glued into both pieces to hold them together (Illus. 5–19). With the plunge router method of cutting mortises, it is quite easy to cut a mortise into the end of the rail (an operation that would be nearly impossible on a drill press). A piece of 2 × 6 clamped to the bench surface as shown in Illus. 5–20 or a mortising jig like the one shown in Illus. 5–15 will help steady the router and keep it square to the edge while you are working the

Illus. 5–16. If you are making a through tenon, you can use the stile to help position the fence.

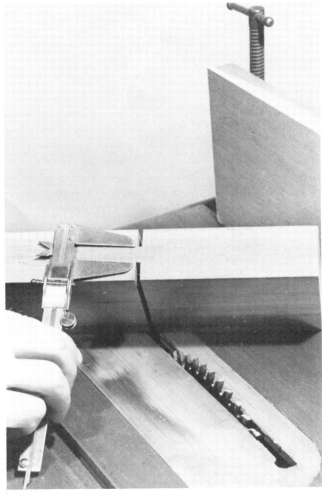

Illus. 5–17. Use the calipers again to check the shoulder cut you made on a piece of scrap to be sure that the tenon will be the precise thickness.

Illus. 5–18. A band saw can be used to remove the waste from the cheeks of a tenon, but be sure to cut to the outsides of the lines, and hand-plane to the final thickness.

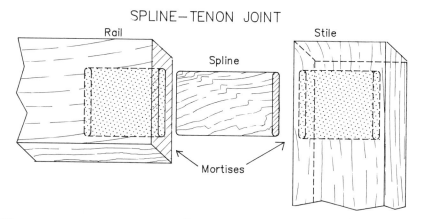

Illus. 5–19. The spline-tenon joint, a variation on the mortise-and-tenon joint, works well with modern weatherproof glues, and greatly simplifies door construction.

Illus. 5–20. When plunge-routing the mortises on the ends of the rails, hold the workpiece in an end vise that is level with the top of a wide piece of two-by material clamped to the bench (check to be sure that the material is perfectly square to the workpiece) to steady the router. The wide piece of two-by is used to lift the router.

shorter rail ends. This method can save considerable time and materials because the splines can be made from scrap or end cuts, and because you won't have to take the time to carefully set up the table saw for at least two different cuts for the tenons. The same setting of the router fence is used on both the stiles and the rail ends. This method is also helpful when you are making cope-and-stick joints because there is no tenon to get in the way of the cope cut.

Dowelling

Dowelling is an acceptable method of joining stiles and rails for interior doors, but it is not recommended for any exterior doors because it lacks the strength to hold the joint firmly through years of weather-induced swelling and shrinking, as well as general use (Illus. 5–21). The good gluing-surface area between the dowel and the stile is minimal because much of the wood in the stile that comes in contact with the dowel is end grain. End grain does not hold well when glued to edge grain. Dowelled joints will often begin to separate within just a few years if the door is not well protected from the elements.

If you are going to use dowels in a door, make sure they are at least ½ inch thick and as long as possible. You can make your own dowels by ripping stock to ½ × ½-inch sticks, and then rounding them off with four passes of a ¼-inch round-over bit on the router table. Finally, drive them through a dowel sizer to groove and size them (Illus. 5–22). Space them about 1½ inches apart, and coat both the insides of the holes and the dowel itself with glue before assembly. Avoid hammering the dowels into their holes, as the sudden blows can cause the lumber to crack. A slot or kerf along the length of the dowel will allow the glue to flow out of the hole without building up enough pressure to cause cracking. Bevelling the tips with a pencil sharpener or disc sander will also ease the assembly.

Use either a dowelling jig and electric hand drill or a horizontal boring machine to bore the holes for the dowels. Dowelling jigs can be slow and tedious to use, but they are accurate, and are cheap compared to a horizontal boring machine.

Clamping and Gluing Techniques

Intricate panel doors can be difficult to assemble even after you have dry-assembled the door several times and have ensured that the joints fit tightly. Here I'll cover some of the basics that apply to clamping and

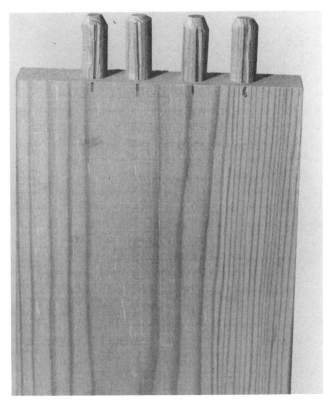

Illus. 5–21. Dowelled corner joints are acceptable for interior doors (which don't swell and contract with the weather), but do not hold well enough for exterior use.

Illus. 5–22. Always drive dowels through a sizer to prevent splitting caused by swollen or oversized dowels.

gluing all frame-and-panel doors. Later, I'll point out good strategies for specific doors. When you are satisfied that the dry pieces fit together properly, make indexing marks across every joint (all on one side of the door) so that you will know when you have the pieces in exactly the right places during the final assembly.

For even a fairly easy panel door, you'll need at least six heavy-duty bar clamps about 3–4 feet long. If the door has vertical mullions, you will probably also need two bar clamps long enough to clamp the door from top to bottom. A layout table or bench with a vise is also very handy, but you may prefer to work on sawhorses with a piece of plywood on top of them to help support the pieces. Begin by covering the meeting surfaces of all the joints and the splines or dowels with urea resin glue (mix according to directions).

One approach is to work flat on the assembly surface, loosely assembling all the rails, panels, and mullions after they have been coated with glue. Slide the panels into their slots, and use bar clamps as necessary to bring the joints close together. If the joinery fits correctly, the joints will slide together without excessive pressure. You can use a mallet to lightly tap the pieces into place, but avoid heavy blows and never apply the mallet to the moulded or shaped areas of the work.

An alternative to assembling the pieces flat on the work surface is to stand one stile held firmly in a vise, or with clamps, on edge, with the outside edge down, and to build up vertically from this stile (Illus. 5–23). This is advantageous for two reasons: you can use gravity to

help fit the pieces together, and it will be easier to get clamps on both sides of the door. A clamping stand like the one shown in Illus. 5-24 will also help expedite the gluing process. This stand can become a permanent fixture in your shop; if possible, keep it in a small room of its own that can be easily heated to about 90F (so that the glue can be cured quickly).

When the joints are almost tight, check your indexing marks to be sure that they are coming together properly aligned; if they aren't, clamp or tap the pieces with a mallet to align them.

If you have vertical mullions, you can get them tight against the rails by clamping from top to bottom with two long bar clamps. To do this, take off all the horizontal clamps and put the long clamps on the same side of the door, near the ends of the rails. Tighten them until the ends of the mullions are all positioned firmly against the rails. Now, measure from top to bottom at both ends of the rails, and tighten any one of the clamps until the distance is the same. This will ensure that the rails are parallel.

Now, with the stiles in place on the ends of the rails put horizontal clamps on the opposite side of the door from the long clamps, one on the top rail, and one on the bottom rail. Tighten both horizontal clamps. Remove the vertical clamps, and add more horizontal clamps to complete the glue-up. Make sure that you put clamps on alternate sides of the door at each rail, and check with a straight edge to be sure that the stiles are flat with the rails.

ASSEMBLING A 4-PANEL DOOR

1.

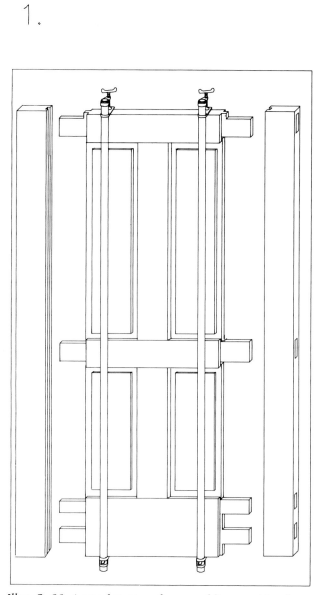

2.

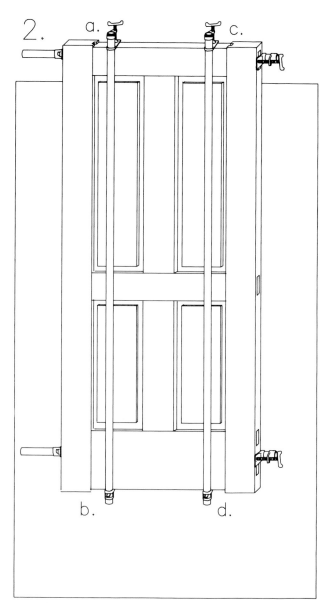

Illus. 5–23. A good strategy for assembling complex frame-and-panel doors like this four-panel door is to first lightly clamp the rails and mullions together and insert the panels. Then work the stiles in place on the tenons, and, when they are in contact, cross-clamp one end tight; use the long clamps to tighten and square the rails on the mullions. Make sure that the mullions are centered on the rails and that the distance from A to B and C to D as shown in the drawing is the same. Then apply another cross clamp at the other end and remove the long clamps. Add more cross clamps opposite the existing ones to even the pressure.

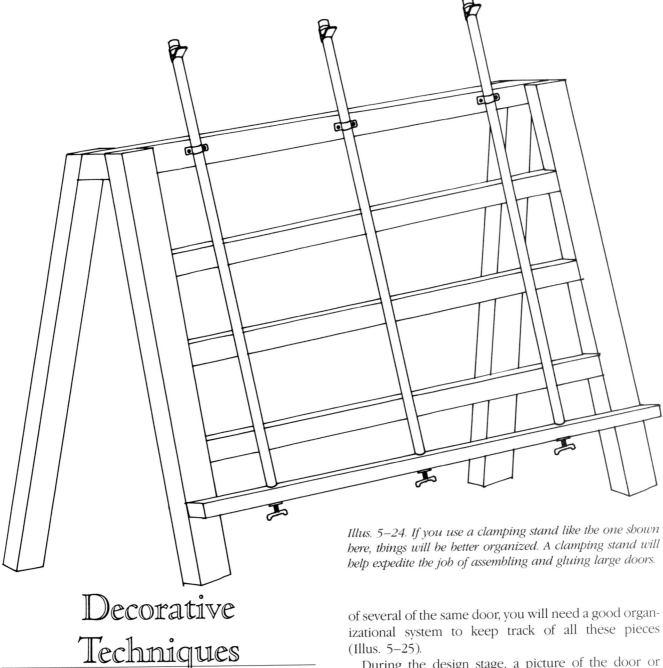

Illus. 5–24. If you use a clamping stand like the one shown here, things will be better organized. A clamping stand will help expedite the job of assembling and gluing large doors.

Decorative Techniques

Once you have mastered the basic joinery methods, you can use any of a number of decorative techniques to achieve the effects you want. The following sections in this chapter examine ways to use these techniques without a shaper. Chapter 7 explores shapers and shaper bits, and shows how doors can be made with cope-and-stick joinery.

Organizing Your Production Run

A standard, four-panel door consists of over a dozen separate pieces, and multi-light French-style doors can have many more. If you are making several doors of varying sizes and designs, or even a production run

of several of the same door, you will need a good organizational system to keep track of all these pieces (Illus. 5–25).

During the design stage, a picture of the door or doors to be built is nearly always drawn. Use this drawing to generate a complete list of all the pieces you will need for each door you will be making during your production run. You can refer to this list as you purchase the lumber for the job, but generally you have to rely on a lot of guesswork at this stage because there are often hidden defects and surprises in the rough boards that won't become apparent until you begin to rip and plane them. For this reason, you should always purchase at least 25% more lumber than you think is needed.

As soon as you have cut all the pieces for a door, lay them out on the workbench and label them with a number to identify the door, and a letter or two to identify the piece and where it goes. Keep the pieces for each door in their own separate piles as you work on them, and be sure to number and name each piece so that you can easily tell which door it belongs to and where it goes in that door (Illus. 5–26). Write the name

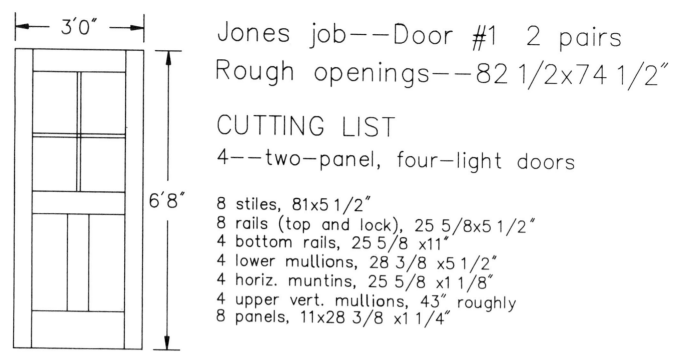

Jones job--Door #1 2 pairs
Rough openings--82 1/2x74 1/2"

CUTTING LIST
4--two-panel, four-light doors

8 stiles, 81x5 1/2"
8 rails (top and lock), 25 5/8x5 1/2"
4 bottom rails, 25 5/8 x11"
4 lower mullions, 28 3/8 x5 1/2"
4 horiz. muntins, 25 5/8 x1 1/8"
4 upper vert. mullions, 43" roughly
8 panels, 11x28 3/8 x1 1/4"

Illus. 5–25. If you use a drawing and a cutting list, especially when making several doors, you will be much better organized.

Illus. 5–26. To avoid confusion, mark and stack the pieces for each door together.

and number on one side of the door only, and always in the same relation to the bottom of the door, so that you can easily reassemble each door in the proper sequence just by looking at the markings. A flat cart on wheels or a dolly will be very helpful in moving the piles of pieces for each door around the shop to the various places where they will be worked on.

How to "Raise" Panels

Yes, panels do grow on trees, but when I say we are going to raise them, I actually mean we are going to lower the edges around the panels by using one of

many possible methods of shaping or wood removal. This makes the central part of the panel look as if it is raised, and thins out the edge so that it will fit into a slot in the framework. Panel raising with shapers is covered in Chapter 7. Here I'll explore several ways to raise panels without shapers.

Only carefully dimensioned lumber should be used for panels. Variations in thickness, length, or width will cause major problems later. There is very little leeway for error when you are fitting panels into slots. They must fit tightly, but not so tightly as to split the wood or prevent the joints from closing. Also, the panels should be ⅟₁₆–⅛ inch shorter and narrower in both directions than the size of the hole (from bottom of slot to bottom of slot), so that the panel can swell a little without forcing the framework apart. The larger the panel, the more it is likely to swell, so avoid making large solid-wood panels. Use exterior-grade plywood if you must make a panel that is more than 12 inches wide.

The simplest type of panel is a flat panel. In some situations, flat panels are fine, but they are plain looking, and, because they are thin, weak. Before power tools were available, panel raising hand planes were used to plane down the edges of raised panels. They had a specially shaped cutting iron, and a spur to score the grain when cutting across the grain (Illus. 5–27).

A simple rabbet, cut with the table saw around the edges on one or both sides of the panel, will often be all that's needed to give the look of a raised panel and improve the panel's strength. The table saw can also be set to cut at an angle so that the panel edge is bevelled, thus wedging tightly in the slot of the framework. The shoulder of the rabbet can also be cut at a bevel to improve the look of the panel.

Whenever you are using the table saw to raise panels, be sure to use the finest toothed blade you have; also, cut so that the panels will be slightly too thick for the slots as they come off the saw. You will still have to plane and/or sand to smooth the saw kerf, and this will thin the panels noticeably. It is also essential that the table insert be perfectly flush with the table. I have a special, extra-tall clamp-on fence that I use for work like this because it is hard to control large panels with a normal rip fence (Illus. 5–29).

Illus. 5–27. Before the advent of power tools, raised panels were made with special panel-raising planes that had a spur to score the grain and a skewed blade to cut cleanly across the grain.

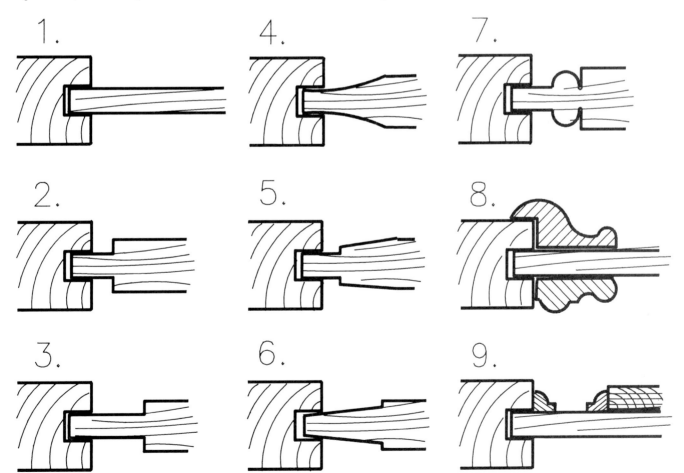

Illus. 5–28. A wide variety of panel and moulding details are possible, even when you are working with simple tools. The details shown here and many more can be made with hand planes, hand or power saws, routers, and shapers, or with applied mouldings.

Illus. 5–29. If you use an extra-tall, clamp-on fence when shaping panel edges on the table saw, you will get more accurate results.

Sawn and routed raised panels

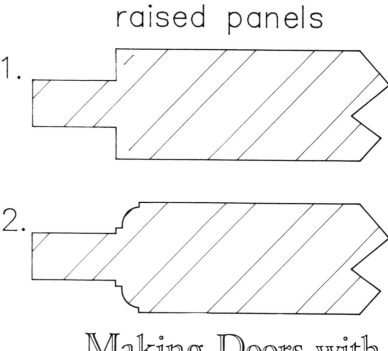

Illus. 5–30. Intricate cuts can be made if you first cut a rabbet with a table saw (1), and then shape the hard edge with a router bit (2).

Panel-raising router bits are available today in many different patterns. They cut very cleanly when sharp, so little or no sanding is necessary. They will often follow curves as well, but are limited as to how deep or wide a cut they can handle. Sometimes the hard edge of a table-saw-cut rabbet can be shaped with a router bit to create interesting effects (Illus. 5–30).

A final method of literally raising panels consists of laminating pieces to a core. Generally, it is best to use plywood or thin pieces of solid wood when doing this. Mouldings can be applied around the raised laminations to give them a fancier look, or the edges of the laminations themselves can be routed. Epoxy glue is the best for this type of laminating, since it holds well, even if the pieces don't meet tightly. Urea resin glues or construction adhesive will also work, but should probably be used in conjunction with nails. Clamping can be difficult, but as long as the pieces make good contact around the edges, the lamination will probably hold.

Making Doors with Mouldings

Applied mouldings were one of the main staples of the pre-router door builder, and this technique offers even more creative potential today than it did 50 or a 100 years ago because of the incredible variety of manufactured mouldings that can be purchased. (Illus. 5–31—5–33.) Router bits are also available now that allow you to create your own custom mouldings of just about any size, thickness, or curvature that you might need (Illus. 5–34).

I've divided mouldings into two general categories: low- and high-profile mouldings. Low-profile mouldings (Illus. 5–35), usually no more than ½ inch thick, can be applied just about anywhere, including around the inner edges of the frame pieces next to panels, around the raised part of a panel, as stops for glass, and

Illus. 5–31 to 5–33. Applied mouldings used around panel and window frames were a staple of old-fashioned door builders.

Illus. 5–32.

Illus. 5–33.

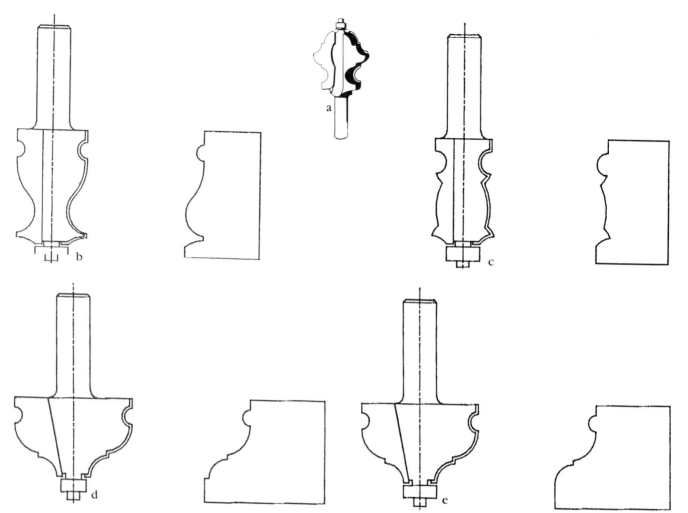

Illus. 5–34. Router bits are now available for making a wide variety of complex mouldings.

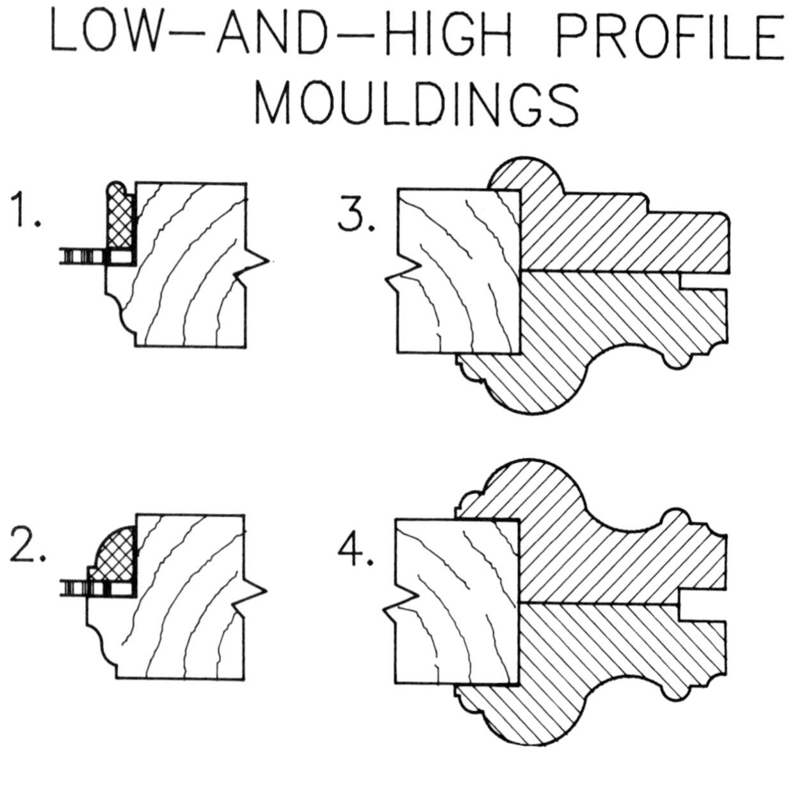

LOW–AND–HIGH PROFILE MOULDINGS

Illus. 5–35. Low-profile mouldings (1 and 2) stay below the surface of the door, while high-profile mouldings (3 and 4) are rabbeted over the framework edge.

BOLECTION MOULDED PANEL

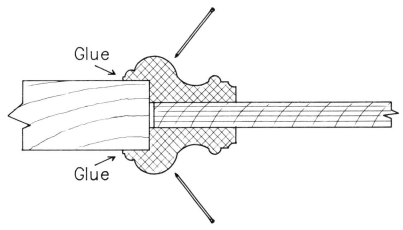

Glue

Glue

Illus. 5–36. High-profile moulding, nailed and glued in place, can be used to hold a panel without the need for cutting a slot in the framework.

even on flush doors to give them the look of panel doors. High-profile mouldings (also called bolection mouldings), on the other hand, are used only around the inner edges of a frame to cover the hard corner of a frame piece, and make a bold and attractive transition from frame to panel or glass. High-profile mouldings can even be used to create a "slot" to hold a panel where none exists (Illus. 5–36).

Mitring Mouldings

Always mitre mouldings where they meet other mouldings. There are several techniques that you can use, but if you follow one rule, you will be able to accurately mitre any type of moulding. The rule is as follows: The angle of the mitre (the cut on the end of each moulding) is always half the overall angle between the meeting pieces. When you apply this rule to your work, you will ensure that all the lines of two pieces of moulding will meet exactly (Illus. 5–37 and 5–38). You can bisect any moulding angle by measuring out a set distance from the vertex on each piece, and then finding the midpoint of a line drawn between these two points. A line from the vertex to this midpoint will give the end cut angle for both mouldings. When curved mouldings meet straight ones, or other curves, the lines of the mitre may actually be curved.

Simple 45-degree mitre cutting can usually be done quite accurately with either a hand or electric mitre box; it is also possible to set up a table or radial arm saw to do this work. Use a fine-toothed saw blade, and be sure that the saw is cutting square in the vertical plane, as

well as cutting an accurate 45-degree angle in the horizontal plane. Cut one end of the moulding first; then hold it up to the space it is to fit into and mark the edge with a sharp knife exactly where it is to be cut. You can usually make the second end cut simply by flipping the piece over rather than resetting the saw for each cut. Cut a little long, if anything, to start with; then, if necessary, recut for the perfect fit. It is often possible to jam a moulding that is slightly too long into the place it is to fit into, but this will make the next piece fit poorly. The only way to get good results is to accurately cut the pieces to length.

Mitring bolection-type mouldings is slightly more difficult, because the marking for the second end cut must be made on the underside of the rabbet on the back of the moulding. To make this mitre cut, start by mitring one end of the stock (Illus. 5–39). Now, lay the moulding in place and mark where the rabbet meets the stile (Illus. 5–40). Remember, your marks must be on the inside edge of the rabbet, not on the outer edge of the moulding that will lap over the frame of the door. Now, flip the moulding over, with the inside face up, for the final cut (Illus. 5–41). You will probably have to tack a strip of wood of the right thickness to your cutting table so that the moulding will be cut flat. Cut the mitre directly through the mark. To get good results, pay careful attention when setting up the saw and support strip.

To cut very complicated mitres, such as curved mouldings or places where several mouldings come together, first make a paper model that shows the lines formed by all the elements of the pieces. Snip the ends of the paper pieces until you find the proper angles, and then transfer them to your work.

MITRING MOULDING AND   MUNTINS

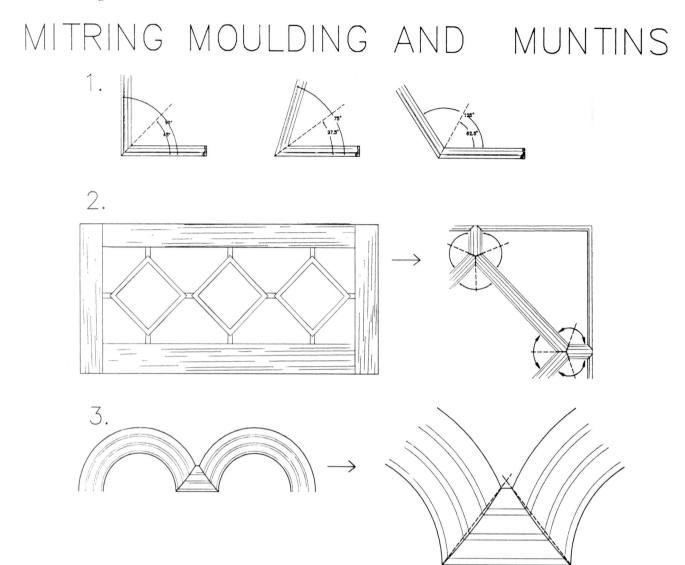

Illus. 5–37. The golden rule in mitring mouldings, as shown in number 1, is that the angle of the mitre should be half the overall angle between the meeting pieces. Number 2 shows how this rule applies when more than two mouldings (or muntins) meet. Number 3 demonstrates that when curved mouldings meet straight ones or other curves, this mitre is often curved. For very complex mouldings, mark the various elements of each moulding on a piece of paper, and find the right mitre angle on the paper before cutting the mouldings.

BISECTING MOULDING ANGLES

Illus. 5–38. To find the right angle for mitring straight mouldings that don't come together at 90 degree angles, bisect the angle by measuring out equal distances on both legs of the angle (AB and BC). Then draw a line between these two points, and find the mid-point of this line (AC). The mitre line will run through this point.

Illus. 5–39. To apply bolection-type mouldings, mitre one end, as shown here, lay the moulding in place, and mark the other end where the back of the rabbet meets the stile.

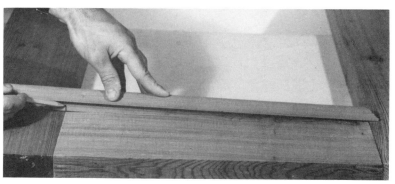

Illus. 5–40. Next, tack a stick of scrap of the right height to the cutoff saw table to support the moulding so that the flat side of it is parallel to the table.

Illus. 5–41. Finally, make the cut through the point you marked.

80 × 36" Moulded Entry Door

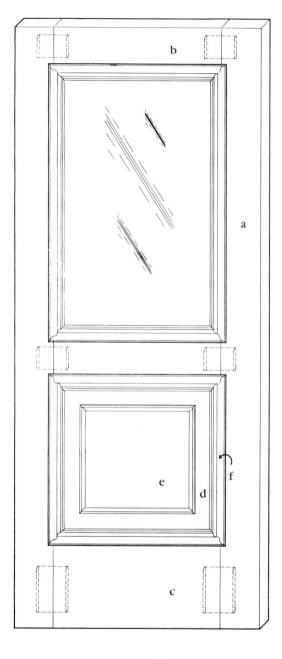

Illus. 5–42 and 5–43. Pattern and photo for 80 × 36-inch moulded entry door.

80 × 36" Entry Door

description	no. of pieces	dimensions
a. stiles	2	80 × 5½ × 1⅝"
b. top and mid rails	2	23 × 5½ × 1⅝"
c. bottom rail	1	23 × 11½ × 1⅝"
d. plywood panel	1	24 × 23 × ½"

description	no. of pieces	dimensions
e. panel laminations	2	14 × 13 × ½"
f. thick moulding	26'	2¼ × 1¼ × ⅞"
g. flat moulding	10'	2⅛ × ⅝"
h. small moulding	10'	⅜ × ⅜"

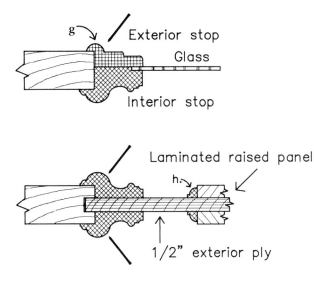

Illus. 5–44. Cross sections of door showing the mouldings and panel construction.

The door shown in Illus. 5–42 and 5–43 is a simple one that combines several different techniques for using mouldings in door construction. The bolection moulding used here is sold as a wainscott cap-moulding, and is available through many specialty moulding dealers. You can also make similar mouldings with various types of router bits. Make the panels from three ½-inch-thick laminations of plywood or solid wood; glue and nail a small applied moulding around the "raised" parts of the panel (Illus. 5–44).

To build this door, first cut the frame pieces to their lengths and widths; then make the joints that hold the rails to the stiles. Position the lock rail so that its top edge is 39 inches above the bottom of the door. Now, carefully dry-assemble the door and clamp it so that all the rails are in the exact positions they will occupy after the final glue-up. Use a slotting cutter in the router to route the slot for the panel in the lower part of the door (Illus. 5–45). Either make two passes with a ¼-inch cutter, or, if possible, stack two cutters to make the cut in one pass. If you make two passes, one from each side of the door, the slot will be exactly centered.

When you have cut the slots all the way around, disassemble the door and square out the ends of the cuts on the stiles by chopping straight in with a sharp chisel (Illus. 5–46). The ends of the rails may need a little attention, too.

Next, measure the hole for the panel; be sure to cut the panel at least ¹⁄₁₆-inch smaller in both directions than the size of the hole. Now, set your marking gauge for two inches and mark the positions for the corners of the panel laminations on both sides of the panel. Use these marks to determine the size of the laminations, and cut them out.

Finally, coat the insides of the laminations with a thick but even coat of glue, and clamp them in place, doing both sides at once. Once the glue has set, nail and glue the mouldings in place on the lower panel. Be sure to completely sand and coat all the panels with an oil or sealer before assembling the door. It is especially important to seal the edges and end grain. You may want to

dry-assemble the door at this point to make sure that the panel will fit into the slots.

When the fit is right, glue the frame together; make sure that all the joints are very flat and won't need much hand planing after the glue is dry. Bolection mouldings are difficult to apply if the framework is not flat and uniformly thick.

After completely planing and sanding the frame, cut the mouldings and apply them with nails and glue. Only the exterior glass stop should not be glued in place. This way, the glass can be replaced, if necessary. Sink and putty all nails.

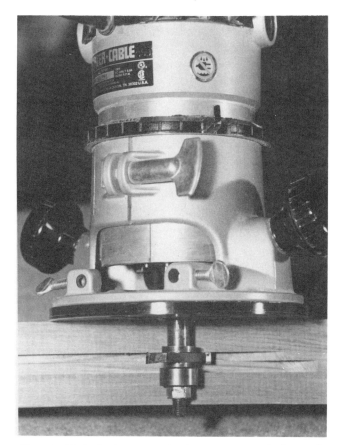

Illus. 5–45. A slotting cutter in the router or a dado can be used to cut the slots that hold the lower panel.

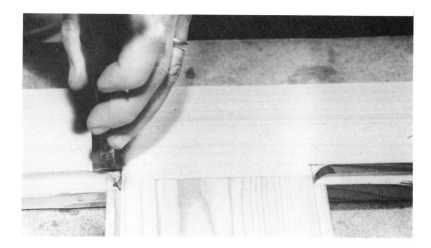

Illus. 5–46. Mark and chop the corners out square with a sharp chisel.

APPLIQUÉS

Appliqués were another favorite technique of past doormakers. You can glue and nail just about any kind of appliqué to a door as long as you do not run a piece that's too long or thick across the direction of the grain. Appliqués were often used in conjunction with mouldings to create very intricate visual effects (Illus. 5–47). Carved pieces, metal work, and plaster can also be applied to both panels and framework.

Certain styles and reoccurring themes developed that utilized appliqués, and although modern doormakers have departed in many ways from these older techniques, some are still fun to use. Dentils, columns, carved floral work, applied sills, caps below and above windows, and fake panels are among the kinds of work in which appliqués can be used. Though the trend today of leaving woods "natural" (unpainted) makes it harder to disguise appliqués, they still can be used in many situations.

Illus. 5–47. Appliqués are often used in conjunction with mouldings.

80 × 36″ Entry Door with Appliqués

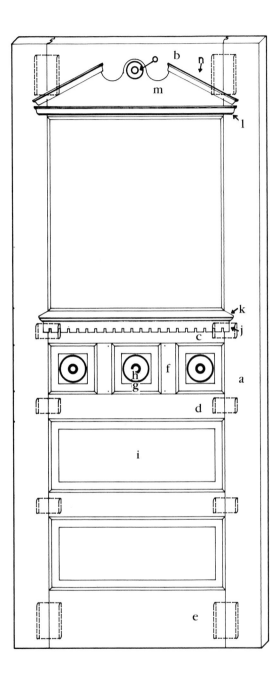

Illus. 5–48 and 5–49. Pattern and photo for 80 × 36-inch entry door with appliqués. See the following page for the building instructions.

80 × 36″ Entry Door with Appliqués

description	no. of pieces	dimensions
a. stiles	2	80 × 4⅞ × 1¾″
b. rail	1	24¼ × 10 × 1¾″
c. rail	1	24¼ × 4⅞ × 1¾″
d. rails	2	24¼ × 4 × 1¾″
e. rail	1	24¼ × 8 × 1¾″
f. mullions	2	6¾ × 2¾ × 1¾″
g. panels	3	6¹¹⁄₁₆ × 6¹¹⁄₁₆ × 1½″

description	no. of pieces	dimensions
h. panel appliqués	3	4 × 4 × ½″
i. panels	2	24³⁄₁₆ × 9¾ × ¾″
j. "dental"	1	25½ × 1½ × ¼″
k. "sill"	1	26¾ × 1¾ × 1¼″
l. long moulding	1	28⅞ × 1⅝ × ½″
m. large appliqué	1	24¼ × 7⅝ × ½″
n. short mouldings	2	11½ × 1⅜ × 1¼″
o. circle	1	2¼″ diameter × ½″

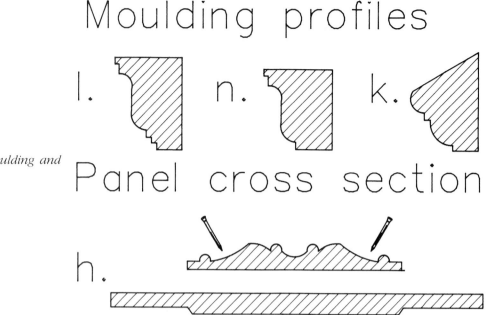

Moulding profiles

l. n. k.

Panel cross section

h.

Illus. 5–50. Cross sections of moulding and applied turned panels.

The jaunty door shown in Illus. 5–48 and 5–49 employs some of the common elements of appliqué work (such as the drip sill and dentil below the window) and some less-common ornaments (such as turned panel appliqués and the somewhat classical-looking appliqué that's located above the window). The effect is dignified, but cheerful.

First, cut the frame pieces to their proper lengths and widths. This door has a cope-and-stick framework (see Chapter 7), and the lengths shown reflect this, but a similar door could be built using routers or applied mouldings. In any case, cut the mortises in the stiles and rails as soon as you have made all the frame pieces. This door has plenty of rails, so there is no need for through mortises.

After you have cut the mortises, run the shaper cuts on all the frame pieces. The panel profile is quite flat, so you can probably set up for a ⅜- or ½-inch slot and still use ¾-inch material for the panels. Note that the three square panels are "raised" only on the inside. Make the turned appliqués, including the square background that appears to be part of the raised panel, separately and apply them with nails and glue after you have assembled the door.

These turned pieces are, of course, applied to the panel pieces before the door is assembled. Urea resin or epoxy glues are best for this type of work. Use small nails to help attach the appliqués in place, and C clamps to hold them tightly until the glue dries.

Now, assemble the door the way you normally would, and, after the glue has cured, smooth and sand the joints. At this point, make and apply the remaining ornaments. Cross sections of the mouldings are shown in Illus. 5–50. You will probably have to use both the table saw and router to make them. Note that the decorative cut goes around both ends of k, l, and n in Illus. 5–48 to give them their finished looks. Make the dentil (j) with repeated cuts with a dado blade on the table saw. You

can avoid breaking out the pieces as you cut by starting with a thick piece of wood (1½ × 1½ inch), and then ripping out the ¼-inch appliqué after you have made the crosscuts.

Apply all these pieces with small nails and a weatherproof glue to the exterior of the door only. You may want to use clamps and nails to secure the appliqués to the frame. Most of these pieces can be reached with clamps applied through the hole where the glass will go, but it is also possible to apply clamping pressure in areas that your clamps normally couldn't reach by clamping a board over the piece that extends out to the edges where the clamps will reach.

ROUTED FRAME-AND-PANEL WORK

One of the simplest ways to make frame-and-panel doors is to rout the slots, rabbets, decorative beads, and raised panels (Illus. 5–51 and 5–52). Doors built in this manner will have rounded corners wherever frame pieces meet at right angles, which will make them look somewhat different than doors made with a shaper. Some people, however, do not find these rounded corners attractive.

One advantage to making routed frame-and-panel doors is that most router bits (with ball-bearing guides) will follow any kind of curving frame member, making it easy to depart from rectangular designs. It is even possible with advanced router and template-cutting techniques (see Chapter 6) to make raised panels with curves that follow the curve of panel members.

The standard procedure for this type of construction

is to cut, mortise, and dry-assemble the frame members, and then rout the slots and beads with the pieces together. Make sure that you position them exactly where they will be in the final assembly, and that they are perfectly flush. In a complicated assembly, you can make some short splines or dowels to help hold the pieces in place. It is also recommended that you use indexing marks across the pieces and a system of numbers or letters to help keep track of each piece.

Since there are no interlocking joints on the areas where frame members meet, as there would be in cope-and-stick construction, you will have to make either a spline, mortise-and-tenon, or dowel joint at every intersection. Narrow mullions and muntins can usually be

dowelled, but a spline joint is not possible here. Be careful to position the dowels so that they won't be cut into by rabbeting for glass.

The rabbets cut to hold glass pieces will also have rounded corners, but you can square these out by chopping straight in with a sharp chisel. You can also make stops to hold the glass in place by routing strips of wood on a router table with a simple clamped-on fence.

You can also use a router on a router table to cut raised panels. There are many "raised panel" router cutters available today. Another method is a combination of table-saw cutting and routing. The door shown and illustrated on pages 88 and 89 incorporates many of these techniques.

Illus. 5–51 and 5–52. Examples of routed frame-and-panel work.

Illus. 5–52.

80 × 36″ Routed Entry Door

Illus. 5–53. and 5–54 Pattern and photo for 80 × 36-inch routed entry door.

80 × 36″ Entry Door

description	no. of pieces	dimensions
a. stiles	2	80 × 6 × 1¾″
b. top & lock rails	2	24 × 5 × 1¾″
c. kick rail	1	24 × 7½ × 1¾″
d. lower muntins	4	5 × 3 × 1¾″
e. lower muntins	2	8 × 3 × 1¾″
f. lower mullions	2	34 × 3 × 1¾″
g. upper mullions	4	5⅞ × 1⅛ × 1¾″

description	no. of pieces	dimensions
h. upper mullions	2	14½ × 1⅛ × 1¾″
i. upper muntins	2	24 × 1⅛ × 1¾″
j. upper muntins	2	5⅞ × 1⅛ × 1¾″
k. panels	4	5⅞ × 5⅞ × 1¼″
l. panels	2	5⅞ × 8⅞ × 1¼″
m. panels	1	8⅞ × 18⅞ × 1¼″
n. panels	2	5⅞ × 18⅞ × 1¼″

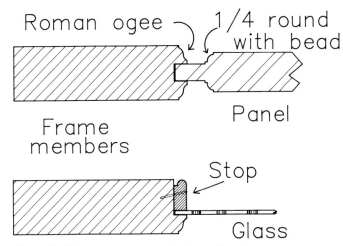

Illus. 5–55. Cross sections of door showing routed ogee cuts and slot.

The complex frame-and-panel door shown in Illus. 5–53 and 5–54 can be made without the use of shapers. Working with routers, a carefully setup table saw, and sharp hand tools, you can obtain beautiful results, even though it may take a little longer.

The framework of this door is built from white oak, while the panels are cut from walnut. Cut all the frame pieces (including the muntins and mullions) to their exact lengths shown in the cutting list. The narrow muntins and mullions for the glazed part of the door will be held in place by dowels, while the wider pieces down below can be held in place by short splines.

After you have cut all the pieces to length and ripped them to width, cut the mortises for the spline tenons at the corner joints and where the lock rail meets the stiles. Now, set up a router table with a ½-inch slotting cutter (you can also flip the pieces over and make two passes with a ¼-inch cutter) to slot the edges and ends of the mullions and muntins in the lower half of the door. Make a test piece with the slot on it, and check to be sure that there will be enough room left on either side of the slot for the ogee cut. If not, use a narrower slot (as narrow as ¼ inch). (See Illus. 5–55).

Cut all the way around the mullions and muntins (d, e, and f in Illus. 5–53) on the router table, and cut the slot on the bottom of the lock rail and the top of the kick rail. You can also cut the slots on the lower half of the stiles this way, too, but be sure to stop the slot cuts on the stiles when you reach the spline mortises so that they won't show on the top and bottom of the door. Cut 1-inch by ½-inch splines one inch narrower than d, e, and f, and glue them into the ends of all these pieces; make sure that you do not leave any excess glue on the ends of the pieces where it will interfere with the joint later.

While the glue is drying, lay out the mullions and muntins for the upper part of the door where they will go—between the stiles and the top and lock rail. Before assembling them, put a pencil mark on the upper face at both ends of each piece so that it is at the center of the 1-inch width. Measure the sizes of the window holes, and check with a square until you have them laid out pre-

cisely; then extend the center marks on to the pieces they meet. These marks will be used to line up the dowel holes. Also, give each piece a number or letter so that you will be able to return it to the same place later. Now, take each piece and bore ⅜-inch dowel holes at all the marks. Set the dowelling jig or boring machine so that the dowels won't be in the part of the mullion or muntin that will be rabbeted later so that the glass can be installed.

At this point, dry-assemble all the frame components of the door. Next, use a router with a rabbeting bit to cut the glass rabbets on the exterior side of the upper part of the door. There is a high risk of "breakout" damage in this operation, so go slowly and be sure the bit is sharp. If you're cutting a very big rabbet, you may want to do it in more than one pass.

The rabbet can vary in depth and width. One that is ¼ inch wide and ½–¾ inch deep will be adequate for regular glass. If you are using stained or leaded glass, or some kind of double glazing, these dimensions may have to be increased.

When the rabbet cutting is completed, chop all the corners out square with a sharp chisel. First use a small square to mark the corners; then chop straight in, first across the grain, then with it. Clamp a square block to the frame when chopping to help guide the chisel.

Now, reassemble the lower part of the door (with the stub-tenons glued into the ends of the mullions and muntins) and cut an ogee or quarter round and bead around the panel frames in it. The depth of the bead cut here should be matched with the slot cut, so that there is enough flat area between them for the guide bearing of the bead cut to ride on.

To make the panels, first cut a rabbet all the way around on both sides so that a tongue is left that will fit snugly into the slot. Cut these rabbets so that they are slightly too thick as they come off the table saw; then plane and sand them so that they look clean and fit perfectly.

Next, set up the router table with a quarter-round-and-bead cutter that has no guide pin or bearing. You may have to grind the guide pin down slightly if you can't find one that is made this way. Set the fence at the proper distance from the bit so that the cutter rounds the corner of the raised part of the panel. Various types of bits could be used here, including cove cutters, chamfers, and other fancy moulding cutters. Before gluing the door together, completely sand the panels and add a finish that has at least one coat of varnish or oil. It is especially important to seal the end grain. Dry-assemble the door with the panels in it to be sure that they will fit properly.

Make sure that you have help when you assemble this door; it is so complex it needs more than two hands. Clamp first the long way, and then across, as explained and illustrated on pages 70–73. After the glue has cured, plane or sand the joints, apply the glazing, cut the stops and nail them in with brass brads, and apply varnish or another sealant.

6
MISCELLANEOUS DOORS

Some of the door patterns in this chapter were chosen to illustrate more advanced applications of the techniques shown in Chapters 4 and 5. Others were chosen because of their designs or because of an especially efficient use of a particular technique. The specific doors I've shown under headings such as Mouldings and Appliqués may employ several different techniques, but I've placed them where they are to illustrate a certain idea or a new twist on an old method.

Also included in this chapter are patterns for specific types of doors, like closet doors, French doors, etc. The requirements for a closet door are much different than those for an entry door (of which we have plenty), and these sections should be of help when you design those types of doors. Finally, the section on catches and handles shows some of the more interesting hand-made types that I have run across.

Illus. 6-1. Photo of three-panel entry door.

DOORS WITH MOULDINGS

80 × 36″ Three-Panel Entry Door

Level Two

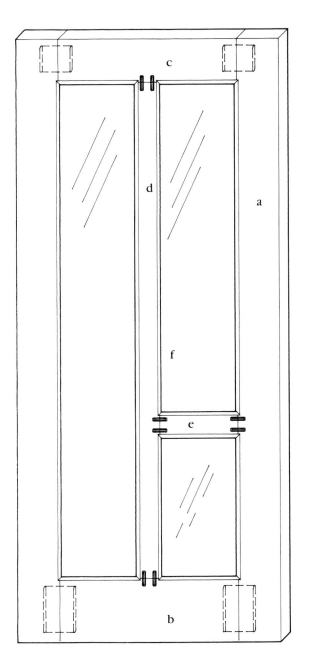

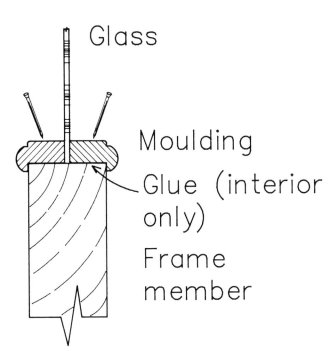

Glass

Moulding

Glue (interior only)

Frame member

Illus. 6-3. Cross section of bolection-moulded, glass-panelled door.

Illus. 6-2. Pattern for three-panel entry door. See the following page for building instructions.

80 × 36″ Three-Panel Entry Door

description	no. of pieces	dimensions
a. stiles	2	80 × 5¾ × 1⅝″
b. kick rail	1	24½ × 8 × 1⅝″
c. top rail	1	24½ × 5¾ × 1⅝″
d. vertical mullion	1	66¼ × 2½ × 1⅝″
e. horizontal muntin	1	10¾ × 2½ × 1⅝″
f. moulding	60 feet	¾ × ½″

This door shown in Illus. 6–1 and 6–2 has a nice design and is very simple to build. It would look much better with wooden panels instead of glass panels—the single, tall panel on one side of the door gives a dramatic touch to an otherwise conventional design. It works especially well when this door is hung in pairs.

To build this door, first cut all the frame stock to the lengths and widths shown in the cutting list. The mullion and muntin can be either dowelled or splined in place. When you assemble the frame, make sure that all the joints are flush. If you have to do a lot of hand planing to flatten them, you will have trouble fitting the bolection mouldings properly.

If you are going to build this door with wooden panels, consider routing a slot in the framework to hold the panels (in which case, you will install the panels as you glue the door together). A slot would only be necessary if the door were going to be hung in an exposed exterior setting. To build the door without the slot, just assemble the frame, and then apply the moulding to the interior side of all the panel holes with glue and nails. If you are building an exterior door, make sure that you glue in the mouldings that will be on the interior side of the door to promote drainage to the exterior side.

When the glue has dried, install the glass by bedding it in a bead of caulk, and proceed to apply moulding to the other side, this time with nails only (Illus. 6–3). Again, if you are using wooden panels glue in the mouldings on both sides of the door, rather than rout the slot.

80 × 30″ Five-Panel Entry Door

Level Two

The pattern for the door shown in Illus. 6–4 and 6–5 is a very common Victorian one that can be used for entry doors as well as for interior passage doors. No shapers are required. Moulding cutters on a table saw were probably used to cut the triple beads on each panel (Illus. 6–6), but even without this cut, this is a fine-looking door.

Old-time doormakers would have cut tenons on the ends of their rails, and would probably have made through mortise-and-tenon joints on a door like this. This door has four sturdy rails and will be very strong even without such extensive joinery, so the through mortising can be excluded. Begin construction by cutting all the frame members to the exact lengths and widths shown in the cutting list. Next, mortise the stiles and rails as described in the section on making spline tenons.

Once you have completed the mortises, cut slots for the panels on the edges of all the frame members. Make a ¼-inch slot, since you need as much space as possible between the slot and the surface of the door for the mouldings. Use either a router or a dado cutter on a table saw to cut slots on both edges of the inner rails and mullions, and around the ends of the mullions too. Insert a short spline into the ends of the mullions that will lock the mullions into the slots in the rails. Stop cutting the slots in the stiles when they reach the mortises, so that they won't show on the top and bottom of the door.

Now, dry-assemble the door and make a mark on the stiles about 1½ inches from the places where the rails meet the stiles, and the same distance from the ends on one side of each piece shown in Illus. 6–4 marked c, and both sides of those marked e and f. These marks are where the chamfer cuts along these edges will be stopped. The actual distance from the corner for these marks will depend on the width of the moulding you intend to use. Transfer the marks to the other side of the door as well, and make the cuts carefully with a router. You can do this with the door still dry-assembled, if you want. And, while the door is still dry-assembled, don't forget to measure for the sizes of the panels.

Now cut the panels to size (use ¾-inch stock), "raise" and groove them if you like, and then sand and finish them. The table saw is probably the best tool to use to shape the edges of these panels. Note that the edge of the panel is flat, not bevelled as on some raised panels. This is so the mouldings can be seated nicely at the ends of the panels (Illus. 6–7). Also, the cutaway area on the ends of the panels is longer than that on the edges, so after you have applied the mouldings, the space around the raised area will be the same all the way around.

Once the panels are ready, glue the door together. This may best be accomplished in two stages. First, glue c, f, and d together, and then also glue b, e, and the other c together. Insert a small piece in the slot of c, against which you can clamp without marring the edge; make sure that the mullions are centered exactly on both rails. Once the glue on these joints has cured, it will be much easier for you to insert the panels, and complete the assembly using only cross clamping.

After the glue has dried, plane the joints, sand the surfaces, and carefully cut and apply the mouldings to complete the door. You can make your own wide, ornate mouldings with router or moulding-head cutters, or you can buy them pre-made.

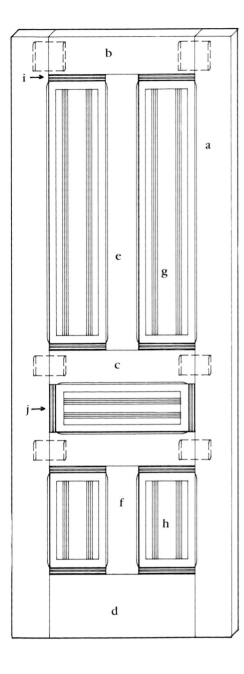

Illus. 6-4 and 6-5. Pattern and photo of 80 × 30-inch five-panel entry door.

80 × 30″ Five-Panel Entry Door

description	no. of pieces	dimensions
a. stiles	2	80 × 5 × 1⅝″
b. top rail	1	20 × 5 × 1⅝″
c. center rails	2	20 × 4½ × 1⅝″
d. kick rail	1	20 × 8½ × 1⅝″
e. upper mullion	1	36½ × 4½ × 1⅝″
f. lower mullion	1	14½ × 4½ × 1⅝″
g. upper panels	2	36⅜ × 8⅝ × ¾″
h. lower panels	2	15⅜ × 8⅝ × ¾″
i. mouldings	8	7¾ × 1 × ⅝″
j. mouldings	2	6½ × 1 × ⅝″

Illus. 6-6. The panels in this door have been grooved and decorated with applied mouldings and stopped chamfer cuts.

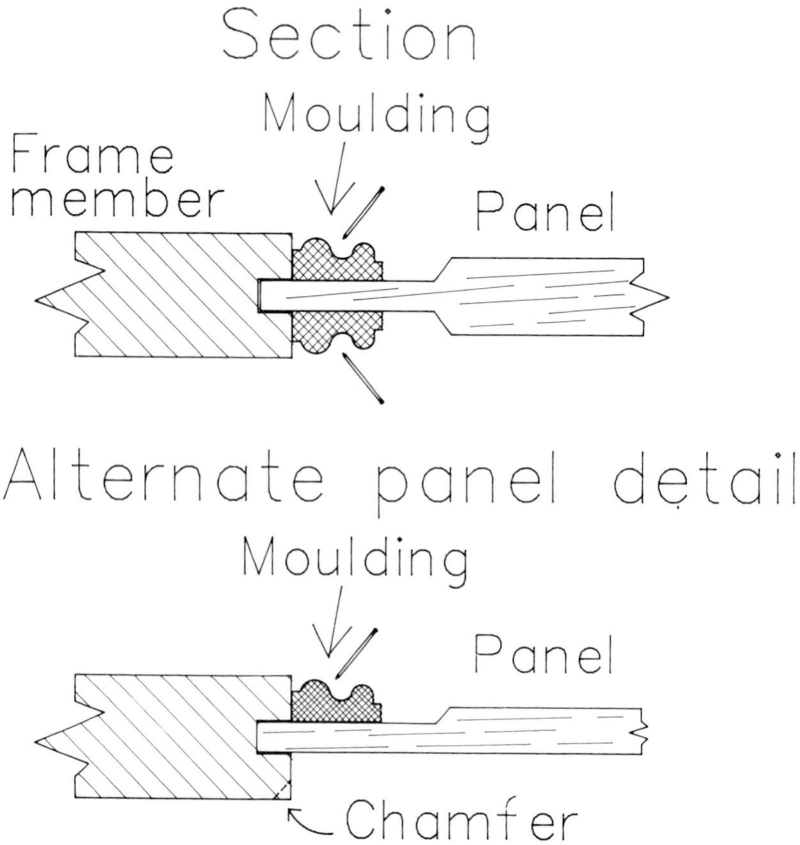

Section

Moulding

Frame member

Panel

Alternate panel detail

Moulding

Panel

Chamfer

Illus. 6-7. Cross section of door that shows applied mouldings.

80 × 36″ Entry Door with Right-Angle Panels

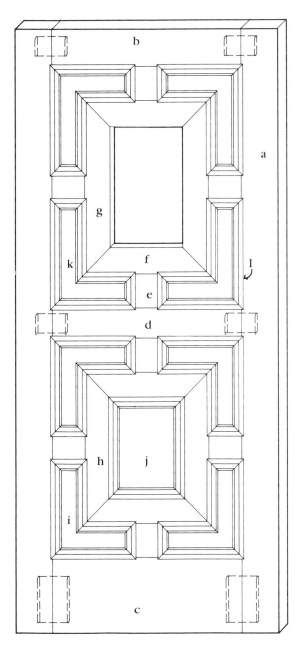

Illus. 6-8 and 6-9. Pattern and photo for 80 × 36-inch entry door with right-angle panels. See the following page for cutting list and building instructions.

80 × 36" Entry Door with Right-Angle Panels

description	no. of pieces	dimensions
a. stiles	2	80 × 5 × 1⅝"
b. top rail	1	26 × 5 × 1⅝"
c. kick rail	1	26 × 10 × 1⅝"
d. lock rail	1	26 × 4 × 1⅝"
e. short frame pieces	8	4½ × 3½ × 1⅝"
f. mitred muntins	4	17 × 3½ × 1⅝"

description	no. of pieces	dimensions
g. mitred mullions	2	23 × 3½ × 1⅝"
h. mitred mullions	2	20 × 3½ × 1⅝"
i. lower panels	4	12⅝ × 11⅛ × 4⅜ × ½"
j. lower panel	1	13 × 10 × ½"
k. upper panels	4	14⅛ × 11⅛ × 4⅜ × ½"
l. moulding	85 feet	1½ × ¾"

There are over 100 pieces of bolection moulding on the door shown in Illus. 6–8 and 6–9! But this shouldn't frighten you. This is basically a straight-forward door to build; it just takes a lot of careful mitring.

First, cut the stiles and rails to the lengths and widths indicated in the cutting list. Clamp them together and make accurate indexing marks across the joints when you have them precisely positioned. Now, set up a stop on your cut-off saw so that you can cut the eight 4½-inch-long pieces all at exactly the same length. Clamp these pieces lightly in place against the rails and stiles, and measure the distances between the opposite ones very carefully. These distances will be the lengths at which you want to make the mitre cuts for the upper and lower frame rectangles.

When you have cut the upper and lower mitred mullions and muntins, and have fitted all the pieces perfectly with them lightly clamped together, you can make indexing marks across all the joints to be used as a guide when you cut the mortises or bore the holes for joining these pieces. Make sure that you label all the pieces so that you don't loose track of where they go while working on them. Join all the rails to the stiles with mortise-and-tenon or spline joints; you can join the rest of the pieces with either spline–tenons or dowels. Even short stub tenons like those used on the ends of the crossbucks on the door shown on pages 115 and 116, will work fine.

It is very important that the frame pieces are exactly the same thickness and that all the joints are perfectly flush when glued. Glue the two inner rectangles together first before assembling the whole door. Mitre clamps are ideal for this, but bar clamps can also be used if you clamp in both directions at once. Put the horizontal clamps on one side of the rectangle pieces, and the vertical clamps on the other side. Position all of them as close to the joints as possible, and tighten each clamp ½ turn at a time to keep the pressure even in both directions.

After you have completely assembled and flattened the framework, cut the panels to fit the holes. The panels in this door were made from ½-inch-thick exterior-grade plywood. Doors with L-shaped panels can also be made by mitring pieces of solid wood for the panels so that the grain runs lengthwise on both parts of the panel.

Use a router and a rabbeting bit to cut a rabbet for the glass in the upper central panel. Then start to cut and apply moulding around the panels. (Refer to pages 76–79 for techniques for cutting bolection moulding.) Cut all the pieces for one side, and glue and nail them in place. Now, flip the door over, drop the panels in, and cut the mouldings for the other side. These mouldings can also be glued and nailed in place. When you have finished this door, you will be an expert at mitring.

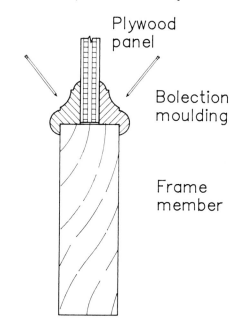

Illus. 6-10. The construction of this door can be simplified if you use bolection mouldings instead of slots to hold the panels.

80 × 30″ Oval-Light Entry Door

Level Three

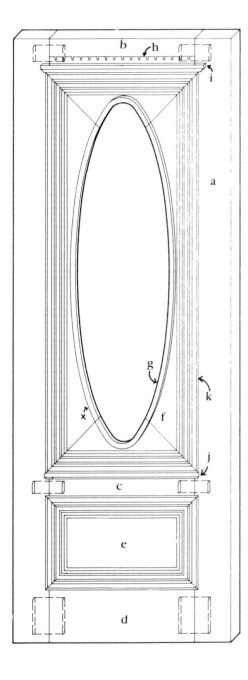

Illus. 6-11 and 6-12. Pattern and photo for 80 × 30-inch oval-light entry door.

80 × 30″ Oval-Light Entry Door

description	no. of pieces	dimensions
a. stiles	2	80 × 5 × 1¾″
b. top rail	1	20 × 5 × 1¾″
c. mid rail	1	20 × 3½ × 1¾″
d. kick rail	1	20 × 7½ × 1¾″
e. lower panel	1	19⅞ × 12 × 1½″
f. upper panel	1	52½ × 19⅞ × 1⅝″

description	no. of pieces	dimensions
g. glass moulding	1	
h. dentil appliqué	1	20 × 1 × ¼″
i. cap moulding	1	21½ × ¾ × ¾″
j. drip sill	1	21 × 1 × ¾″
k. moulding	35 feet	

Illus. 6-13.

The door shown in Illus. 6–11 and 6–12 has some of the most intricate moulding patterns and raised panels I've ever seen. The upper panel with the oval light is es-

pecially tricky because of the raised rim around the oval light. Most craftsmen would have made this rim by applying a thin strip to the face of the panel, but on this door, the surrounding areas were actually removed instead (Illus. 6–14).

To build this door, first cut the frame pieces to the lengths and widths indicated in the cutting list. Join the three rails to the stiles with either mortise-and-tenon or spline–tenon joints, but make sure that all the pieces are exactly the same thickness and that the joints come out perfectly flush. If the joints aren't flush, you can hand plane them, but then you will probably have to plane the mouldings to get them to fit tightly.

The mouldings themselves can be made with one of the large multi-profile router bits shown in Chapter 5, or you can buy similar mouldings. They do not have to be exactly the same. It is also possible to make these mouldings by gluing two separate moulded strips of wood together.

You could house the panels in this door in slots in the framework, but with such large bolection mouldings, there's really no need. Just glue and nail the mouldings in on one side, drop the panels in, and then glue and nail the mouldings in on the other side.

The lower panel is fairly easy to make. Cut the four separate steps from the edge to the face of the panel with either router bits or a table saw. If you use a table saw, use a blade that leaves very little kerf.

Make the upper panel from four separate pieces, mitred at the corners (Illus. 6–15). Use a spline to attach these pieces together, and drive pegs into holes bored through the spline to lock these joints. You'll have to make two separate templates for the oval light in this panel. The first one will be the oval shape itself, only about 1½ inches bigger than the hole you will cut out. This one will be used just to remove the wood from the face of the panel outside of the ridge around the oval. You will later use this first template to make a rectangular template out of high-quality ½-inch plywood to use in trimming the oval hole.

To draw an ellipse for the first template, draw a straight line through the vertical axis of a piece of ¾-

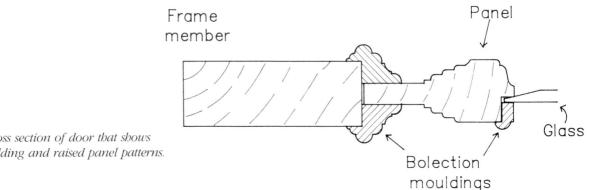

Illus. 6-14. Cross section of door that shows complex moulding and raised panel patterns.

Illus. 6-15. This mitred panel construction is similar to the method used for the 80 × 32-inch oval-light entry door.

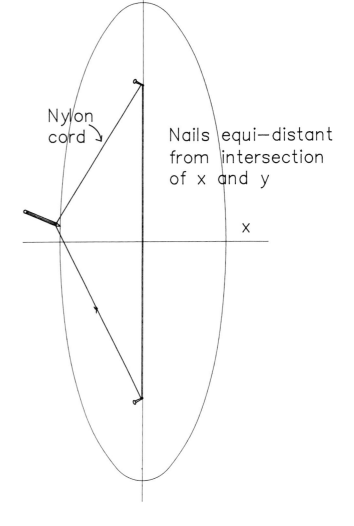

Illus. 6-16. Two nails and a loop of cord can be used as a fairly accurate method of drawing an ellipse.

inch plywood that is large enough for the oval (illus. 6–16). Find the center of this line, draw a line at right angles for the horizontal axis, and drive two nails, equal distance from the center on the vertical line, into the plywood. Now, make a loop of heavy nylon cord, drop it over the two nails, and use it to guide your pencil as you draw the ellipse. You will have to experiment with the nail positions and the size of the loop to get the ellipse required. Remember, the ellipse should be 1½ inches longer and wider than the hole will be. Also, the extremities of this ellipse should come to within ½–¼ inch from the edges of the raised part of the panel. This is labelled X in Illus. 6–16.

After you have cut out the oval and have carefully faired the edges by planing and sanding, position it on top of the panel lamination using the axis as indexing marks. Screw it down near the window hole, driving the screws into areas that will later be trimmed off. Now, use a router with a flush-trimming bit to remove about ⅛ inch of wood from the surface of the panel all around the template. As shown in the cross section, do this only on the outside of the door. A bit with a slightly rounded corner will work best. Just cut a swath about 2–3 inches out from the template with the router. Don't try to go all the way out to the corners. Use a plane to remove the wood from the corner areas; this way, you won't cut too deeply when the router base gets to the edge of the template. Flatten and smooth these areas afterwards, and proceed to cut the steps for the raised parts of the panel as before.

Now, use a marking gauge set at ¾ inch to mark a line ¾ inch in from the edge of the oval template, and cut the template down to this size. Use this smaller template to mark the oval hole you will cut out of the second rectangular ½-inch-thick plywood template. If you don't have a scroll saw to make the cut, use a band saw and glue the starting cut back together. This piece of plywood should be 2 inches larger in both directions than the panel, so that you can screw battens around the edges of it to hold it in position on the workpiece. Attach it to the workpiece by screwing through the bottom into the ends or edge of the panel where the holes won't show later. Use this template to guide a 1¾-inch long flush-trimming bit for trimming the inside of the oval cutout.

Now that you have finished cutting out the elliptical window, use a rabbeting bit with a ball-bearing guide to cut out the rabbet that will hold the glass. Next, make a stop. It will probably be easiest to saw the moulding for the glass stop. Start by marking the outside cut of the stop cut from the rabbeted side of the cutout onto the

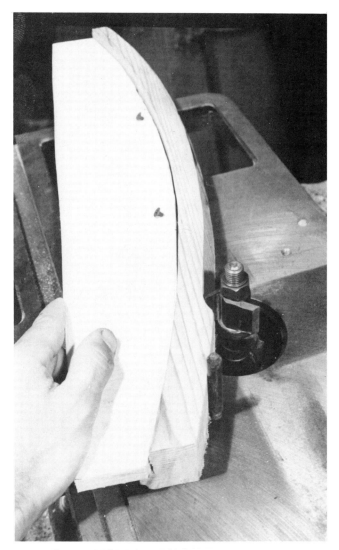

Illus. 6-17. When you are shaping thin, curved pieces, make sure that you attach a holding jig to the workpiece.

stock, and cutting and sanding until it fits. It doesn't have to be perfect, since this is a bolection moulding.

Before making the inside cut, rout the bead and the rabbet on the outside cut. Make sure that the pieces are a bit long, because you are going to have to bend them slightly to make them fit tightly. Make two pieces, one for each side. Now, mark the inside line and cut it. Attach the moulding to a holding jig with glue or nails before smoothing and routing the inside cut (Illus. 6–17).

After you have installed the panels and nailed and glued in the outside moulding, cut the three appliqués and nail and glue them in place. You can simplify the oval window panel greatly by leaving the ridge around the oval off. This door, painstaking to make, is exquisite.

Illus. 6-18–6-21. Oval lights work nicely on many different types of doors.

Illus. 6-19.

Illus. 6-20.

Illus. 6-21.

80 × 32" Gothic Four-Panel Entry Door

Level Two

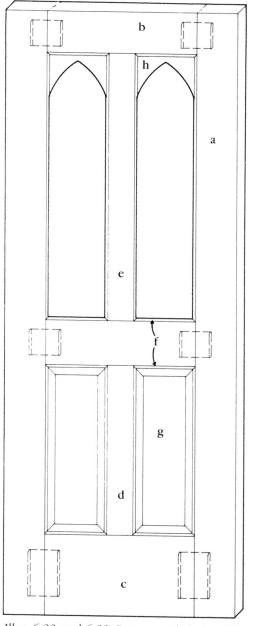

Illus. 6-22 and 6-23. Pattern and photo of 80 × 32-inch gothic four-panel entry door.

80 × 32" Gothic Four-Panel Door

description	no. of pieces	dimensions
a. stiles	2	80 × 5½ × 1½"
b. lock and top rails	2	21 × 5½ × 1½"
c. kick rail	1	21 × 11 × 1½"
d. lower mullion	1	22½ × 4½ × 1½"
e. upper mullion	1	35½ × 4½ × 1½"
f. stop stock	56 feet	⅝ × ½"
g. lower panels	2	22½ × 9⅜ × ¾"
h. arched inserts	8	5 × 4¾ × ¼"

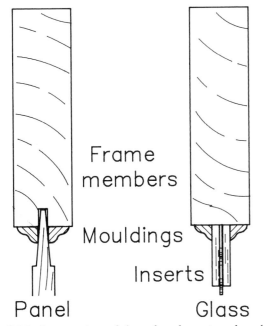

Illus. 6-24. Cross section of door that shows panel and glass installation.

Illus. 6-25. The inserts make an otherwise plain-looking door interesting.

The simple but intriguing panel door shown in Illus. 6–22 and 6–23 can be made with low-profile mouldings. The thin pieces for the gothic arches at the top of each light are notched in under the mouldings that hold glass in place.

To build this door, first cut the frame pieces to the lengths and widths shown in the cutting list. Then dry-

assemble them and cut slots around the lower two panel holes to hold the wooden panel. There are no rabbets for the glass in the upper panels; the glass is held by mouldings on both sides. It should be centered between the faces of the frame pieces, and the slots for the panels should be only ¼ inch wide and centered on the edge of the frame. Be sure to glue and nail the inner mouldings in so that they will be weathertight.

Disassemble the door and square out the ends of the slots for the wooden panels. The panel material used on this door is only ¾-inch thick, but could be made thicker. The edges, however, must stay thin so that there is room for the low-profile mouldings around them. Finish the panels completely and seal the end grain before assembling the door.

Before applying the glass mouldings, cut the gothic arches out of ¼-inch-thick stock and glue them to both sides of the glass with silicone caulk (Illus. 6–26–6–28). You can round the outside lower edges slightly, but all the other edges will be covered up by the mouldings. Now, notch the eight side mouldings to fit over the arch appliqués, and cut the four top pieces down so they will fit in place too.

After gluing up the pieces, apply the low-profile mouldings on both sides of the lower panels and glue them in place on the insides of the uppers.

Illus. 6-26–6-28. Some other uses of gothic arches.

Illus. 6-27.   *Illus. 6-28.*

ROUTED FRAME-AND-PANEL DOORS

Illus. 6-29–6-32. These various doors were made by routing beads and slots for raised panels. The doors illustrated and discussed on pages 106-124 incorporate the same techniques.

Illus. 6-30.

Illus. 6-31.

Illus. 6-32.

80 × 36″ Six-Panel Arch-Top Entry Door

Level Three

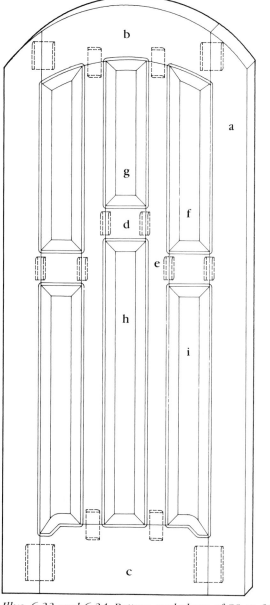

Illus. 6-33 and 6-34. Pattern and photo of 80 × 36-inch six-panel arch-top entry door.

80 × 36″ Six-Panel Arch-Top Entry Door

description	no. of pieces	dimensions
a. stiles	2	80½ × 5½ × 1¾″
b. top rail	1	25 × 11½ × 1¾″
c. kick rail	1	25 × 10 × 1¾″
d. muntins	3	6 × 5 × 1¾″

description	no. of pieces	dimensions
e. mullions	2	66 × 3½ × 1¾″
f. panels	2	26⁵⁄₁₆ × 5¹⁵⁄₁₆ × 1½″
g. panel	1	21¹¹⁄₁₆ × 5¹⁵⁄₁₆ × 1½″
h. panel	1	41⁷⁄₁₆ × 5¹⁵⁄₁₆ × 1½″
i. panels	2	36⁵⁄₁₆ × 5¹⁵⁄₁₆ × 1½″

The elegant entry door shown in Illus. 6–33 and 6–34, which has contrasting woods and an attractive design, can be made without the use of shapers. The panel slots and beads are cut with router bits, and the panels are "raised" with the table saw.

First, cut the stiles and rails to length and width on the table saw. Rip the long upright mullions to width, and rough-cut them a few inches long for now. You can cut the upper and lower rails from one solid piece or edge glue two narrower pieces to make one wide enough if you don't have wide stock.

When you have cut these two rails to length, carefully mark the arch on the top and bottom of the top rail, and the curves near the ends on the upper edge of the bottom rail, and cut these shapes out with the band saw. Cut as accurately as possible, and use a cabinet scraper, rasp, sander, or compass plane to fair out the curve on the lower edge of the top rail before proceeding. The other curves can be cleaned up easier later, but this one must be dealt with now so that good joints can be made where the mullions meet it.

When the curve is right, lay out all the frame pieces except the top rail on the worktable and lightly clamp them so that they fit snugly together. Now, lay the top rail in place on top of the two long mullions and mark with a knife or a very sharp pencil the cuts that will be made on the upper ends of these mullions (the lower ends of the mullions should already have been trimmed off square so they fit tightly against the lower rail). Make the cuts carefully with the band saw and use a sharp block plane to smooth the cuts so that they fit perfectly against the upper rail. You should now be able to dry-assemble the framework so that all the joints go tightly together.

Now, cut the mortises for the splines that will hold the framework together. Since this door has no interlocking cope-and-stick joints, it will rely totally on the splines to hold it together, so make them strong. Dowelling is not recommended, but you can use the same technique that was used for the crossbuck door on pages 114–118 to hold the mullions and muntins in place with short splines.

After you have cut the joints, dry-assemble the door again. Then rout the slot for the panels. Cut either the bead or the slot first; before making the cut experiment on a piece of scrap to ensure that there will be room for both, and that whichever one is done last will have a solid edge for the guide bearing to ride on (Illus. 6–35). If you use a large ogee bit, the widest slot that you will probably be able to cut will be ¼ inch wide. After the routing is done, square out the slot in the corner of each panel with a sharp chisel (Illus. 6–36). If you cut the slots through, as in the crossbuck door, you'll only have a few slots to square out.

Before disassembling the door, make templates for the panels. Probably the best way to do this is to lay a piece of plywood or particle board under each panel hole and mark the exact size and shape of the opening. Then draw a new line on the template about ⁷⁄₁₆ inch outside of the first line. This will be the actual edge of the panel. Cut this line and use the template to mark the lines on the actual panel stock.

To make the panels, first plane the panel stock to a thickness of about 1¼ inch. Cut the slight curves on the upper edge of the upper panels as straight lines when first cutting out the panels; also cut the bottoms of the lower panels off straight so that these panels are the lengths indicated in Illus. 6–37. After you have made the bevel cuts to "raise" the panels, cut these edges more accurately. Set the table saw blade at the angle that will give you the bevel wanted and make the cut all the way around both sides of all the panels. Then use a block plane to smooth these areas and shape them slightly.

When you have cut and planed all the panels, dry-assemble the door again to make sure that everything fits. Make pencil marks across the joints to help keep the pieces aligned when you glue them. Make sure that you have someone to help you when you are ready to glue the pieces, as this door is tricky. To ensure that the joints are tight, clamp them from across the middle. It will also help to leave the stiles long on the top until after the glue dries, so that you can clamp across the middle of the upper rail. You may also need to tap the short center muntins up or down to get them in the right place. Use a wide block of a softer wood to do this; place it against the bead and tap it with a hammer.

When the glue is dry, plane the joints, sand, and apply the finish. This arched top needs a head jamb cut from a solid piece or bent into an inside form. The stop will also have to be bent; you can do this most easily by laminating several thin strips.

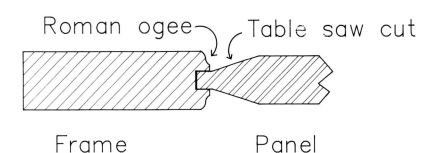

Illus. 6-35. Cross section of door showing routed ogee and slot.

Illus. 6-36. The corners of routed slots must be squared out with a chisel after routing.

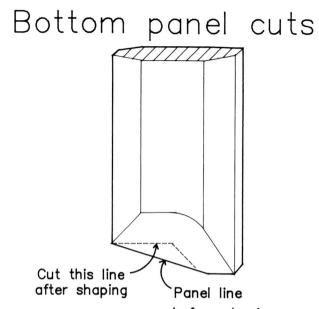

Bottom panel cuts

Cut this line after shaping

Panel line before shaping

Illus. 6-37. First cut the bottoms of the panels straight across; then shape them, recut them to the dotted line, and finally reshape the raised part with a plane or chisel.

80 × 42" Round-Panel Dutch Door

Level Three

The door shown in Illus. 6–38 and 6–39 is one on which a whole range of technical skills are used. Oak or mahogany are good woods to use for this door because they don't break easily where the grain is short. Note that this door is divided in the center so that the top can open while the bottom remains closed. Dutch doors, as they are commonly called, allow for plenty of ventilation while keeping kids in and pets out, but they may not be the most practical type of entry door in most cases. Besides needing extra hinges and hardware, and being less weathertight, they can also be difficult to hang straight. In addition, unless they are sheltered, they must be hung so that they open outward, or else the interlocking rabbet between the two parts will force dripping moisture inward instead of shedding it outward.

If you do make this door as a Dutch door, remember that you must add an extra ½ inch to its height at the beginning to compensate for the overlapping rabbets where the two parts meet. If you choose to make it a one piece door, just start with regular 80-inch stiles and use an extra-wide lock rail.

This door was built without the use of cope-and-stick cutters. The only place where shapers were probably used was where the three panels were raised in the lower part of the door, and router bits are now available that would allow you to make similar cuts without having to use shapers.

To build this door, first cut the stiles and rails to the lengths and widths given in the cutting list. The lower frame piece (g in Illus. 6–38) will be made from two pieces that are 22½ × 9¾ × 1¾ inches. These pieces will be edge-joined in the center (dotted line in Illus. 6–38) to trap and hold the circular panel in the center. Also cut the two upright mullions (f in Illus. 6–38), to their proper lengths and widths. Rout the mortises for the stile-to-rail joints as soon as you have figured the positions of the rails.

Now, lay the upper part of the door (c, d, and f and the two stiles) out on the assembly table, and position the mullions between the rails. Position them carefully, and mark the half circles that extend up from the edges of the top rail. You can also mark the indexing lines where the dowels will go that hold the mullions in place on the rails.

Now, either cut these lines very carefully with the band saw, and, later, after the door is glued together, rout the rabbet and bead, or assemble the door before cutting the half circles out of the top rail (c), and then later (after glue-up), use a template and a long flush-cutting router bit to make the arches. If you use the second method, rough-cut the arches after the glue-up (staying an ⅛ inch or so outside the lines) with a hand-held jigsaw, and make sure that the template runs down the mullions and stiles an inch or so past where you will start and stop the cuts, so that you don't cut into them. If you use the second method, there is less chance you will break the wood on the top rail, where the grain is

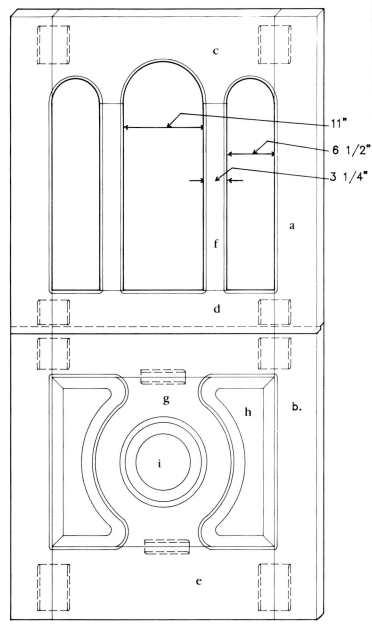

Illus. 6-38 and 6-39. Pattern and photo of 80 × 42-inch round-panel Dutch door.

80 × 42″ Round-Panel Dutch Door

description	no. of pieces	dimensions
a. upper stiles	2	42 × 5¾ × 1¾″
b. lower stiles	2	38½ × 5¾ × 1¾″
c. top rail	1	30½ × 11½ × 1¾″
d. lock rails	2	30½ × 5¾ × 1¾″
e. kick rail	1	30½ × 9¾ × 1¾″
f. upper mullions	2	23¾ × 3¼ × 1¾″
g. lower frame piece	1	22½ × 19½ × 1¾″
h. side panels	2	23½ × 11 × 1½″
i. circle panel	1	13″ diameter × 1½″

very short; however, the first method may be quicker if it is done very carefully. Either way, take your time to prevent breaking out pieces of the top rail.

To make the bottom half of the door, first lay out the stiles and two lower rails, with the two blocks that will form the lower frame piece (g in Illus. 6–38) in place in the middle (Illus. 6–41). Find the halfway point on the line where the two pieces of the lower frame piece meet, and use a compass to make a 12-inch-diameter (6-inch-radius) circle on the two pieces. Now, from the same center point, draw a 24-inch-diameter (12-inch-radius) circle on the lower frame pieces.

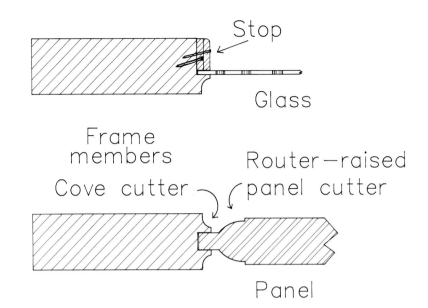

Illus. 6-40. Two layers of thin material are used for the glass stops.

At this point, cut the inner circle out of the two lower frame pieces, clamp them together, and rout the beads and slot for the panel. You can cut the panel to a perfect circle with a 13-inch diameter by pivoting or freehand cutting on a band saw; the profile cut around the edge can be made with either router or shaper bits (Illus. 6–42). Now, glue the two parts of the lower frame piece together around the panel (i), and retrim the ends of the lower frame piece so that they are perfectly straight and square.

Next, draw two lines, parallel to the ends of the lower frame piece, about 4½ inches in from each end. These lines intersect with the 24-inch-diameter circle at the area where the circle will start curving back outward to form the rounded corners of the panels. So, finally, draw four more short lines parallel to the edges, two inches in, and find the point halfway between the ends of the lower frame piece and the first line. Use this point as the center of the circular section at each corner. Now, freehand cut the outside edges of the lower frame piece on a band saw, and dry-clamp the lower half of the door (without the two outer panels) together.

You may have to do some fairing with rasps or sanders to get the curves to flow smoothly from the edges of the rails and the large circle on the lower frame pieces to the small curves in the corners. You can do this much more easily after you make one pass with the bead and

slot cutters around the space that will hold the side panels (h). After making the first pass with the router, fair the curves where necessary (you now have only the thin edge on either side of the slot to shape); then make another pass with the router to recut the areas where wood was removed. Once again, be careful not to break off the corners on the lower frame piece where the grain is short. You will have to chop out the corners of the slots where the rails meet the stiles so that they are square.

Now draw the shapes of the two side panels (h) on the pieces of wood that will be used, by placing the pieces under the clamped-up frame, and carefully drawing the inner edges of the frame pieces on them. Redraw these lines on the panels ⁷⁄₁₆ inch farther out all the way around and cut the outer lines. Use the same profile cutter that you used on the circle panel (i) to shape the edges of these panels.

Now you are ready to glue the door together. This is not as tricky as it looks, but you still have to clamp from top to bottom before applying the edge clamping.

When the glue has cured, plane and sand the door. Square out the lower corners of the glass rabbets with a sharp chisel, and install the glass in a bed of caulk. Bent laminations were used for the curved parts of the stops on this door, but you can also cut them from a layered lamination or use glazing putty.

MAKING LOWER FRAME MEMBER

1.

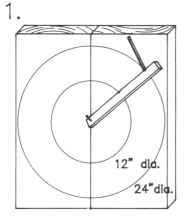

12" dia.

24" dia.

2.

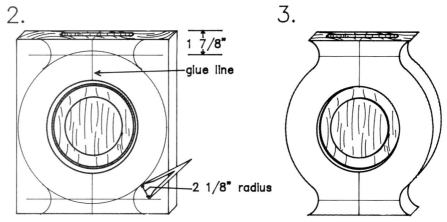

1 7/8"

glue line

2 1/8" radius

3.

Illus. 6-41. First mark out the lower frame member on two separate pieces of wood. Then cut and shape the inside and, with the finished panel in place, glue it together.

Afterward, mark and cut out the outer edge (3), and retrim and mortise the ends.

Illus. 6-42. Use a pivot-cutting jig like this one (except make sure that your jig has a nail for the pivot center) to cut out the round panel.

84 × 36″ Entry Doors

Level Two

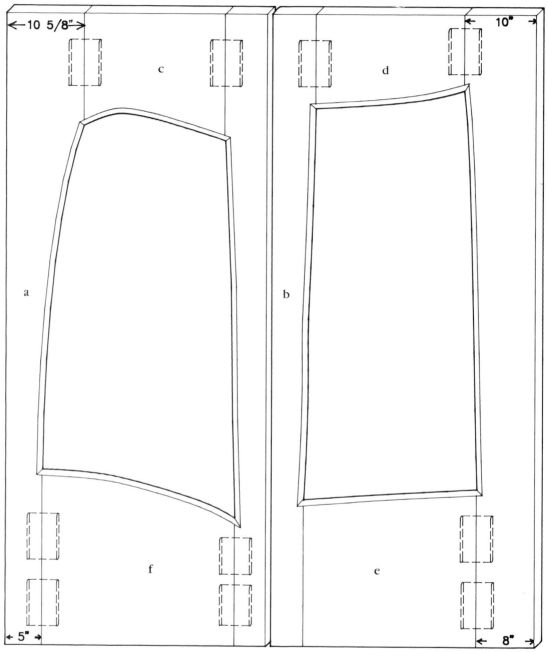

Illus. 6-43. Pattern for 84 × 36-inch entry doors.

84 × 36″ Entry Doors

description	no. of pieces	dimensions
a. hinge stiles	2	84 × 10¾ × 1⅝″
b. lock stiles	2	84 × 6 × 1⅝″
c. top rail	1	19½ × 17 × 1⅝″
d. top rail	1	20¼ × 12½ × 1⅝″
e. kick rail	1	23½ × 21 × 1⅝″
f. kick rail	1	26¾ × 24 × 1⅝″
stop laminations	90 feet	¼ × ¾″

Illus. 6-44. Photo of 84 × 36-inch entry doors.

The wild-looking set of restaurant doors shown in Illus. 6–43 and 6–44 should destroy any preconceived notions you have about how doors should look. These doors are actually quite simple to build, but they catch the eye with their bold, unusually shaped glass panels.

To build these doors, you will need wide pieces of 1¾-inch-thick wood for the rails and the hinge stiles. You will probably have to edge-glue pieces to get material of the proper width for them. When edge gluing to make pieces that are wider than the planer you have available, plane all the stock to the thickness you intend to use before making the laminations. Then clamp the edge-gluing laminations together very carefully so that you will not have to hand plane them much to get them flat after the glue has cured. After gluing and hand planing them, trim the rails to length with a sliding crosscut table on the table saw. With pieces this wide, you can even run the ends over the jointer (set for a very light cut) to get them perfectly straight and square.

The next step involves cutting the hinge stiles to different widths at each end, and getting the areas that will butt against the rails straight and square. Probably the best approach is to start with a board that is wide enough for the wide end, joint the edge carefully, and then (with your best 60- or 100-tooth blade and a good guide fence) rip the cut in from the narrow end far enough for the joint at the narrow end of the stile. Stop the cut and pull the board up off the blade to avoid damaging the joining surface of the stile. Now, mark the freeform curve that will form the edge of the glass panel, and cut this part out with the band saw.

Now, lay the pieces out on the worktable, and mark the curves for the rest of the cuts that will form the edges of the glass panels. At this point, measure across the top and the bottom of the door to ensure that your calculations for the stile widths and rail lengths at each end add up to the same overall width for the door top and bottom. You may have to do some hand planing or jointing to get everything to come out precisely.

After you have made the remaining band-saw cuts for the glass panels, cut the mortises in the ends of the rails and the edges of the stiles. Don't worry about fairing out the band-saw-cut curves yet; this will be done after the first router cutting is done. With wide pieces like these, it is best to divide the spline mortises into sections not more than 8–10 inches long to lessen the stress caused by wood expansion and contraction.

Now, dry-assemble the roughly cut out door frames, and use a rabbeting bit in your router to rout the rabbet for the glass (Illus. 6–45). You can also rout a bead or ogee on the inside of the doors at this time. This will reduce the width of the edge around the glass panels to less than half the full 1⅝ inch thickness of the door, and make it a lot easier to fair out the curves. Now, go back with the hand plane, rasp, sander, disc grinder, or whatever tool works, and smooth any uneven spots in the curves. After this is done to your satisfaction, go back once again with your router bits and recut the areas that were altered when you smoothed out the curves.

Now, glue the doors and, when the glue has cured, plane and flatten the joints. When this is done, take a

sharp chisel and chop the corners of the glass rabbet out so that the lines of the curves continue to a sharp corner, rather than to a rounded corner, which would be left by a router.

Make the stops on this door by laminating in place two ⅛-inch-thick strips (this is easier than trying to bend strips of the full thickness). After the fairing is done, cut and fit the first strip all the way around, and then nail it in with small headless brads that are set below the surface. Mitre the corners by bisecting the angle of the curves where the stops meet. Now, repeat the process with the second lamination and apply a coat of glue between the two.

Be sure to use tempered or safety glass for a door like this. You will probably want to make patterns for the glass pieces with thin plywood or pressed board and take them to your glazier.

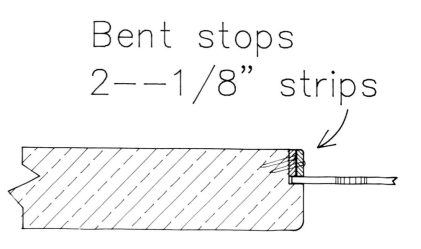

Bent stops
2——1/8" strips

Illus. 6-45. Cross section of door that shows glass rabbet and stops.

80 × 34″ Cross-buck Doors

Level Three

At first glance, one would think the doors shown in Illus. 6–46 and 6–47 were made with shapers because there are no radii at the corners, but this is not the case. Interesting frame shapes and a simple panel rabbet that creates a thin "accent" line between the frame members and the raised parts of the panels keep these doors from appearing hard-edged, even though neither shapers nor routers were used to soften the edges of the various parts. To take the hard corner off the panels and the frame members, just hand-sand lightly.

This is a technique that could be used much more widely than it is by builders who like intricate frame-and-panel patterns, but don't want to invest a lot of money and time in shapers and cutters. The clean ⅛-inch line between the panels and the frame members is

in keeping with a more modern look. A logical extension of this technique is to hand sand the ends of the rails and the stiles (where they meet the rails) slightly round so that when they are joined, a slight groove separates these pieces as well.

To build these doors, first cut the rails and stiles to the lengths and widths indicated in the cutting list. The arch on the top rail has a radius of 11 inches. You can mark it on the rail with a stick-and-nail compass and carefully cut it with a band saw. The best way to smooth this curve is with a compass plane, but if you don't have one use rasps and sanding blocks that are cut to the right arch; while smoothing the curve, keep the edge as square as possible.

Note that the area that holds the cross bucks and the

four triangular panels is perfectly square. Whatever length you use for the rails, place the center rail so that the distance from the bottom of it to the top of the kick rail is the same as its length. When you have made the three rails and the stiles, lay them out and position the

lock rail so that the bottom area is square; then mark the places for the mortise cuts.

At this time, take the long cross-buck piece (e in Illus. 6–46) and place it in position under the clamped-up frame. Mark a center line down the length of the piece;

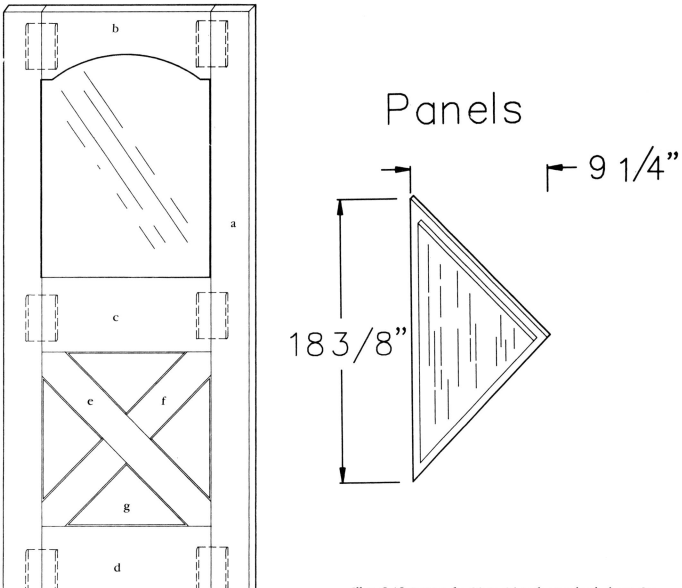

Panels

⌐ 9 1/4"

18 3/8"

Illus. 6-46. Pattern for 80 × 34-inch cross-buck doors. See the following page for a photograph.

80 × 34″ Cross-Buck Door

description	no. of pieces	dimensions
a. stiles	2	80 × 5¼ × 1¾″
b. top rail	1	23½ × 9 × 1¾″
c. lock rail	1	23½ × 10 × 1¾″
d. kick rail	1	23½ × 11½ × 1¾″
e. cross buck	1	33 × 4½ × 1¾″
f. cross bucks	2	14¼ × 9¾ × 1¾″
g. panels	4	19½ × 9¾ × 1½″

Illus. 6-47. Photo of 80. × 36-inch cross-buck doors.

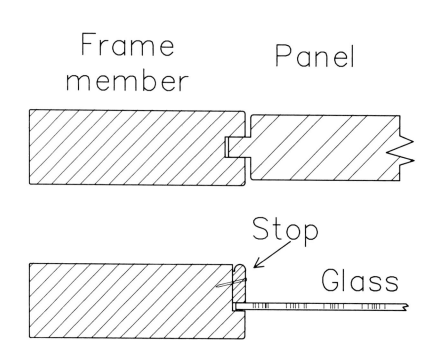

Illus. 6-48. Cross section of the door that shows the simple raised panel construction used.

make sure that this line goes right through both corners of the frame laid over it (Illus. 6–49). Now, very carefully mark the right-angled cutoff lines on the long cross-buck piece with a knife. Cut this piece and fit it in place. Repeat the marking and cutting procedure with both of the smaller cross-buck pieces (f in Illus. 6–46).

Now, disassemble the doors and use a slotting cutter in a router table to cut slots all the way around all the cross-buck pieces (including the ends) and around the inside edges of the square lower frame section. Make two passes, one from either side, so that you have a ½ × ½-inch slot that is centered on the edges of the pieces. Glue short splines into the ends of the cross-buck pieces (Illus. 6–50).

Next, cut the panels to fit the holes, and use a box-core router bit or dado cutter on a table saw to cut the rabbets on both sides of the panels. The rabbets should leave a tenon all around the edges of the panels that will fit tightly into the slots; these tenons should be approximately ⅛–¼ inch wider than the ½-inch-deep slot. Sand all the sharp corners and edges round on both the raised parts of the panels and the frame pieces, but be careful not to sand where frame pieces meet unless you want a groove at all the joints.

When the panels have been completely sanded and finished, and you have dry-assembled the pieces to ensure that all the joints will close tightly, glue up the door. After the glue has cured and you have flattened all the joints, use a rabbet cutter to cut the rabbet for the glass. Make either a bent or sawn stop for the arched rail. Make an astragal to seal the closure where the double doors meet (Illus. 6–51).

Illus. 6-49. Marking the end cuts for the cross bucks.

Illus. 6-50. Shown here is the end of a cross buck which has been slotted and which has a short spline glued into it that will fit into the slot in the framework.

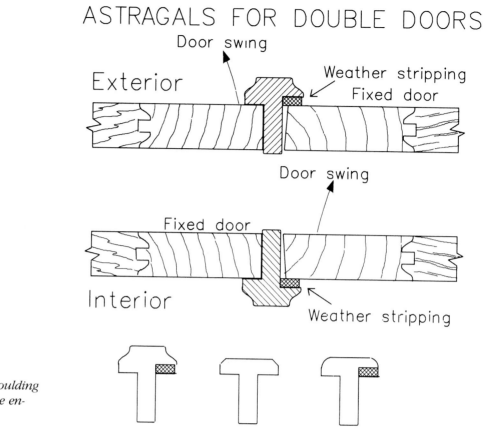

ASTRAGALS FOR DOUBLE DOORS

Door swing

Exterior

Weather stripping
Fixed door

Door swing

Fixed door

Interior

Weather stripping

Illus. 6-51. Use an astragal or T moulding where double doors meet to seal the enclosure.

80 × 30″ Arch-Top Entry Doors

Level Two

The pair of arched-top glass doors shown in Illus. 6–52 and 6–53 can be made without shapers. They work nicely as passage doors from a solarium to an interior room. Because there is no cope-and-stick joint where the mullions and muntins meet the frame, you must make dowel joints to hold them in place. Also, on this door, you will leave the corners of the rabbets cut with the router to hold the glass round, and will round the stops off at the corners to fit them.

Begin construction by cutting the outer frame pieces to length and width, leaving the hinge stiles (a in Illus. 6–52) square at the top end. Cut the top rails from a piece of 2 × 8. Cut the angles on the ends at the distance shown in the cutting list, and lay the pieces out where they will go. Now use a stick of wood 44 inches long with a small nail in one end and a pencil held in a notch at the other end as a compass, and swing this arc across the tops of the stiles and rails (Illus. 6–54). Next, shorten the pencil end of the stick by 4½ inches and, with the nail in the same place, mark the inside edges of the top rails. Now cut these rails carefully to their proper widths with the band saw.

Next, cut the vertical mullions to their proper widths,

leaving them a few inches long, and lay them in place centered between the stiles on top of the rails. Butt the square-cut lower ends against the lower rails and draw a line across the upper end where it will butt up against the inside edge of the rail. Also check your measurements on the horizontal muntins at this time, and cut them to length.

Now, cut the dowel holes for the joints that will hold all the muntins and mullions (Illus. 6–56). Dry-assemble the door and cut the routed beads and rabbets. A ⅜ × ⅜-inch rabbet cut for the glass will work well for standard glazing.

Once you have completed these cuts, glue the doors. After the glue has dried, true the arch at the top by trimming the stiles and hand planing the arch. Though it is quite possible to square out the corners of the rabbets with a sharp chisel before cutting the stops, on this door they are left rounded, and the stops are sanded round to fit them. This takes a lot of hand fitting and is very time-consuming.

As with most gently curved tops, it is easiest to make the jamb for this door using the built-in form method.

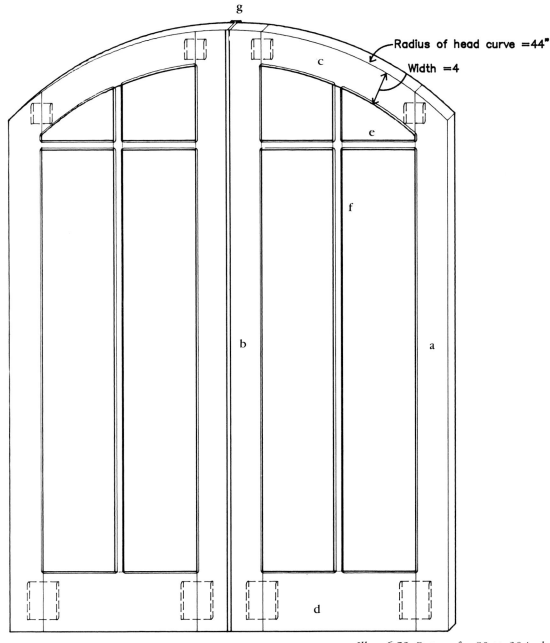

Radius of head curve =44"

Width =4

Illus. 6-52. Pattern for 80 × 30-inch arch-top entry doors. See the following page for a photograph.

80 × 30" Arch-Top Entry Doors

description	no. of pieces	dimensions
a. short stiles	2	72 × 4½ × 1½"
b. long stiles	2	80 × 4¼ × 1½"
c. top rail blanks	2	25 × 7 × 1½"
d. kick rails	2	21 × 8 × 1½"
e. horizontal muntins	4	10⅞ × 1¼ × 1½"
f. vertical mullions	2	65¾ × 1¼ × 1½"
g. astragal	1	2 × 1¼ × 80"

Illus. 6-53. Photo of 80 × 30-inch arch-top entry doors.

Illus. 6-54. Use a long stick, with a nail driven into one end that acts as a pivot, to draw the arch-top rails for these doors.

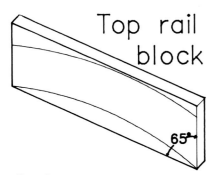

Illus. 6-55. Top rail block.

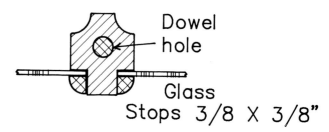

Illus. 6-56. This cross section of a muntin shows the dowel holes in the ends of the muntins and mullions.

80 × 36″ Door with Template-Cut Curved Raised Panels

Level Three

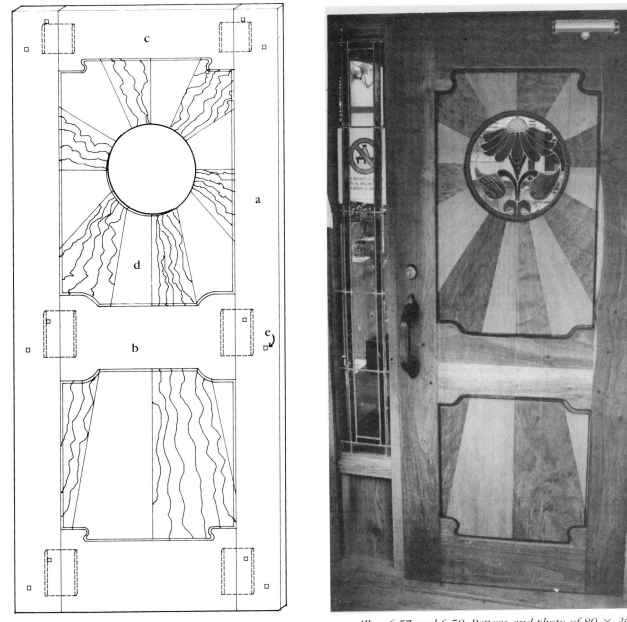

Illus. 6-57 and 6-58. Pattern and photo of 80 × 36-inch door with template-cut curved raised panels.

80 × 36″ Door with Template-Cut Curved Raised Panels

description	no. of pieces	dimensions
a. stiles	2	80 × 6 × 1¾″
b. kick and lock rails	2	24 × 11 × 1¾″
c. top rail	1	24 × 8 × 1¾″
d. contrasting panel lumber	10 square feet	1½″ thick
e. square peg caps	24	⅜ × ⅜ × ¼″

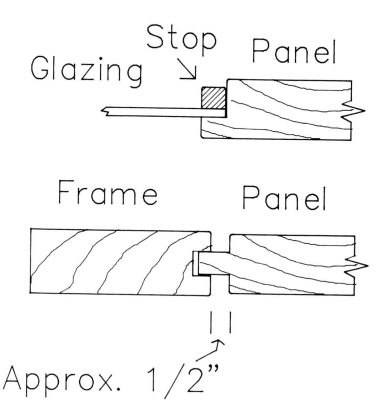

Illus. 6-59. Cross section of the door showing the panel and glass constructions.

By using templates and straight-cutting router bits with different-sized guide bearings, you can make a raised panel that follows the curve of the frame members that surround it. It is also possible to perfectly edge-join two boards that have totally arbitrary curves along their edges. This technique will open up a whole new realm of possibilities for the doormaker. For example, it can be used to make curving corner joints that match each other perfectly.

The door shown in Illus. 6–57 and 6–58 has two large panels made from alternating pieces of curly redwood and straight-grained Douglas fir. These pieces are tapered and joined so that they convey the idea of rays of sunlight emanating from the round window in the upper panel. The darker outer framework is made from black walnut wood. You can cut out the panel stock on a table saw with a tapering jig, or mark and cut it freehand on a band saw. In either case, carefully straighten the edges of each piece on the joiner. The upper panel is the most complicated, and must be glued up in stages; clamp from both directions at once (Illus. 6–60).

Once you have completely glued up the upper panel, roughly cut the lines to size; then extend it out to find the tapers for the lower panel. Be sure to include the width of the lock rail in your calculation of the angles for the tapers. To get the exact angles, totally complete the upper panel and the framework before cutting the pieces for the lower panel.

Start all the rails as straight boards, and cut tenons on their ends to fit them into the mortises that you have worked into the stiles (or mortises for splines). Now, make two templates, one for the middle rail and one for both the top and bottom rails. Make the templates from ¼ inch or thicker plywood with as many laminations as possible, and no voids. Particle board or Masonite can be used, but it is more likely to get soft along the edge.

Make the template pieces an inch or two longer than the rails, and attach them through half-inch spacer pieces to either the ends of the rails or the tenons, any place where the screw holes won't show in the finished piece. First, mark the lines to be cut on the rail, and cut as close as possible to them with the band saw or jigsaw. Now, attach the template securely to the workpiece, and it is ready to be trimmed with the router.

You will use a couple of different router bits and bearings in the construction of this door. For this cut, you will need a 2-inch long, ½-inch straight cutter, with a ½-inch-o.d. (outside diameter) bearing (Illus. 6–61). You can place the bearing on either end of the cutter for this trimmer bit; just make sure that it rides firmly on the edge of the template and that the cutters are not cutting any of the template.

When you reach the part of the curve where the bit is cutting against the grain of the wood and is in danger of breaking it out, take the bit away from the work, move ahead of the curve, and very carefully cut backwards through the curve. The bit will try to pull itself in the direction of the cut, but if you brace yourself carefully and go slowly, you can make this part of the cut this way without danger of breakout.

Once the rails have been trimmed to shape, assemble the framework and position the panel stock under it, so that you can draw the first set of lines to guide you in cutting out the panels. When you have traced all the way

ASSEMBLING PANEL FROM TAPERED PIECES

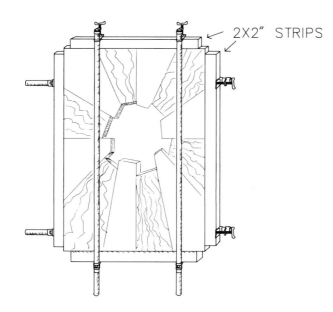

2X2" STRIPS

Illus. 6-60. Trim the outer edges of the upper panel carefully, and clamp from both directions at once. The window hole will be trimmed later with router cuts.

Illus. 6-61. Use a 2-inch-long flush-cutting bit to trim thick stock to a template shape. A flush cutter with an inboard bearing is necessary for cutting panel shapes to follow the framework.

around the insides of the frame on the panels, remove the frame and draw the second set of lines, ⁷⁄₁₆ inch outside of the first set. Cut these lines to cut the panels to their final sizes.

Now, make a template from the templates used to cut the rails; this template will fit over the panels and guide you in cutting the curves that follow the curves on the rails. One simple way to accomplish this is to assemble the framework and lay it over a piece of template stock that has been ripped to the exact width of the panels. The straight lines on the edges of the panels are very important, because they will help you to keep the template straight and square. Be sure that the template stock is perfectly aligned under the frame by marking ⁷⁄₁₆ inches in from each edge, top and bottom, and then simply drawing a line with a very sharp pencil along the

rail, so that the line is ⅛ inch from the rail at all points along the curve. Mark both ends, but don't worry about the straight sides; they will be cut afterwards with either a dado or a router bit and fence.

Next, cut and shape the template exactly to the line. Position the template on one side of the panel using the lines that were traced from the framework as guides. Screws can be screwed into the edges of the panel, where the side rabbets will later be cut, to hold the template in place. Now it is a simple matter to cut the curves on the ends of the panel using a straight cutter with an inboard bearing. Figure the depth you will need from the thickness of the panel stock and the width of the panel groove, and, if necessary, space the template up from the panel so that the cutter cuts to the right depth with the bearing riding solidly on the template.

Before removing the template from the first side of the panel, make indexing marks at the corners to help you get the end-to-end alignment right when you move the template to the other side. Be careful not to flip the template over when you move it to the other side of the board. The side of the template facing away from the panel on the first cut will now be towards the panel on the second side.

Use the indexing marks you made to align the panel, and repeat the process on the second side. After you have cut both ends, cut the straight sides to the same depth with the dado or a router and fence guide. Now, lightly round over all the hard edges on both the panel and the framework by sanding them. The door is ready for final fitting and assembly.

You can get more precise following curves with this method if you make a second template from the first, and use it as an intermediate template for making a matching template (Illus. 6–62). Align the first template on top of the stock for the intermediate template, with the piece that will actually be used for the intermediate template on the off side. When making the cut for the intermediate template, make sure that the bearing rides solidly on the first template at all times. Any deviation will cause a defect in the intermediate template.

The intermediate template will match the curves of the first, but only when the two templates are held apart the width of the router bit. To get a template that exactly matches the first one, you must use the intermediate template and a router cutter with a bearing that is 1 inch wider in its o.d. (outside diameter) than the cutter. The bearing will follow the intermediate template, and the cutter will cut the final matching template ½ inch away from the intermediate template so that the curves match perfectly. By using a bearing that is ⅞ inch wider than the cutter, you could get matching lines that are ¹⁄₁₆ inch apart.

You can buy bearings for this type of work in many sizes for both the inside bore and the outside diameter. The bearing should have an inside diameter exactly the same as the shank of the router bit you are using, and can be dropped onto the bit from the shank end before it is put in the router collet. Bearings are sized by thousandths of an inch. A .500-inch i.d. (inside-diameter) bearing will fit very snugly on most ½-inch shank router bits, sometimes so snugly that heat must be applied to the bearing to expand it, or cold (a couple of hours in the freezer) applied to the router bit to shrink it enough to slip the bearing on. These techniques can be used to cut curving joints where the rails and stiles meet, or to join contrasting woods along curved lines for panels.

MAKING MATCHING TEMPLATES

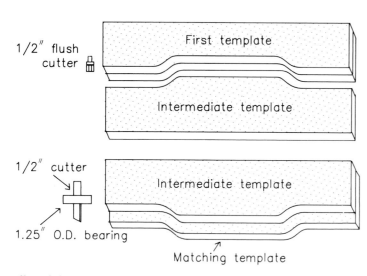

TEMPLATE CUTTING MATCHING RAILS AND PANELS

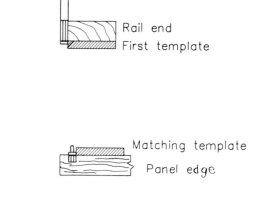

Illus. 6-62. Intermediate templates and cutters with various sized bearings can be used to make precise following curves or edge joints along curved lines.

DOORS WITH APPLIQUÉS

Illus. 6-63–6-65. Appliqués—whether carved, turned, or simply cut out and applied to panel or frame pieces—can create intricate decorative motifs or give the illusion of complex frames or panels. The doors shown and discussed on pages 126-131 all feature appliqués.

Illus. 6-64.   *Illus. 6–65.*

80 × 30″ Entry Door

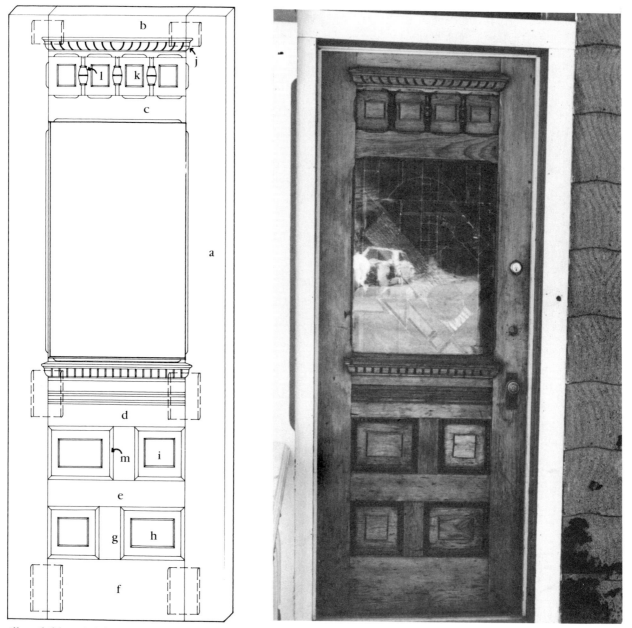

Illus. 6-66 and 6-67. Pattern and photo of 80 × 30-inch entry door.

80 × 30″ Entry Door

description	no. of pieces	dimensions
a. stiles	2	80 × 5½ × 1⅝″
b. top rail	1	19 × 5½ × 1⅝″
c. rail	1	19 × 3½ × 1⅝″
d. lock rail	1	19 × 9 × 1⅝″
e. rail	1	19 × 3½ × 1⅝″
f. kick rail	1	19 × 8 × 1⅝″
g. mullions	2	7½ × 3½ × 1⅝″

description	no. of pieces	dimensions
h. panels	2	8¾ × 7 × ¾″
i. panels	2	7 × 7 × ¾″
j. dentils	2	20¾ × 2 × 1″
k. upper panel	1	20 × 6 × ¾″
l. spindles	3	6 × 1½ × ¾″
m. panel moulding	20 feet	½ × ½″

The door shown in Illus. 6–66 and 6–67 is one in which not all is as it appears to be. The panel section above the glass appears at first glance to be four separate panels, but on closer inspection you will note that it is actually one piece of wood with three "spindle" appliqués positioned between four raised rectangles. The stopped bevels on the edges of the frame pieces also contribute to this illusion. The upper dentil appliqué which has curved lines that match the curves of the end cuts, was most likely hand-carved. The lock rail has nice detail routed into it, and the four lower panels are oddly shaped and positioned.

Start by cutting the frame pieces to the lengths and widths shown in the cutting list. Dry-assemble the door and use a chamfering router bit to cut the chamfers around the glass panel and the upper panel. Before breaking the door down, make indexing marks for all the joinery. Use either dowels or splines for the mullions and muntins.

After you've cut the joinery, dry-assemble the door again and cut slots to house the upper panel. You can also house the lower panels in slots or simply hold them in place by gluing the mouldings in.

Before gluing the framework together, complete the panels that are housed in the slots. Start the upper panel with the four separate raised areas like a normal raised panel. Then remove the sections between the raised areas either by cutting down at a bevel through the raised parts with a small hand saw and planing the remainder away with a rabbet plane, or by using router bits (or a combination of the two). Also, before gluing up the door, cut the moulding in the lock rail, or laminate the lock rail as shown in Illus. 6–68.

After you have glued the frame and flattened the joints, cut the spindle pieces (either turn them yourself or buy them premade) in half with a fine-toothed hand saw, and then glue and nail them in place on the outside of the door only. As with many appliquéd doors, the fancy work is only on the outside; the inside is rather plain. At this time, also apply the two dentils and the beaded mouldings around the lower panels to the outside. To bring out the intricate detail of this door, stain the grooves and beads.

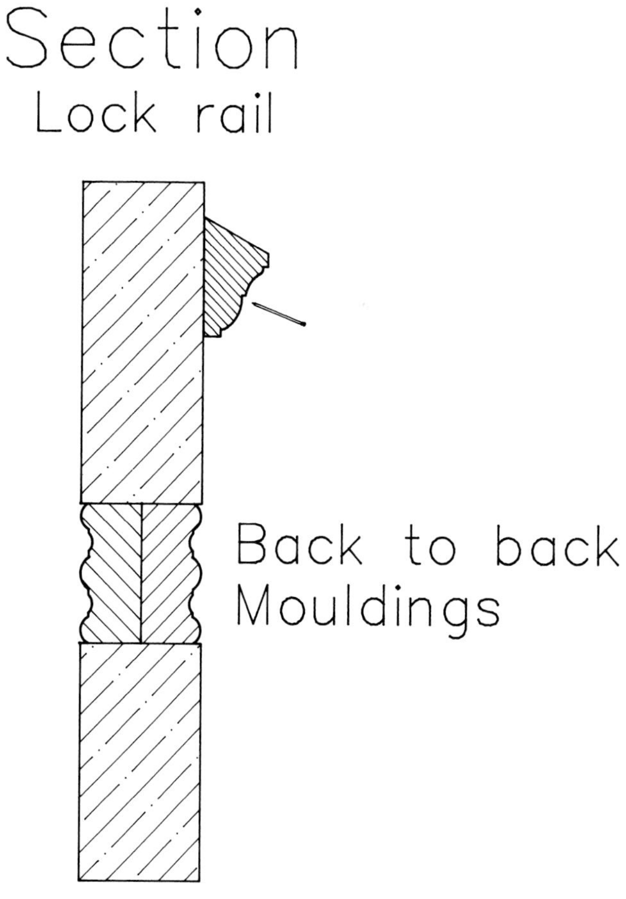

Section
Lock rail

Back to back
Mouldings

Illus. 6-68. Back-to-back mouldings can be edge-joined between frame pieces.

Illus. 6-69. Cross sections of dentil mouldings that also serve as a drip cap and sill on this door.

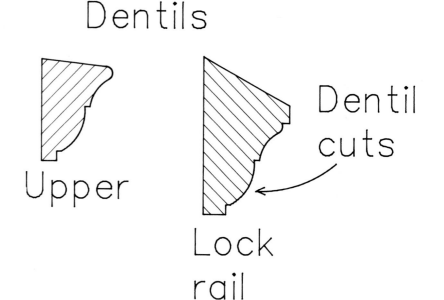

Dentils

Upper

Dentil cuts

Lock rail

80 × 32″ Solid-Core Entry Door

Level Two

Look closely and you will note that the door shown in Illus. 6–70 and 6–71 is really a solid core door that has been made fancier with appliqués. The dark stain used on the door makes it look older, and conceals the fact that it is not really a panel door.

To build this door, start with a solid-core, exterior-grade, birch panel door. Make a template out of high-quality, ½-inch plywood which you will use to cut out the oval window. Cut the piece for the template so that it is 2 inches wider than the door and about four inches longer than the height of the window (37 inches in this case). Draw your ellipse on the template as described on page 99, carefully cut the template out, fair the curves with rasps and sanders. Apply battens to both edges of the template so that you can clamp or screw it to the sides of the door to hold it securely.

Position the template so that the top of the window is 12 inches from the top of the door, and mark the oval on the door. Remove the template and use a jigsaw to roughly cut the hole out; stay about ¼ to ⅛ inch inside the line. When this is done, use a rabbeting bit to cut a rabbet about ¾ inch deep around the rough window hole. This will make the thickness of the wood that has to be trimmed with the flush cutter and template about half what it would have been.

Now, reposition the template and use a long flush cutter (Illus. 6–61) to trim the window hole to the template. After this has been done, use the rabbet cutter again to recut the rabbet so that it follows the line of the template cut. You can make a stop for the oval window glass according to the method used on the door described on pages 97–101.

Now cut the two rectangles of moulding that suggest panels and apply them with nails and glue. Epoxy glue would work best here, but urea resin glue is easier to clean up where it squeezes out. You may not be able to obtain mouldings made from the same wood as the surface of the door, so, if you plan to stain it, experiment to make sure that the stain absorption is similar to that on the door shown in Illus. 6–71. Mitre the mouldings in the lower rectangle, and butt the vertical pieces in the upper rectangle against the horizontal pieces. Apply a hint of a cap and apron above and below the upper horizontals.

Cut two turned pieces into quarters for the upper rectangle corners, and cut a half piece for the lower rectangle. Cut the "rays" for the upper area freehand from ⅛-inch stock with either a band saw or scroll saw, and glue and nail them in place. The rays for the lower "panel" are ¼ inch thick, and have a small cove routed around their edges. Do this with a ball-bearing-guided router bit in a table-mounted router.

Illus. 6-70 and 6-71. Pattern and photo of 80 × 32-inch solid-core entry door.

80 × 32″ Solid-Core Entry Door

description	no. of pieces	dimensions
a. solid-core door	1	80 × 32 × 1½″
b. lower mouldings	80″	1½ × ½″
c. upper vertical mouldings	2	37 × 1½ × ½″
d. appliqué strips	2	24½ × 1½ × ½″
e. cap strip	1	25½ × ¾ × ½″
f. apron	1	22½ × ¾ × ½″
g. ¼ circle appliqués	4	1½ × ⅜″
h. ½ circle appliqué	1	8 × ½″
i. upper cutouts	16	⅛″ thick
j. lower cutouts	7	¼″ thick

80 × 36″ Arch-Top Entry Door

Level Two

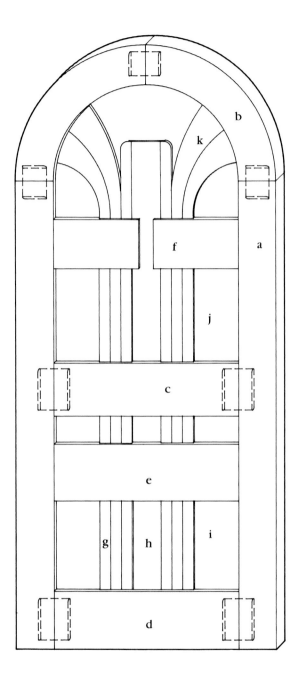

Illus. 6-72 and 6-73. Pattern and photo of 80 × 36-inch arch-top entry door.

80 × 36″ Arch-Top Entry Door

description	no. of pieces	dimensions
a. stiles	2	62 × 5¼ × 1⅝″
b. arch pieces	2	26 × 9 × 1⅝″
c. lock rail	1	25½ × 7 × 1⅝″
d. kick rail	1	25½ × 8 × 1⅝″
e. rail appliqués	2	25½ × 7½ × 1⅝″
f. appliqués	4	11¾ × 6½ × 9⁄16″

description	no. of pieces	dimensions
g. appliqué strips	30 feet	1½ × ¼″
h. appliqué strips	8 feet	4 × ¼″
i. lower panel	1	26⅜ × 24⅛ × ½″
j. upper panel	1	26⅜ × 37 × ½″
k. fan appliqués	8	16 × 5 × ¼″

The magnificent door shown in Illus. 6–72 and 6–73, built by Al Garvey, of Fairfax, California, illustrates the potential of appliqué work for modern door building. A true lock rail helps strengthen the door, and divides the upper and lower sections into two panels. An appliqué that appears to be a rail and other vertical and horizontal appliqués function solely as design elements. This combination produces a door that is strong, stable, and completely distinctive in design.

Make the stiles, rails, and appliqués from solid wood, and cut the two panels from ½-inch-thick plywood. Cut the two halves of the arch that forms the top of the door from 11-inch-wide pieces of lumber. First join them to each other with a spline–tenon joint and then true the arch with either a compass plane or sanders.

When you are satisfied with the curve on the inner edge of the arch, cut the mortises for all the remaining spline–tenon joints; then use a slotting cutter to cut ½ × ½-inch slots around the inner edges of the arch, the stiles, and the kick rail. Cut a slot in the lock rail on both sides.

Now, assemble the main body of the door and, after the glue dries, flatten the joints and sand the frame. At this point, cut out the various appliqués and apply them to the surfaces of the panels with glue and screws. It is important to use screws or nails as well as glue, because glue alone may not hold if the door is exposed to harsh weathering.

Plug the screws, and then, if you like, texture the door using epoxy autobody fillers; then paint it. Al's doors are truly works of art, each designed specifically according to how and where it will be used. His combination of frame-and-panel and appliqué techniques allows him to create lines and forms that are a pleasing and unique synthesis of existing elements.

Illus. 6–74–6–77 show more doors by Al Garvey.

Illus. 6-74–6-77. These doors, made by Al Garvey, show a distinctive style of appliqué work.

Illus. 6-75.

Illus. 6-76.

Illus. 6-77.

COPE-AND-STICK DOORS
80 × 36-Inch Nine-Light, Two-Panel Entry Door

Level Three

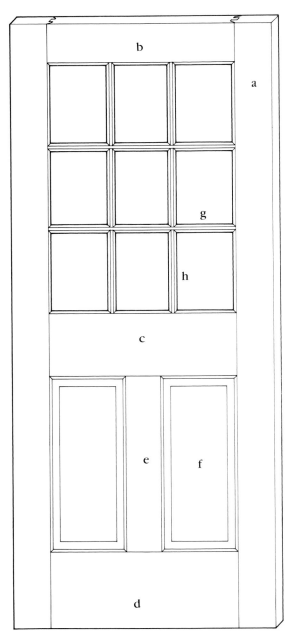

Illus. 6-78 and 6-79. Pattern and photo of 80 × 36-inch, nine-light, two-panel entry door. See the following page for building instructions.

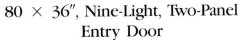

80 × 36″, Nine-Light, Two-Panel Entry Door

description	no. of pieces	dimensions
a. stiles	2	80 × 5½ × 1⅝″
b. top rail	1	25¾* × 5½ × 1⅝″
c. lock rail	1	25¾* × 9 × 1⅝″
d. kick rail	1	25¾* × 10½ × 1⅝″
e. lower mullion	1	23¼* × 5½ × 1⅝″

description	no. of pieces	dimensions
f. panels	2	23⅛ × 10⅜ × 1¼″
g. horizontal muntins	2	23²⁵⁄₃₂* × 1⅛ × 1⅝″
h. vertical mullions	6	11* × 1⅛ × 1⅝″
stop stock	21 feet	⅜ × ½″

*Lengths based on cope cut depth of ⅜″

Making cope-and-stick doors with both glass and wood panels, like the one shown in Illus. 6–78 and 6–79, presents one small difficulty: Two different profiles are needed—one with a slot between two beads to hold the panels, and the other with just one bead and a rabbet for glass and stops. It is possible to stop the shaper cut on the stiles and reset the cutters, or even use routers for part of the door, but a simpler solution is simply to cut the panel slot all the way through and then, after assembling the door, use a flush trim router bit to remove the bead from one side of the slotted areas that will have glass instead of wooden panels (Illus. 6–80).

Most of the pieces in the upper part of this door, where the glass is, don't need two bead cuts. All the stick cuts for the mullions, muntins, and rails can be cut with just one bead. Either reset the shaper after cutting the panel-slot parts or cut the bead and slot on just one side, and then rip the waste away from the rabbet with a table saw.

To build this door, cut all the stiles, rails, muntins, and mullions to the lengths and widths indicated in the cutting list. When you have all the pieces cut to length, cut the mortises for the joints. If the cope cut is not exactly the same depth as that indicated, you will have to adjust the lengths of these pieces to compensate. If you want to use sash cutters that cut a very narrow rabbet, you can deepen the panel slot afterward with a slot cutter.

Now, make the cope cuts first, using a backer block to keep the cutters from breaking out the wood at the end of each cut. Make a double bead-and-slot cope cut on the rails because you are going to make the double cut all the way along the stiles. Use only a single bead cope cut on the upper mullions and muntins and the top rail.

When this is done, make the stick cut by cutting a double bead-and-slot on the stiles and all the edges that hold panels in the lower part of the door. Now, either remove one bead cutter (if your set cuts both at once) or remove spacers (if you have only one bead cutter and have to make two passes), and then use a straight cutter on the spindle to cut the rabbets for the glass on all the mullions and muntins and the two rail edges in the upper part of the door. As mentioned before, an alternate method is to just cut one bead and the slot, and then use the table saw to complete the cut.

Now, dry-assemble the door without the upper mullions and muntins, and use a flush trim bit to remove the bead from the stiles in the upper part of the door. When this is done, you should be able to completely dry-assemble the door. Check the sizes of the panel holes and make the panels, completely sanding and finishing them before gluing the door together.

After the glue has cured, flatten the joints and sand and trim the door. Bed the glass in a bead of caulk to weatherseal it. Make the stops either with router or shaper bits, and then mitre and nail them into place.

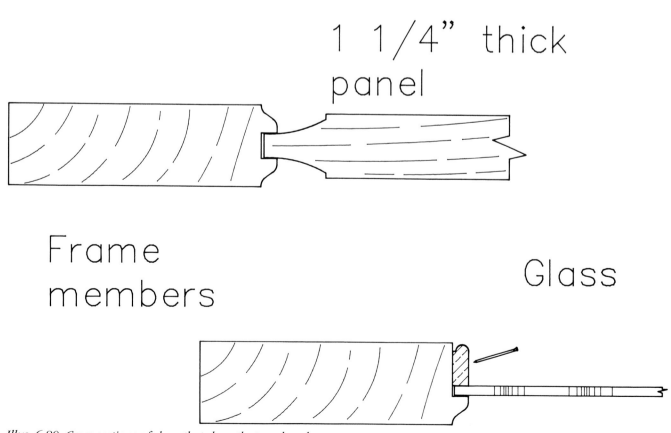

1 1/4" thick panel

Frame members

Glass

Illus. 6-80. Cross sections of door that show the panel and glass construction.

80 × 32″ Entry Door with Stopped Shaper Cuts

Level Three

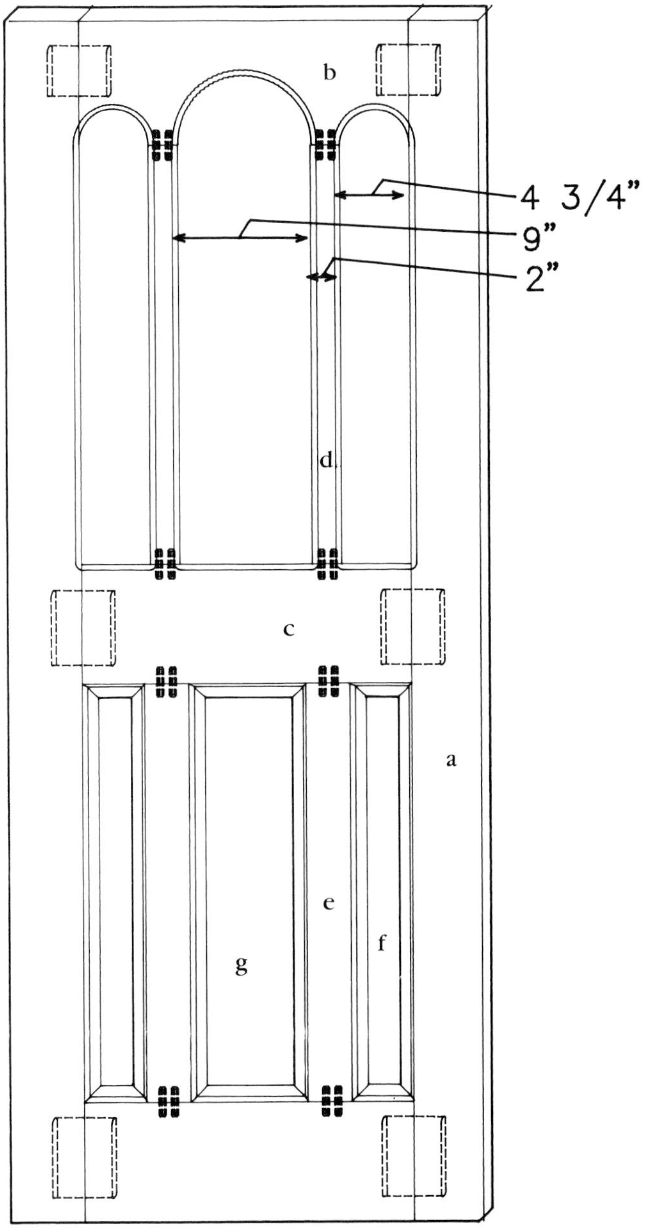

Illus. 6-81 and 6-82. Pattern and photo of 80 × 32-inch entry door with stopped shaper cuts.

80 × 32″ Entry Door with Stopped Shaper Cuts

description	no. of pieces	dimensions
a. stiles	2	80 × 4¾ × 1½″
b. top rail	1	22½ × 8¼ × 1½″
c. lock and kick rails	2	*23¼ × 8¼ × 1½″
d. upper mullions	2	27½ × 2 × 1½″
e. lower mullions	2	*27¾ × 3⅝ × 1½″
f. panels	2	27^{11}⁄16 × 4⅜ × ¾″
g. panel	1	27^{11}⁄16 × 8¼ × ¾″

*Lengths based on cope cut depth of ⅜″

As with most frame-and-panel doors, begin making the door shown in Illus. 6–81 and 6–82 by ripping and crosscutting all the frame pieces to their proper lengths and widths. Before cutting, however, note that shaper cutters are used to form the slot and bead around the panels in the lower part of the door, and router bits are used to make the rabbet and bead for the glass panels in the upper part of the door. This means that you have to stop the shaper cuts on the stiles just at the place where the top of the lock rail will be. This sounds tricky, but it really isn't. You can also make a very similar door without shapers by simply slotting the lower frame pieces with either a router or table saw, and either applying moulding around the panels or using a panel detail that does not require moulding.

If you do decide to make cope and stick cuts on the lower part of the door, remember when cutting out the pieces to add twice the depth of the coping cut to the length of the two lower rails and mullions to compensate for the undercut. The top rail, on the other hand, does not have an undercut on it, and, as shown at b in Illus. 6–81, is shorter than the lower rails. First, cut the top rail out square from a solid piece of wood 8¼ inches wide; then mark the three half circles on it and cut them out carefully with either a band saw or by using a template and a flush-trimming router bit. Be very careful near the ends, as the corners can easily break away. You may find it easier to cut the circles with a template after you have glued the door together to avoid this problem.

When you have cut out all the pieces, lay them out on the table according to where they will go on the door, and mark the places where you will be cutting mortises for the splines that hold the joints together. If you want to, you can use one or two dowels to hold each of the upper mullions in place, and dowels or a spline to hold the lower mullions in place. They are not absolutely necessary, though, because the interlocking cope-and-stick joints will hold them in place quite well.

Before cutting all the mortises with a shaper, accurately mark the spot where the top of the lock rail will meet the stiles on both sides of the stiles. When you shape the stiles, you will want to stop as close to this mark as possible without cutting past it. You will have to drop the stile into the shaper cutters precisely at the mark on one side, and pull it out precisely at the mark on the other side. The end of the shaper cut will be rounded from the radius of the cutters, but a few careful cuts with a sharp ½-inch chisel will square the end of the cut out so that the rail will fit up against it perfectly (Illus. 6–84). Make the shaper cuts on the lower rail and the two upright mullions in the usual manner.

Once you have made the shaper cuts and have squared-out the stop-cuts, dry-assemble the door and determine the sizes of the panels. Completely shape the panels and finish the door before gluing it together.

Begin the final glue-up of the door by laying out the rails, mullions, and panels on the assembly table, applying glue to all the meeting surfaces of the joints, and

clamping from top to bottom with long bar clamps. Apply these clamps to just one side of the door; do not overtighten them. Now, work the stiles into place and apply clamps across the door on the side opposite the long clamps. When you have clamps across the top and bottom of the door and all the joints are tight, remove the long clamps and apply more clamps across the door to ensure that the pressure is even. Check with a straight edge to be sure that the stiles are not twisted or tilted by uneven pressure.

After the glue has cured and you have planed the joints flat, use an ogee or quarter-round bit on the interior side of the window holes, and a rabbeting bit to form the seat for the glass (Illus. 6–85). Then square out lower corners of the rabbets with a chisel, and make stops to hold the glass in place. Cut the stops for the half circles at the upper ends of the windows from laminated material so that they won't break where the grain is short. Shape the edges of these stops with a small quarter-round bit and a guide bearing set up in a router table.

Illus. 6-83. This door was also made using cope-and-stick cutters for the lower panels, and router cutters for the glazed areas.

Stopped shaper cut at lock rail

Alternate panel cross section

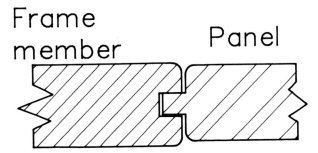

Frame
member

Panel

Illus. 6-85. You can make this door without shapers by simply slotting the lower frame pieces and slightly rounding the corners.

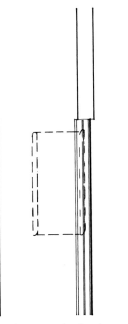

Illus. 6-84. After you have made the shaper cut, use a sharp chisel to square off the end of the cut, so that the rail can fit snugly against it.

80 × 34″ Entry Door

Level Two

The cope-and-stick door shown in Illus. 6–86 and 6–87 is nicely proportioned and easy to build. Begin by cutting all the frames pieces to the lengths and widths indicated in the cutting list. Leave the rails long (twice the depth of the cope cut) for the interlocking joints; do the same for the wide lower mullion and the two narrow upper mullions. If your cutters cut differently than the depths indicated, change the lengths of the pieces accordingly.

Once you have cut all the pieces, lay the door out and mark across the joints for the mortises where the rails meet the stiles. The muntins and mullions don't need splines or dowels because the interlocking cope and stick will hold them together. Glass and stops will also help lock these pieces in place.

After you have cut the mortises, run all the pieces that need cope cuts first, and then those that need stick cuts. When making cope-and-stick doors that have both glass and panels, I usually run the panel cut on all pieces, and

then go back with a flush cutter or the table saw to remove the bead on one side of the pieces that will hold the glass. This turns the slots into rabbets for the glass without you having to reset the shapers. Now, dry-assemble the door to check the joinery and to measure the widths of the panels. Make the panels about ⅛ inch shorter than the length of the lower mullion, and about ⅛ inch narrower than the widths of the spaces from side to side.

When you are sure that all the cope-and-stick cuts fit tightly, break down the stick cutter and set up for cutting the panels. Check your cut on a scrap of the same thickness as the panels until you get it perfect—if anything, slightly thick. Sand if necessary around the edges, and completely finish the panels before gluing the door together. Use the method described on pages 70–73 to assemble this door. After the glue has dried, flatten the joints and trim and sand the door.

Illus. 6-86 and 6-87. Pattern and photo of 80 × 34-inch entry door.

80 × 34″ Entry Door

description	no. of pieces	dimensions
a. stiles	2	80 × 5½ × 1⅝″
b. top and lock rails	2	*23¾ × 5½ × 1⅝″
c. kick rail	1	*23¾ × 9½ × 1⅝″
d. lower mullion	1	*38½ × 5 × 1⅝″
e. panels	2	38⅜ × 9⅝ × 1¼″
f. upper mullions	2	*22 × 1 × 1⅝″
g. muntins	4	*5¼ × 1 × 1⅝″
h. stop material	20 feet	⅝ × ⅜″

*Lengths based on cope cut depth of ⅜″

80 × 30″ Entry Doors

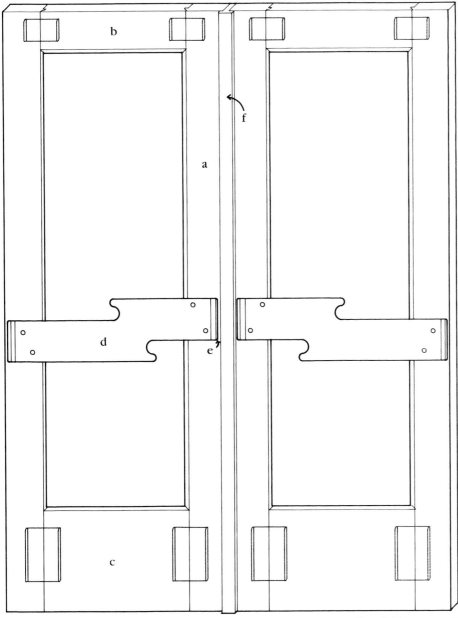

Illus. 6-88. Pattern for 80 × 30-inch entry doors. See the following page for a photo and building instructions.

80 × 30″ Entry Doors

description	no. of pieces	dimensions
a. stiles	4	80 × 5½ × 1⅝″
b. top rails	2	20 × 5½ × 1⅝″
c. kick rails	2	20 × 14 × 1⅝″
d. applied rails	4	29 × 7½ × ¾″
e. spacer pieces	8	5½ × 5 × ¼″
f. astragal	1	80 × 2 × 1½″

Illus. 6-89. Photo of 80 × 30-inch entry doors.

The pair of simple doors shown in Illus. 6–88 and 6–89 do not cost a lot to glaze with tempered glass, and yet have more visual appeal than a door with single rectangular light. The applied middle rail works both functionally as a handhold for opening and closing the door, and aesthetically as an interesting design element.

This idea can be taken a step further if you carve, inlay, or shape the hand rail any way you choose (Illus. 6–90–6–93). Carved hand rails provide a good opportunity for those who have the urge to carve, but lack the time or inclination to decorate an entire door. Homemade catches and lock plates can also be used to embellish doors.

This door also works nicely as an entry and exit door because it is operated simply by pushing or pulling—you don't have to turn a knob every time you use it. Use a bullet catch or pivot hinge to hold the doors shut most of the time, and install a deadbolt lock to lock them.

To build these doors, first cut out two stiles and a top and bottom rail. Double the numbers of pieces shown in the cutting list if you are making a pair of doors. The

doors shown in Illus. 6–88 and 6–89 were made with cope-and-stick cutters on shapers, but a simple door like this could also be made with a router-cut bead and rabbet as long as a strong mortise-and-tenon joint is used at each corner.

If you use shaper cutters, remember to make the rails longer than indicated to compensate the undercut of the cope. Once you have assembled, planed, and sanded the door, install the glass. You can slip it into place after applying the hand rails, but it will be less troublesome if you do it before.

Glue the glass in by laying it in a thick bead of silicone caulk. This is especially important if you use double glazing, or are building an extra wide door, because the weight of the glass can cause weak joints to fail if it is not borne evenly by the entire frame. Any type of stop will do as long as it doesn't project above the edge of the rabbet.

Now, make the hand rails by cutting out the pattern. The rails could be made from a single piece of wood, but these doors have ¼-inch spacer pieces glued to the

Illus. 6-90—6-93. Handles and catches can be incorporated as interesting and functional elements on custom-made doors.

Illus. 6-91.

Illus. 6-92.

Illus. 6-93.

ends where they attach to the stiles to give slightly more finger room between the rail and the glass (Illus. 6–94).

Bevel the ends of the rails to 45-degree angles, but keep the ends of the spacers square. Remember that if you are making a pair of doors, the rails will have to be positioned far enough back from the edges to allow for the astragal and stops.

Glue the spacers on to the rails after trimming the

ends to their right lengths; then round over the edges all the way to the ends on the outside, and just up to the spacer pieces on the insides.

Now, drill and countersink two screw holes in each end and apply the rails to the doors at approximately doorknob height with #12 × 2-inch screws. Also use glue if you haven't yet applied a finish to the doors.

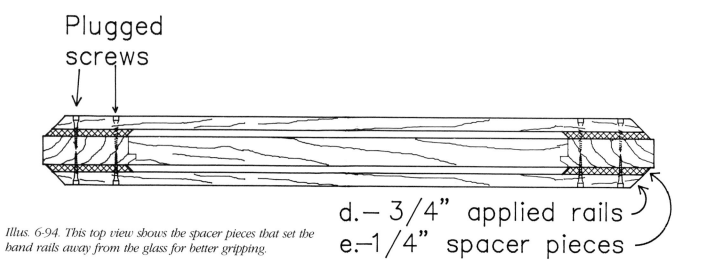

Plugged screws

d.— 3/4" applied rails
e.—1/4" spacer pieces

Illus. 6-94. This top view shows the spacer pieces that set the hand rails away from the glass for better gripping.

80 × 30" Entry Door with Arched Light

Level Three

Both the cope-and-stick cuts and the raised panels on the simple but aesthetically pleasing door shown in Illus. 6–95 and 6–96 are made with shaper cutters. You can make a similar door without having to use shaper cutters by moulding the lower panels and routing the bead and rabbet for the glass.

If you do use cope-and-stick shaper cutters, the slightly curved top rail will present an additional difficulty. When you shaper-cut on curved edges like this, you have to use a guide template and a bearing of the right diameter both inside and out to guide the cutters along the template.

To build this door as it is shown, first cut the frame pieces in the cutting list to size. Remember to add twice the depth of the cope cut to the length of the rails and the ends of the upright mullion. Next, cut the spline mortises for all the structural joints. The upright mullion can either be dowelled or splined in place.

When you have made the mortises, go to the shaper. Note that the lower panels have a bead on either side which forms the slot that holds the panels, while the glazed area just has one bead and an applied stop (Illus. 6–97). The simplest way to do this is to make the double cut all the way through the shaping sequence, and then, after assembling the door, use a flush trimming router bit to remove the bead from one side of the glass panel.

The side you remove the bead from should become the exterior side of the door. Square out the corners with a sharp chisel.

With a very shallow curve like the one on the inside of the upper rail in this door, you need not worry that the short grain at the ends of the cut will break away. On the other hand, if the wood you use tends to break easily, or you begin to increase the angle of the curve, you can prevent breakage by leaving short, straight sections at the ends, as demonstrated by the "alternate curve" shown in Illus. 6–98.

The panels present no special problems, and can be made in a number of ways with either the shaper or table saw. Remember, they must be totally finished and sealed before you assemble the door.

Once you have done all the shaping and have completed the panels, assemble the door in the usual manner. After the glue has cured, flatten the joints with a hand plane and then cut the glass rabbet with a flush trimming router bit. Carefully saw the curved stop for the upper rail and sand it to fit. If you continue the curve all the way to the ends of the rail, you will have to draw a line tangent to the curve at the end of the rail, and then bisect the angle formed by the tangent line and the stile, to find the angle at which to mitre the upper stop to the sides.

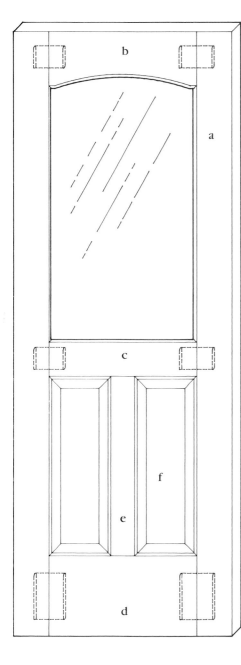

Illus. 6-95 and 6-96. Pattern and photo of 80 × 30-inch entry door with arched light.

80 × 30″ Entry Door with Arched Light

description	no. of pieces	dimensions
a. stiles	2	80 × 5¼ × 1⅝″
b. top rail	1	*20¼ × 7½ × 1⅝″
c. lock rail	1	*20¼ × 5¼ × 1⅝″
d. kick rail	1	*20¼ × 11 × 1⅝″
e. lower mullion	1	*23¾ × 4 × 1⅝″
f. panels	2	23¹¹⁄₁₆ × 8⁷⁄₁₆ × 1⅜″

*Lengths based on cope cut depth of ⅜″

Illus. 6-97. Cross sections of door that show cope-and-stick panel and glass rabbet.

Illus. 6-98. With a very shallow arch, you can continue the curve all the way to the ends of the piece, but for deeper curves it may be safer to leave straight sections at the ends to keep the grain from breaking.

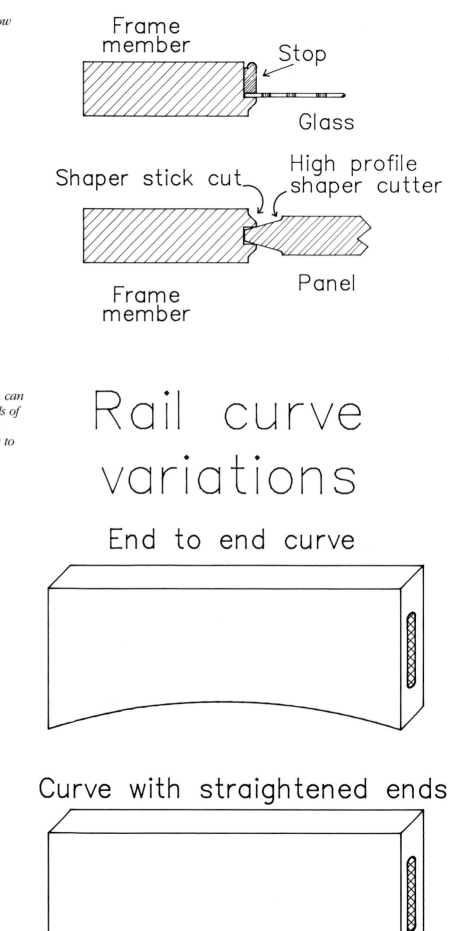

Frame member

Stop

Glass

Shaper stick cut

High profile shaper cutter

Frame member

Panel

Rail curve variations

End to end curve

Curve with straightened ends

80 × 36″ Entry Door

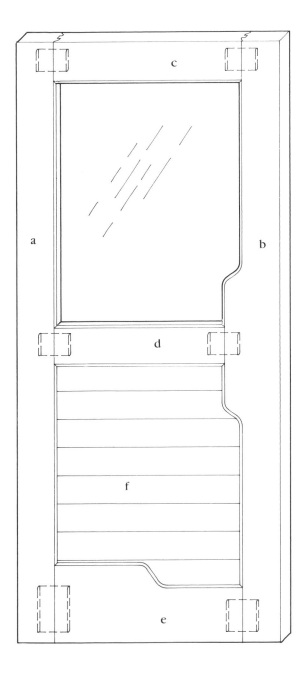

Illus. 6-99 and 6-100. Pattern and photo of 80 × 36-inch entry door. See the following page for building instructions.

80 × 36″ Entry Door

description	no. of pieces	dimensions
a. stile	1	80 × 5½ × 1¾″
b. stile	1	80 × 7½ × 1¾″
c. top rail	1	25¾* × 5½ × 1¾″
d. lock rail	1	23⅜* × 5½ × 1¾″
e. kick rail	1	25¾* × 11 × 1¾″
f. tongue-and-groove pieces	8	25⅝ × 3¾ × ⅝″

*Lengths based on cope cut depth of ⅜″

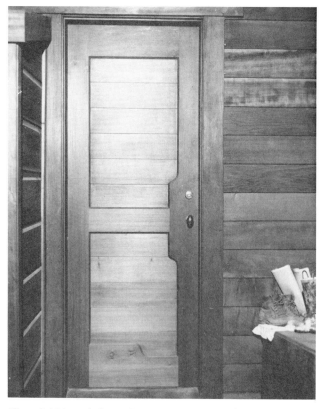

Illus. 6-102.

Illus. 6-101 and 6-102. Two variations on the same pattern.

The simple-looking door shown in Illus. 6–99 and 6–100 is actually quite tricky to build; it requires the use of templates for shaping the lock stile and the bottom rail. Also, you have to cut and fit a stop that follows the line of the curve in the upper part of the stile. This can be quite timeconsuming, especially if you use glass panels at the top and bottom.

First, cut the frame pieces to the sizes shown in the cutting list. Note that the lock stile (b in Illus. 6–99) is two inches wider than the hinge stile (a). Before proceeding, make templates for the two irregularly shaped pieces. Screw these templates into the ends of the rail and stile so that the screw holes won't show later. The stile, because of its length, should also have a backing piece that runs the full length of the outside edge of the piece. Drive a couple of screws through this piece into the outer edge of the door to stabilize the template on the piece.

Cut the stile template from a carefully jointed piece of plywood that is two inches longer than the stile and one inch wider. Cut in from both ends using the rip fence on a table saw to get the straight parts of the template perfectly straight and parallel. Stop where the curve begins; cut the curves with a band saw, and then fair them into the straight parts of the template. It is very important that the straight parts be perfectly straight so that the joints will be tight.

This template will ride on a guide bearing that you should mount either above or below the cutters on your stick shaper. The bearing must be the right diameter for your cutters. If your cutters cut on only one side of the piece at a time, as mine do, you will have to do one of the following: reverse the rotation of the cutters (with a

reversing switch on the shaper) so that you can make both sides of the stick cut without moving the template; or flip the piece over with the template on the bottom, move the bearing to the bottom, reset the height of the cutters, and make the cut. If you choose to flip the piece over, be sure that there are no protruding screws or nails on the surface of the template. Another approach that avoids this problem is to cut just one bead like the cross section of the bead with glass (shown in Illus. 6–103), and then make a moulding to hold the tongue-and-groove panel in.

When you have made the templates, use them to mark the finished shapes on the stile and rail, and cut as closely as possible along the outside of these marks. Now, cut the mortises for all the corner joints before going to the shaper.

Make all the end or coping cuts first. Then set up the stick cutter with a fence and cut all the straight pieces with the stick cut. Lastly, remove the fence, mount the bearing on the spindle, and a guide post on the table to help steady the work, and make the template cuts. Dry-assemble and check to be sure that everything fits.

The panel in the lower part of the door is made from tongue-and-groove material that is the same thickness as the slot in the frame. You can make your own tongue-and-groove material if it is not available in the type of wood or thickness you want.

After you have glued the door together, use a flush trimming router bit to remove the bead from one side of the slot in the upper part of the door so that you can install glass (if you have made two bead cuts). Make the curved stop by carefully marking the curve on a piece of wood of the right thickness, cutting it out with a band saw, and sanding or planing it until it fits tightly. Now, cut and sand the outside edge, and, finally, mitre the ends. Use a small, quarter-round bit in a router table to round the outer edge of the stop. Be careful, as it will be delicate where the grain is short on the curved part.

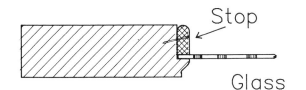

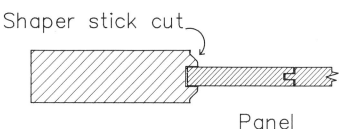

Illus. 6-103. Cross sections of door that show glass and panel construction.

FRENCH DOORS

Level Two

Multi-light window-doors, commonly called French doors, can be made in various widths and with various configurations of lights (Illus. 6–104–6–107). For clarity's sake, French doors are defined here as doors that have only glass panels and a sash-like frame, no wooden panels. They are often installed in pairs in areas leading to a deck or backyard patio. They are also commonly used between greenhouses or solariums and the living area of a home. The configuration of the lights can be regular or irregular. Generally, the door looks better if the lights are taller than they are wide.

It is possible to make French doors without cope-and-stick joinery by using stub tenons to hold the pieces together, but this is a slow, tedious way to build them. The best approach is to use sash-cutting bits—the same type used for making windows—on a shaper or router. The interlocking end cuts on the muntins and mullions will then hold the pieces in place in the rigid frame formed by the stiles and rails, and the glass and stops will add strength to the construction (Illus. 6–108). On some French doors with irregular light patterns, you may still want to strengthen certain mullions with tenons or splines.

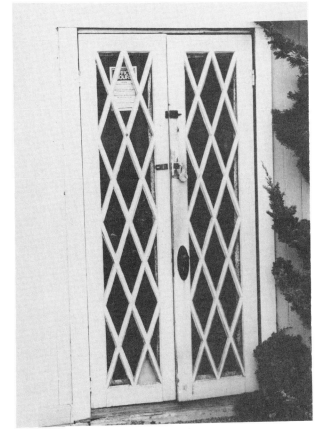

Illus. 6-104–6-107. French doors—glazed doors without panels—can be hung in pairs or singly, and can be made in a wide variety of designs. The doors illustrated and described on pages 149-155 are French doors.

Illus. 6-105.

Illus.6-106.

Illus. 6-107.

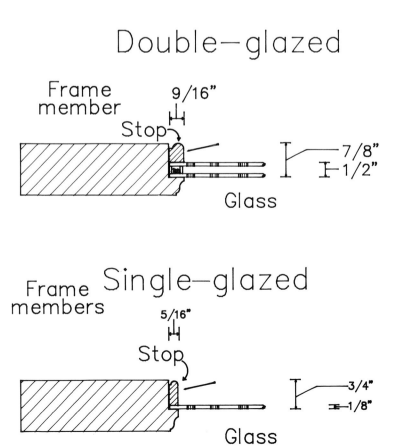

Illus. 6-108. Double-glazed French doors require a wider mullion and wider stops because of the spacer and sealant around the edges of the pieces.

80 × 36″ 15-Light Door

Level Two

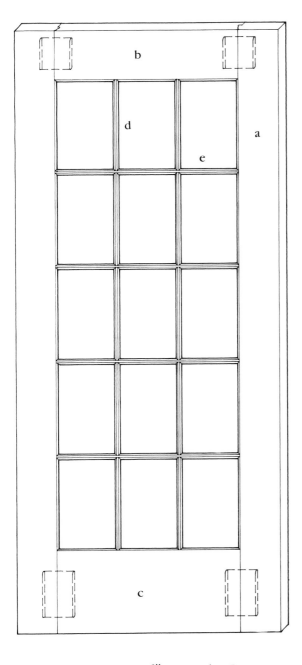

Illus. 6-109 and 6-110. Pattern and photo of 80 × 36-inch 15-light door. See the following page for building instructions.

80 × 36″ 15-Light Door

description	no. of pieces	dimensions
a. stiles	2	80 × 5½ × 1½″
b. top rail	1	25⅝* × 5½ × 1½″
c. kick rail	1	25⅝* × 11¼ × 1½″
d. vertical mullions	10	12¼* × ⅞ × 1½″
e. horizontal muntins	4	25⅝* × ⅞ × 1½″

*Lengths based on cope cut depth of 5⁄16″

To build a regular French door like the one shown in Illus. 6–109 and 6–110, first cut the stiles and rails to the lengths and widths indicated in the cutting list. Make an extra rail like the top one, from which you will eventually cut the horizontal muntins (see Illus. 6–109). This piece should be, if anything, just slightly longer than the top and bottom rails. Later, you will rip it into ⅞-inch-wide strips for the muntins, but not until after the cope cut is made on the ends. If you are unsure of the lengths of the upright mullions, cut them later. The lengths on these pieces must be exact, because any error will be amplified five times.

Once you have cut the stiles, rials, and the piece for the muntins, cut the mortises for the corner spline joints. Now, make the cope cut on the rail ends, and cut the ends of the piece for the muntins. Next, rip the muntins to their proper widths (they may vary, depending on the type of the cutters you are using, but you should have at least ¼-inch left between the two stick cuts), and run the stick cut on the stiles, inside edges of the rails, and both edges of the muntins. Use a holder to push these thin pieces past the shaper cutters.

Now, calculate the length of the upright mullions by measuring from the rabbet on the top rail (b in Illus. 6–109) to the rabbet of the kick rail (c in Illus. 6–109), subtracting the width of the space left between the stick cuts on the muntins (times this figure by the number of muntins you have), and dividing by the number of lights. Once again, you will save yourself some tricky cutting if you cut a wide piece of this length, run the cope cut on the ends of it, rip out the pieces for the mullions, and finally run the stick cut on them.

Before assembling the door, lay the rails and muntins out edge to edge, with their ends perfectly aligned, and mark the places where the centers of the mullions will butt to them (Illus. 6–111). Then assemble the door by laying out the grid work of mullions and muntins on the table and clamping up the frame of the stiles and rails around it. Apply just enough glue to the ends of the muntins and mullions to coat them without causing a lot of extra glue to squeeze out. Clean off any glue that does squeeze out in the corners with a small, stiff-bristled brush and water.

Check with a straight edge and/or square to ensure that the mullions are lined up straight, and that the muntins are not bent. After the glue has cured, plane the outer frame joints and sand the muntin and mullion joints to get them completely flat. Mitre the stops and apply them with small nails to hold the glass in place. Be sure to apply a bead of caulk around the bottom of the glass rabbet to seal the glass to the wood and prevent leaking.

Illus. 6-111. Line up all the rails and muntins, and use a square to mark the positions of the mullions across them.

80 × 32″ Double-Glazed Door

Level Two

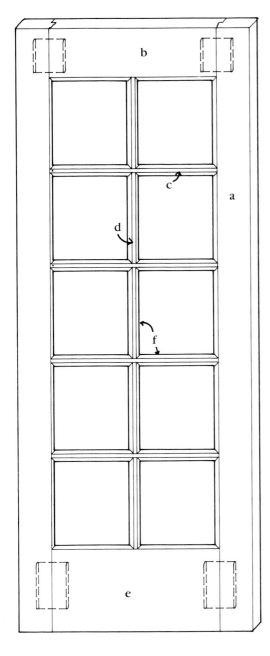

Illus. 6-112 and 6-113. Pattern and photo of 80 × 32-inch double-glazed door.

80 × 32″ Double-Glazed Door

description	no. of pieces	dimensions
a. stiles	2	80 × 5 × 1⅝″
b. top rail	1	23* × 7 × 1⅝″
c. horizontal muntins	4	23* × 1½ × 1⅝″
d. vertical mullions	5	12¹¹⁄₁₆* × 1½ × 1⅝″
e. kick rail	1	23* × 11½ × 1⅝″
f. stops	40	12 × ½ × ½″

*Lengths based on cope cut depth of ⁹⁄₁₆″

Double glazing has become a necessary means of controlling heat loss through windows. Double glazed French doors are essential for those who live in cold climates and burn expensive heating fuels. A wooden-framed, double-glazed French door like the one shown in Illus. 6–112 and 6–113 can be built in one of two ways. Both methods are discussed here.

If you are going to use real mullions and muntins to divide the lights, they will have to be somewhat wider and heavier looking than those that would be necessary for single glazing. This is because double glazing is made with an aluminum spacer around the edge that is sealed with a black neoprene glue. The neoprene totally seals the space between the panes of glass, and a desiccant in the aluminum spacer absorbs all the moisture in the air that is trapped between the panes. This prevents fogging of the glass.

Therefore, make the rabbet for the glass at least ½ inch wide and at least ⅞ inch deep so that the spacer and neoprene are completely hidden from view. Also, you must take special precautions to protect the neoprene glue from direct sunlight, and from contact with chemicals that can ruin it. Even regular glazing putty contains agents that will break down the neoprene seal, so wooden stops are generally used to hold the glass in place. Some, but not all, silicone, butyl, or acrylic caulks can be used to bed the glass and prevent leaking.

The construction method for building a double-glazed French door is basically the same as that outlined for single-glazed French doors, except that wood at least 1⅝ inch thick must be used, and special, longer, straight shaper cutters must be used to cut a deeper rabbet. Some builders prefer to make this cut in two passes—one on the shaper, and one on the table saw—to prevent large pieces from accidentally breaking out, but I have found that as long as several narrow cutters are used and stacked so that the cutting edges are offset, this is not a problem.

An alternative method of French door construction when double glazing is necessary is to use a single large

panel of glass, and then make a light, narrow grid that you will apply to the glass on one or both sides to give the appearance of separate panes (Illus. 6–114).

Illus. 6-114. An alternative construction method when using double glazing is to use one large piece of glass, and then make a light framework to give the illusion of separate panes.

80 × 30", 18-Light Door with Bevelled Glass

Level Three

Illus. 6-115 and 6-116. Pattern and photo of 80 × 30-inch, 18-light door with bevelled glass. See the following page for building instructions.

80 × 30" 18-Light Door with Bevelled Glass

description	no. of pieces	dimensions
a. stiles	2	80 × 5⅞ × 1½"
b. top rail	1	19* × 5⅞ × 1½"
c. kick rail	1	19* × 16¼ × 1½"
d. vertical mullions	12	9¼* × ¾ × 1½"

description	no. of pieces	dimensions
e. horizontal muntins	5	19* × ¾ × 1½"
6 × 9" bevelled glass panes	18	

*Lengths based on cope cut depth of ⅜"

The door shown in Illus. 6–115 and 6–116 is built with the same construction methods as the previous door, except that the size of the lights (the glass panels) is predetermined. Bevelled glass is, as a rule, quite expensive, but you can purchase small pieces (the pieces used in this door being the largest available) from stained glass suppliers quite cheaply. Circles, teardrops, diamonds, and other shapes are also available for use as peepholes or as other ways to accent the doors.

Since the bevelled area of the glass is only ½ inch wide, make the mullions and muntins so that there is at least ⅛ inch extra space all around each piece of glass—this is so you can show as much of the bevel as possible (Illus. 6–117).

If you add another 6½ inches to the length of all the rails and horizontal muntins, and add six mullions, you can make a 24-light bevelled glass French door that is 36 inches wide.

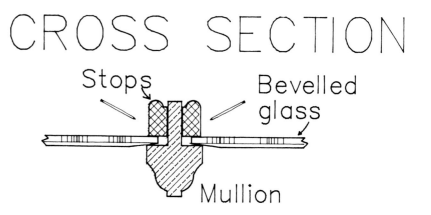

Illus. 6-117. Leave at least ⅛ inch of space all around each piece of glass to show as much of the bevel as possible.

80 × 24″ Curved-Rail Doors

Level Three

You can make the set of narrow cope-and-stick French doors shown in Illus. 6–118 and 6–119 more intriguing by cutting mirror-image curves into the top and bottom rails. One template can be used for all four of the curved pieces.

First, make the template from a piece of high-quality, ½-inch plywood. Leave the template about two inches longer than the rails you will be making so that you can screw battens to the ends of it, and then drive screws through the battens into the ends of the rails to hold it securely in place. You may have to apply battens to both sides of this template, since you will have to flip it over to make the mirror image cuts for the second door. If you have a reversing switch on your shaper, you may not need to do this.

When you start, the template should also be about 1 inch wider than the widest part of the kick rail. Also, screw in battens along the straight edge of the template to totally lock the template in place on the workpiece. After making the kick rails, screw in battens to both sides of template two inches in from the edge to fit the narrower top rails.

When the template is done, cut all the frame pieces to the lengths and widths indicated in the cutting list. Crosscut a block that is wide enough so that you can get

all the horizontal muntins for one door out of it; if anything, it should be a little longer than the rails. You may want to wait and cut the vertical mullions later, since any slight inaccuracy in their lengths (or your cope cutters) will be repeated several times, adding up to a large error.

Use a band saw to cut the rails about ⅛ inch outside the line you marked on them from the template. Now, make all the cope cuts on the rails and muntins. When the cope cuts are done, either set up the stick cutter with a fence for the straight cuts, or without it for the curved cuts. When you make the curved cuts, be sure to use a guide pin and a bearing that's the right size for the depth of cut your shapers make. The outside diameter of the bearing should be slightly smaller than the outside diameter of the cutters.

When you have made the cope-and-stick cuts on the stiles, rails, and muntins, dry-assemble the door and carefully check the length you will need for the mullions (see page 155). When these have been cut, assemble the door and allow it to dry. Flatten and sand it in the normal manner, and then bed the glass and cut the stops. Cut and fit the curved stops in the same way as the stops for the door on page 151.

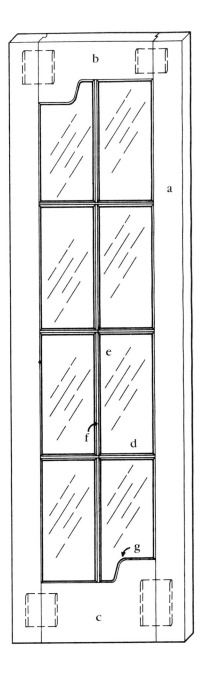

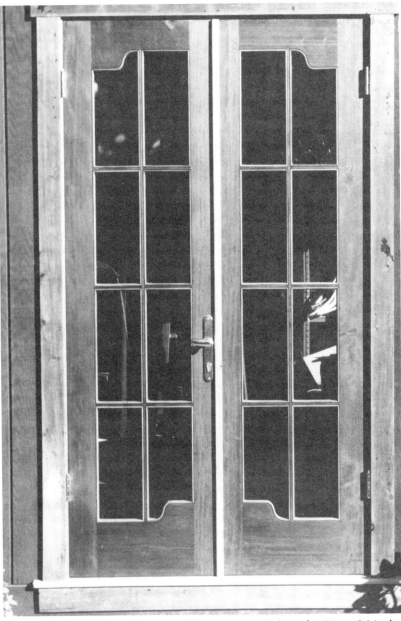

Illus. 6-118 and 6-119. Pattern and photo for 80 × 24-inch curved-rail doors. Note that the cutting list below contains materials for one door.

80 × 24″ Curved-Rail Doors

description	no. of pieces	dimensions
a. stiles	2	80 × 4⅜ × 1½″
b. top rail	1	*16 × 8 × 1½″
c. kick rail	1	*16 × 11 × 1½″
d. muntins	3	*16 × ⅞ × 1½″
e. mullions	4	*16⅜ × ⅞ × 1½″
f. straight stops	20 feet	⁵⁄₁₆ × ⅝″
g. curved stops	2	8 × ⅝ × ⁵⁄₁₆″

*Lengths based on cope cut depth of ⅜″

CLOSETS

Beautiful closet doors can add a lot of style and elegance to a room (Illus. 6–120 and 6–121). They do not have to be built of thick, heavy material, and there is no need to worry about damage from weather, so simple joinery can be used. The hardest thing about building closet doors is finding material that is the right thick-ness. Material that is ¾ inch thick will be fine for some closets, but often material 1–1¼ inch thick is more desirable, and since lumber isn't normally sold in this thickness, you are forced to plane down thicker material.

Illus. 6-120 and 6-121. Closet doors can be beautiful without being difficult to build.

76 × 34″ Fabric-Panel Closet Doors

Level Two

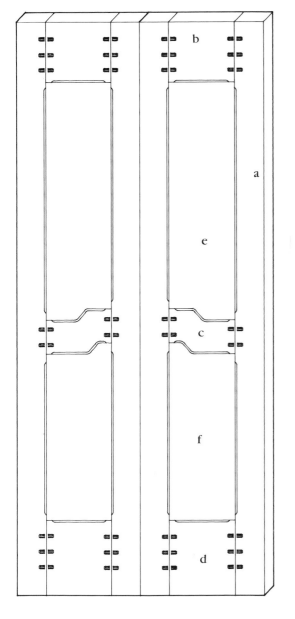

Illus. 6-122 and 6-123. Pattern and photo of 76 × 34-inch fabric-panel closet doors. See the following page for building instructions.

76 × 34″ Fabric-Panel Closet Doors

description	no. of pieces	dimensions
a. stiles	4	76 × 4 × 1½″
b. top rails	2	9 × 8 × 1½″
c. middle rails	2	9 × 6 × 1½″
d. kick rails	2	9 × 10 × 1½″
e. upper panels	2	32½ × 10 × ¼″
f. lower panels	2	23½ × 10 × ¼″

The beautiful closet doors shown in Illus. 6–122 and 6–123 are made by gluing fabric to ¼-inch-thick wood or pressed board panels. The doors shown here are mounted as bifolds, but this design would also work for swinging closet doors. It's possible to mount two panels back to back for a door that would be viewed from either side, but the fabric will be hard to clean, so this might not be a good idea if the closet is going to be used a lot.

To build these doors, cut the frame pieces to length and width, and use a sliding T square and compass to mark the cuts on the center rail. Then cut this rail out on the band saw. To simplify the making of the panels, cut the rabbets on the back sides of the center rails through with the table saw so that the panels can be rectangular

(Illus. 6–124 and 6–125). First decide on the depth of the router cut that will hold the panels, and then cut out the backs of the rails to this depth.

For a closet door, you can use dowels for the corner joints. Once you have cut the dowel holes, assemble the frames and allow the glue to dry. Then plane and sand the doors before making the stopped chamfer cuts around the outer edges with a router. Draw marks 1 inch from the corner on all the edges of every panel, and stop or start the router cuts here. Also make the rabbet cuts for the panels with the router, and square out the upper and lower corners with a chisel.

Use a spray adhesive to glue the fabric to the panels, and trim the edges carefully. Apply wooden stops to hold the panels in.

Illus. 6-124. Marking the cloud-lift patterns onto the rails.

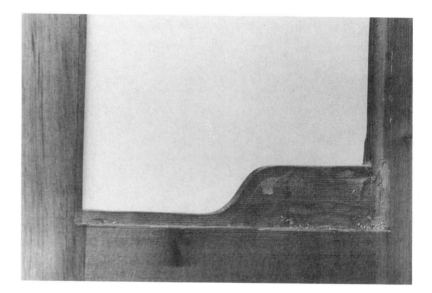

Illus. 6-125. Cut the rabbet on the inner sides of these rails straight through so that the panels can be simple rectangles.

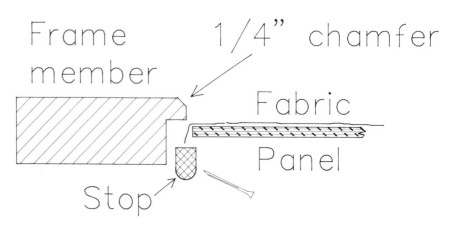

Illus. 6-126. This cross section of the door shows how it is constructed.

SCREEN DOORS

80 × 36″ Victorian Screen Door

Level Three

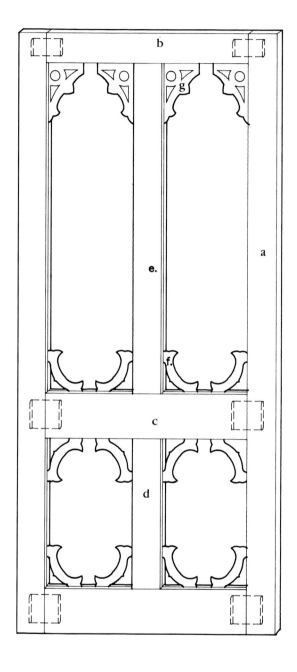

Illus. 6-127 and 6-128. Pattern and photo of Victorian screen door. See the following page for building instructions.

80 × 36″ Victorian Screen Door

description	no. of pieces	dimensions
a. stiles	2	80 × 4 × 1″
b. top rail	1	28 × 4 × 1″
c. lock and kick rails	2	28 × 6 × 1″
d. lower mullion	1	20 × 4 × 1″

description	no. of pieces	dimensions
e. upper mullion	1	44 × 4 × 1″
f. brackets	6	7½ × 3½ × ¼″
g. brackets	4	8½ × 5½ × ¼″
h. stop stock	32 feet	¼ × ¼″

The door shown in Illus. 6–127 and 6–128 is really very simple to make but it requires strong joinery because of its lightness. The stock is milled down from a thickness of 1½ inches to 1 inch. Mortise-and-tenon joints at the corners are necessary to give strength to such a light door, especially since screen doors often take the brunt of the weather, and are slammed a lot because of the springs that people put on them. Cut the corner brackets from ¼-inch marine plywood, and glue them and nail them into their slots; this will also help strengthen the door, as well as support the screen somewhat.

Begin by cutting the frame pieces to size, leaving enough extra length on the rails for the tenons (unless you choose to make spline–tenon joints). The vertical mullions do not have to be tenoned. Dowels or a short spline–tenon joint will serve here. Glue up the frame and allow it to dry before cutting the rabbets for the screen.

When the assembled frame has dried, use a rabbeting bit with a ball-bearing guide to cut a ⅜-inch-deep by ¼-inch-wide rabbet around each of the "panels" on what will be the inside of the door. Square out the corners with a sharp chisel. Go slowly with the routing to avoid chipping out the material.

Now, mark out the corner brackets on the ¼-inch material and cut them out carefully with a scroll saw. Leave ¼-inch tabs on the ends of the brackets so that you can attach them to the door. Take each bracket and from the corner of the frame measure a set distance out to where the mortise will start that the tab will fit into. Position the tabs for each bracket on the door, and mark around it; then use the router with the same rabbet cutter, but set the tab mortises ¼ inch deeper (Illus. 6–129 and 6–130). You will have to square out the mortises by hand with a sharp chisel, but the router will help get the depth right.

Glue and nail the tabs in place (use a good weatherproof glue), and paint or finish the entire door before applying the screen. First staple the screen in place, and then apply wooden stops to cover the edges of the screens (Illus. 6–131).

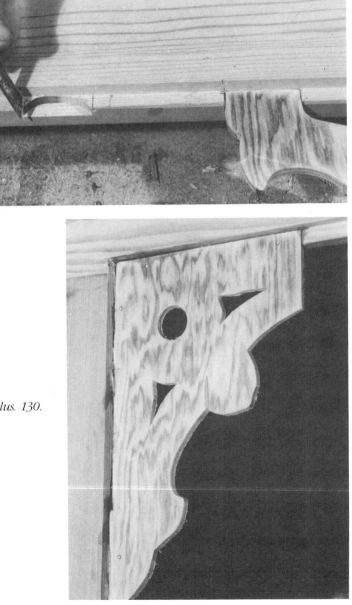

Illus. 6-129 and 6-130 (below). Attach the upper and lower corner brackets to the corners of the framework by routing mortises into the screen rabbet.

Illus. 130.

Stops

h.

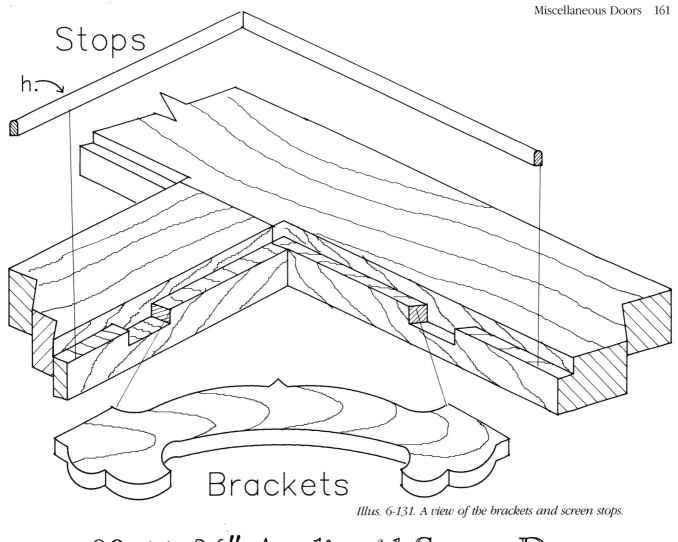

Brackets

Illus. 6-131. A view of the brackets and screen stops.

80 × 36″ Appliquéd Screen Door

Level Three

The door shown in Illus. 6–132 and 6–133 will certainly promote an attitude of good cheer. It also makes a nice project for someone who has his own lathe. Some of the turned spindles can be found in specialty catalogues, but the larger ones applied to the stiles will probably have to be custom-made.

To build this door, first cut the stiles, rails, and the half-lapped pieces for the "X" in the lower part of the door; also cut the quarter circle-shaped pieces in the upper corners of the door. Then glue the quarter circles in place on the ends of the rail; you will retrim the ends afterward. You may want to key the pieces for the X shape into place with small splines, but if your joinery is tight, you can probably just glue them in, and then later drill and drive an 8d finish nail through to hold it.

Now, clamp the assembly together tightly and rout the chamfer around all the areas where it is shown on the outside in Illus. 6–132; also rout the screen rabbet around the two large and two small screened areas on the inside of the door. Position the two narrow rails in the upper part of the door the correct distance from the larger rails to get the length of the spindles you plan to

use. Put indexing marks on all the joints to help you align the pieces accurately at glue-up time.

While the door is still clamped together, find the places where the holes will be drilled for the spindles in the pieces lettered in Illus. 6–132. Copy the marks from one rail to another with a square to be sure that they are aligned with each other. Use a drill press or dowelling jig to drill these ½-inch-deep holes.

You'll probably find it easier to do the carving on the lock rail before assembling the door. The bulk of the relief cutting here was probably done with a router, but the flower in the center definitely looks as though it was chiselled by an expert.

Now, with all the spindles ready, assemble the door. It might be helpful to glue the spindles into both sets of rails in a separate, previous step, but, on the other hand, that might make it hard to get the rail ends perfectly tight against the stiles. If you can, do it all at once, except for the applied spindles on the stiles that can be added at any time. After painting, staple the screen into the rabbets and apply stops to complete the door.

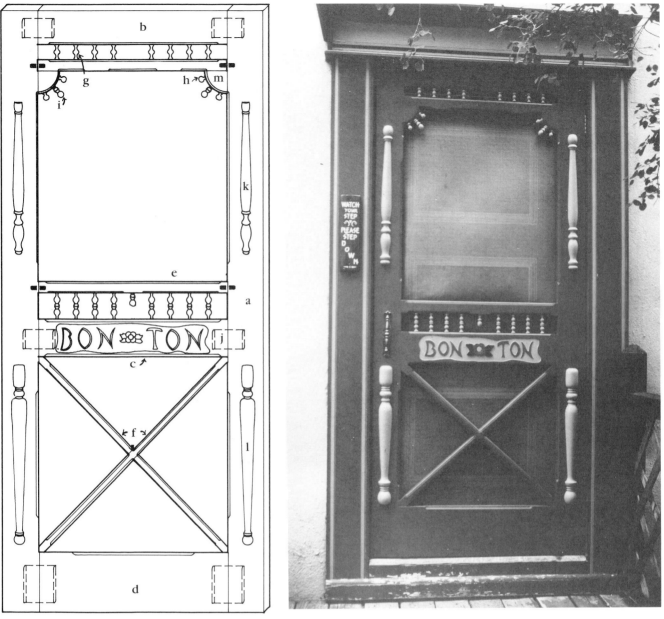

Illus. 6-132 and 6-133. Pattern and photo of 80 × 36-inch appliquéd screen door.

80 × 36″ Appliquéd Screen Door

description	no. of pieces	dimensions
a. stiles	2	80 × 5 × 1″
b. top rail	1	26 × 4½ × 1″
c. lock rail	1	26 × 5 × 1″
d. kick rail	1	26 × 8 × 1″
e. muntins	2	26 × 1½ × ¾″
f. cross pieces	2	36¾ × 1 × ¾″
g. spindles	8	2½ × ¾″ diameter
h. spindles	4	2 × ¾″ diameter

description	no. of pieces	dimensions
i. spindles	8	2¼ × ¾″ diameter
j. spindles	8	4 × ¾″ diameter
k. upper appliqués	2	20 × 1¾ × ¾″
l. lower appliqués	2	24 × 1¾ × ¾″
m. quarter circles	2	3 × 3 × ¾″
stop stock	20 feet	¼ × ¼″
muntin stops	2	26 × 1 × ¼″
cross-piece stops	2	36¾ × 1 × ¼″

80 × 36" Screen Door

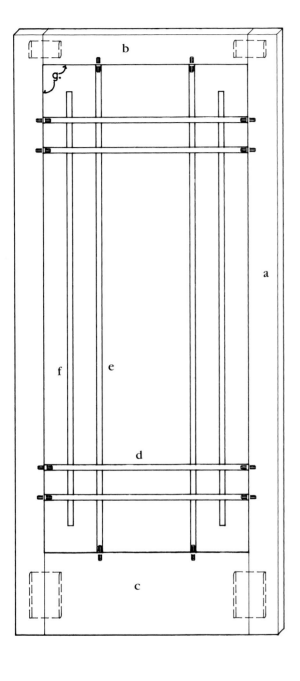

Illus. 6-134 and 6-135. Pattern and photo of 80 × 36-inch screen door.

80 × 36" Screen Door

description	no. of pieces	dimensions
a. stiles	2	80 × 4 × 1″
b. top rail	1	28 × 4 × 1″
c. kick rail	1	28 × 11 × 1″
d. muntins	4	28 × ¾ × ¾″
e. mullions	2	65 × ¾ × ¾″
f. mullions	2	58 × ¾ × ¾″
g. stop stock	15 feet	¼ × ¼″

The screen door shown in Illus. 6–134 and 6–135 is an easy-to-make one that suggests all kinds of variations on the design used (Illus. 6–136 and 6–137). The same simple technique used on the Victorian door is used on this one. The pieces that crisscross in the screened part of the door are either dowelled or mortise-and-tenoned into the framework, and half-lapped where they meet. They have to be the depth of the screen rabbet (¼ inch)

thinner than the frame wood so that you can apply stops around the edges on the inside.

Staple the screen into the screen rabbet about every 3 inches, and attach it to the thin pieces with either staples or by nailing stop pieces over all the thin pieces on the inner side of the door. Stops will add considerable strength to a rather delicate construction.

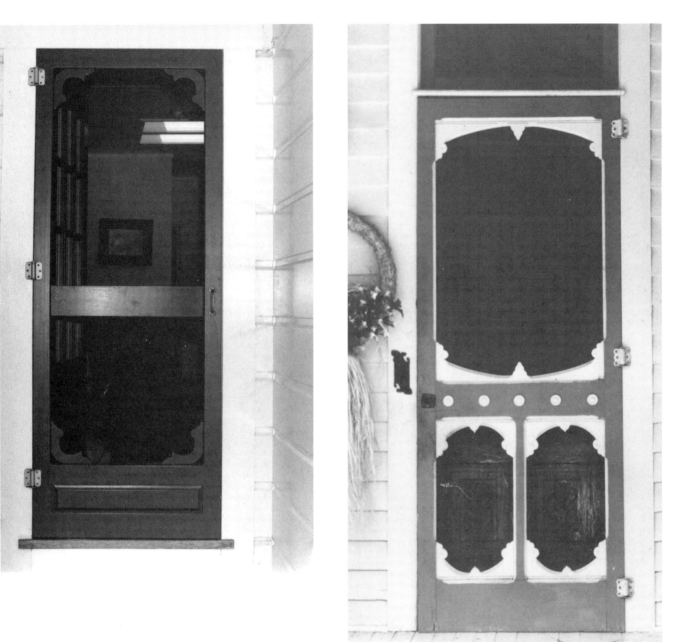

Illus. 6-136 and 6-137. More variations of a screen door.

UNUSUAL DOORS

80 × 30″ Louvered Door

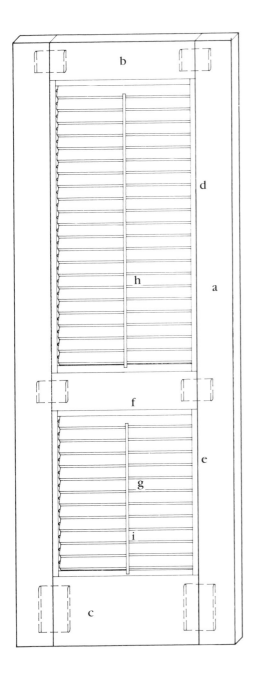

Illus. 6-138 and 6-139. Pattern and photo of 80 × 30-inch louvered door.

80 × 30″ Louvered Door

description	no. of pieces	dimensions
a. stiles	2	80 × 5 × 1½″
b. rails	2	20 × 5 × 1½″
c. kick rail	1	20 × 10 × 1½″
d. louver holders	2	38 × ¾ × 1½″
e. louver holders	2	20 × ¾ × 1½″
f. blocks	4	18½ × ¾ × 1½″

description	no. of pieces	dimensions
g. louvres	34	19 × ¼ × 1½″
h. connecting strip	1	38 × ⅜ × ¾″
i. connecting strip	1	20 × ⅜ × ¾″
small eye hooks	68	

Louvered doors, as shown in Illus. 6–138 and 6–139, are useful wherever ventilation is desirable. In very warm climates, they can be used as interior passage doors, and in normal climates you may want to use one as a closet door or in a cellar, furnace room, pantry, or similar location. They are actually quite easy to make, although somewhat timeconsuming.

To build this door, first cut the frame pieces to length and width and rout the mortises that will hold them together. Once this is done, glue the frame together; after the glue has cured, plane and sand the frame's surfaces.

The next step is to cut the louvers. Before doing this, however, note that they are ½ inch longer than the space between the louver holders. This is because a ¼ × ¼-inch tenon is cut on each end of each louver to hold it in place in its hole in the louver holders. These tenons can be "gang cut" on groups of louvers (Illus. 6–140). If you are starting with wide stock, cut it to length, and then set the table saw (using either the fence or a crosscutting jig with a stop block) to make both the shoulder and cheek cuts on the ends of the wide stock. Then rip the louvers to ¼-inch widths (leave them slightly thicker than needed). Round the corners of the tenons with a coarse file. Also plane the louvers themselves to remove saw marks, and sand them to smooth them and round their edges.

Drill a series of ¼ inch or slightly larger holes at intervals of 1¼ inches down the middle of the louver holder pieces. Use a drill press to ensure that the holes are square. Drill them in a piece of 1½ × 1½-inch stock before ripping it to make the two opposite louver holders. This will save time and ensure that the holes will be perfectly lined up with each other. Start the first holes 1¼ inches from the end and measure carefully to keep the spacing even.

If you plan to varnish, oil, or otherwise finish this door, do this now, before it is assembled. You may need additional assistance to get all the louvers in their holes in the holders. Work on a flat surface. First attach all the pieces on one side. Now, work from one end to the

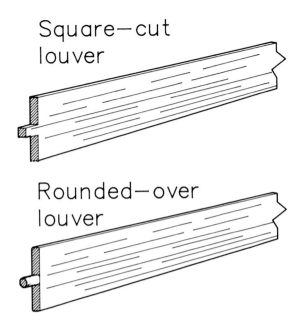

Illus. 6-140. Cut all the tenons on the louvers square, rip the louvers, and, finally, round the tenons with a file.

other to get the other side in. If you need to, you can plane some thickness off the louver holders so that the louvers are held loosely enough between the stiles so that they work easily.

Now, nail the louver holders in place using small finish nails; add blocks at the ends to help keep the louver holders tightly against the stiles, and to fill the spaces at the ends. Now, using the smallest eye hooks you can find, screw one into the edge of each louver at its center point. The connecting strips, h and i in Illus. 6–138, will have eye hooks every 1¼ inches; start these strips an inch or so from the end to avoid splitting the wood near the end. Use a pair of pliers to open all the eye hooks on the connecting strips slightly, interlock them all with the hooks on the louvers, and close them again. You are now finished, though you may find it necessary to hollow out a little place in the center of each end block for the connecting strip to fit into when the louvers are fully closed.

80 × 36" Seven-Panel Entry Door

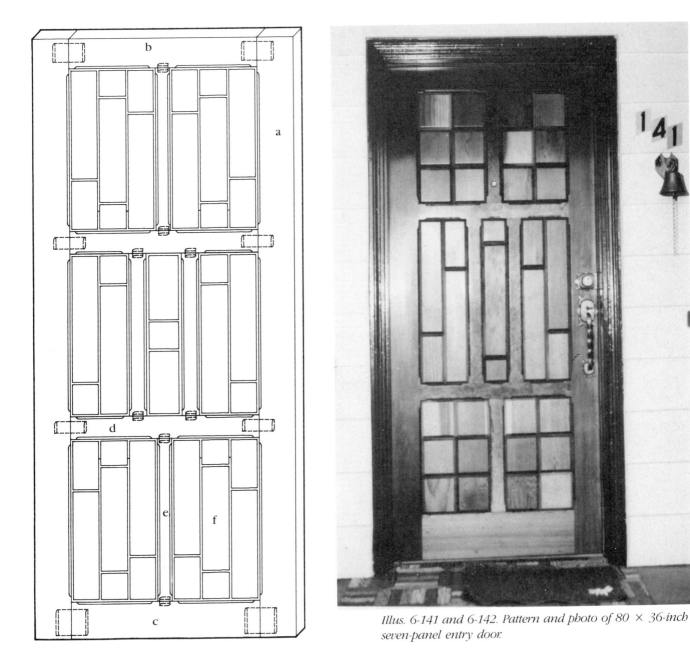

Illus. 6-141 and 6-142. Pattern and photo of 80 × 36-inch seven-panel entry door.

80 × 36" Seven-Panel Entry Door

description	no. of pieces	dimensions
a. stiles	2	80 × 5 × 1½"
b. top rail	1	26 × 4 × 1½"
c. kick rail	1	26 × 5 × 1½"
d. muntins	2	26 × 3 × 1½"
e. mullions	6	26 × 2 × 1½"
f. panel pieces	34 feet	3½ × 1½"

As shown in Illus. 6–141 and 6–142, Mr. Harry Christian, of Fort Bragg, California, developed his own unique style of door building based on the availability of short scraps of redwood lumber from the local mill. He built most of his doors for friends and neighbors.

The unique thing about his doors is the way he created panels by dowelling together scraps that had been routed around the edges with either chamfer or round-over bits. The routed edges separate the pieces so the joints don't show, and create interesting patterns. Many of his doors have panel material that is the same thickness as the frame material, making it hard to distinguish between the two.

To build a door like the one shown in Illus. 6–141 and 6–142, first square off the ends of all the panel pieces. Next, rout the panel pieces all the way around on both sides. Use a router bit with a ball-bearing guide in a table for best results. Now, join the pieces into strips, using two dowels at each end-to-end joint. Use

weatherproof glue. When the glue has dried, joint the strips lightly to make sure that the edges are perfectly straight from piece to piece. If you have to take much off the edge of one or more piece, run these edges on the router again to make them even.

Now, join the strips edge to edge with the end joints offset. Use dowels every six inches or so on these joints, too. When the glue has dried, trim the panels to size to fit the frame holes. Prepare the framework in the usual manner—use spline–tenon joints at the corners.

Use a router with a slotting bit to cut slots to hold all the panels. Also slot the edges of the panels all the way around;, this is where you will glue in the splines to hold the panels in the framework. It is possible to cut the edges of the panels to fit in the slots, but you would have to plan ahead so that all the panel pieces, including the ones that fit into the framework, appear to be the same width. Whichever method you use, finish and seal the panels before gluing the door together.

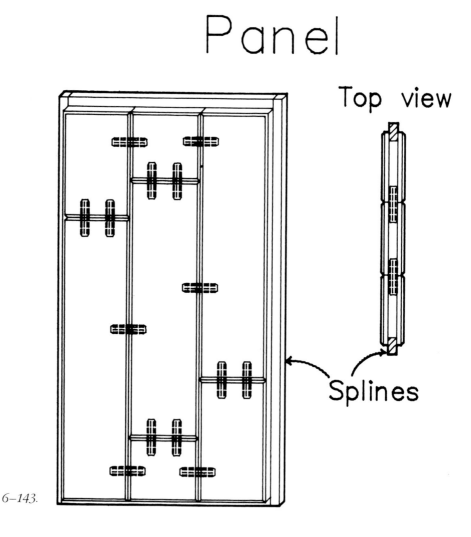

Panel

Top view

Splines

6–143.

7
BASIC SPINDLE SHAPER TECHNIQUES FOR DOORMAKING

Certainly, the most important and versatile tool in the doormaker's shop is the spindle shaper (Illus. 7–1–7–4). The shaper is like a large router in an inverted position (the way the router would be on a router table) except that instead of having a collet that accepts the arbor of a cutting bit, the spindle shaper has a spindle on which are stacked two- or three-wing-cutting bits that are hollow-bored in the middle. You can stack several cutters, spacers, and bearings on the spindle at once so that the shaper can cut the complete profile of a frame member, including both beads and the central slot or a bead and a rabbet, in one pass (Illus. 7–5). Cutters commonly come in matching sets for cope-and-stick joinery so that the ends of the rails, muntins, and mullions can be undercut to match the bead cut and slot of the stile, forming an interlocking joint that appears to be mitred in the corners. This joint is stronger than a straight butt joint because it is intricate; it is also cleaner looking than the rounded corners caused by routed beads, and much quicker to make.

Most production shops have at least two shapers set up for each type of cut, so that both the stick or bead cut and the matching cope or end cut can be made without having to break down and reset the cutters on the shapers. A third shaper, with a larger table and a more powerful motor, is often used solely for cutting the profiles for raised panels. Power-feed units, auxiliary tables so that two sets of bits can be stacked on one shaper for making both cope and stick cuts, and many other options are available for shapers.

In recent years, the trend has been to use smaller, less powerful shapers. Many types of cutters are now becoming available for ½-inch spindles that were once available only for larger shapers with 1-inch or larger spindles.

Generally, a well-constructed ½-inch-spindle shaper can handle the forces generated in cope-and-stick cutting, as long as the feed is slow and steady and the rotation speed of the cutters is high enough. A ½-inch spindle is light enough to flex slightly, causing "chatter" and rough, inaccurate cutting if it is not driven by a powerful enough motor and a heavy, steel-drive pulley. Chattering can also cause the spindle bearings to fail rapidly. The drive pulley must also be carefully balanced to prevent unnecessary vibration (Illus. 7–6).

If you plan to invest in one or more ½-inch shapers,

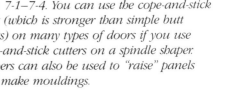

Illus. 7-1–7-4. You can use the cope-and-stick joint (which is stronger than simple butt joints) on many types of doors if you use cope-and-stick cutters on a spindle shaper. Shapers can also be used to "raise" panels and make mouldings.

Illus. 7-2.

Illus. 7-3.

Illus. 7-4.

VARIOUS SHAPER CUTTER SETS
FOR DOORS AND WINDOWS

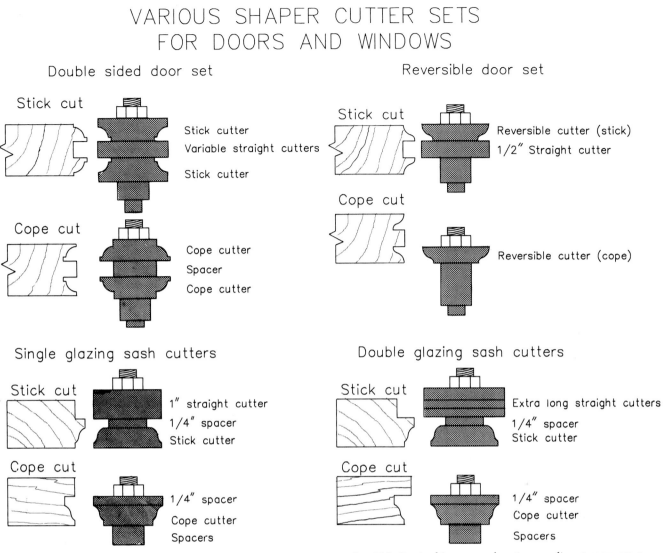

Double sided door set

Stick cut

Stick cutter
Variable straight cutters
Stick cutter

Cope cut

Cope cutter
Spacer
Cope cutter

Reversible door set

Stick cut

Reversible cutter (stick)
1/2″ Straight cutter

Cope cut

Reversible cutter (cope)

Single glazing sash cutters

Stick cut

1″ straight cutter
1/4″ spacer
Stick cutter

Cope cut

1/4″ spacer
Cope cutter
Spacers

Double glazing sash cutters

Stick cut

Extra long straight cutters
1/4″ spacer
Stick cutter

Cope cut

1/4″ spacer
Cope cutter
Spacers

Illus. 7-5. By stacking several cutters and/or spacers on a shaper spindle, you can cut the complete profile of a frame member in one or two passes.

SHAPER DRIVE COMPONENTS

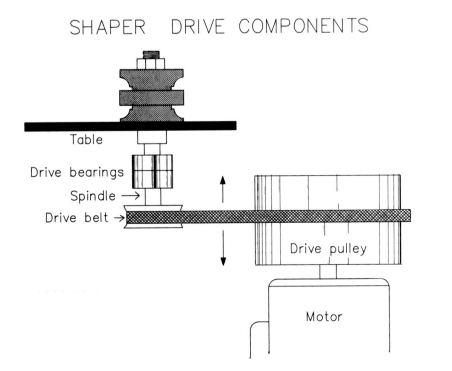

Table
Drive bearings
Spindle →
Drive belt →
Drive pulley
Motor

Illus. 7-6. Drive pulleys for shapers are flat (not V-grooved) and several inches wide so that the drive belt can move up and down when the spindle is moved. A carefully balanced cast-iron pulley will drive the spindle smoothly and quietly.

make sure that the drive components are of the heaviest quality and are in good condition if you plan to do production-type work with them. Panel-cutting makes even heavier demands on the machinery, but it can also be accomplished with ½-inch shapers if care is taken.

Shaper Use in Door Production

The use of spindle shapers in door production makes it possible to work in a more efficient, assembly-line-like manner. The tedium of carefully dry-assembling the

Illus. 7-7. The ends of rails, mullions, and muntins are "coped" or undercut to fit over the matching "stick" cut.

Illus. 7-8. When the joint is assembled, the beads appear to be mitred in the corners.

door and making multiple passes with the router is eliminated, as well as all the hand work of squaring out the corners, applying mouldings, etc. Instead, the pieces can be taken separately to the shaper for the cope and stick cuts, which will allow them to fit cleanly together with a stronger joint that looks like a perfect mitre in the corners (Illus. 7–7 and 7–8). Panels can be raised with various profiles on the shaper much more cleanly and quickly than on the table saw or by hand, and large, high-profile mouldings can also be made with one or more shaper cutters. It is also possible to use a shaper with a guide bearing to cut curved pieces and to follow templates much as you would with a router.

All this and more is possible with shapers, but be forewarned: Shapers are among the more dangerous tools in the workshop. The cutters rotate at speeds of up to 10,000 RPM, and motors of up to five horsepower are used. Use extreme care and follow proper safety procedures, especially when shaping small pieces like the ones that are needed for multi-light doors and windows.

A large variety of carbide-tipped cutters is available even for the smaller ½-inch machines these days, including cope-and-stick cutters and many types of panel cutters (Illus. 7–9). If you are considering investing in a carbide cope-and-stick set, make sure that it will handle a variety of door thicknesses ranging from 1⅜ to 1¾ inches, and that you can use it with various straight cutters and spacer collars both for slotted doors, to hold panels, and for rabbeted doors, to hold glass. If you are ordering by mail, make sure that you have the option of returning the merchandise if the cutters are poorly matched or if the sharpness and workmanship are not of high enough quality.

Grinding Your Own Cutters

High-speed steel cutters are much cheaper to purchase, and are available from companies such as Greenley and Delta. Even though steel cutters won't stay sharp nearly as long as carbide cutters, you can easily sharpen them yourself and regrind them if they don't match perfectly. You can lightly sharpen them without changing the profile by grinding only the flat side of the cutters on either a small carbide grinding wheel or a 1-inch belt sander like the one shown in Illus. 7–10.

Reshaping the profile of the cutter may be necessary from time to time, and can be done by grinding the bevelled side of the cutters on a fine carbide grinding wheel that has a slightly rounded edge for getting into tight corners and curved areas (Illus. 7–11). The grinding wheel should be run at a slow speed, not over 1,750 RPM. High-speed grinders are unsafe for this type of work, and can also quickly ruin your cutter profiles.

Keep in mind that you can only grind away the cutters; you can't add to them. Also remember that the cutters are the negative to the positive finished piece. By grinding away the cutters, you add to the profile of the workpiece.

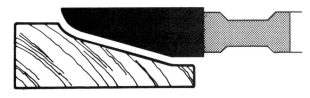

Illus. 7-9. A wide variety of panel-raising cutters and cope-and-stick cutters are available, even for smaller spindle-diameter shapers.

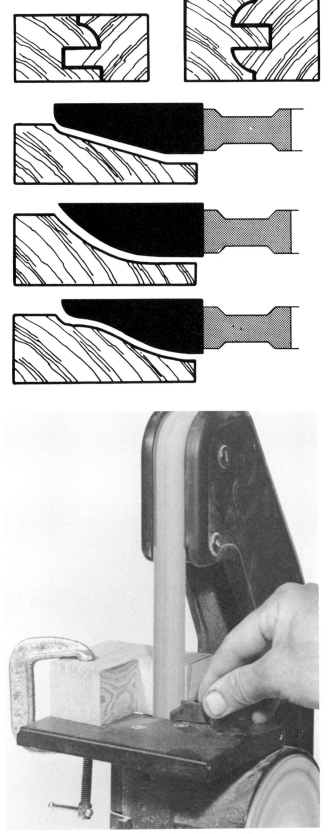

Illus. 7-10. Grinding the flat sides of high-speed-steel cutters will help sharpen them without changing their profiles noticeably.

Illus. 7-11. More extensive resharpening and reshaping can be done on a fine carbide wheel.

When grinding matched pairs of cutters, make a pair of test cuts first; then grind only in the areas where the test pieces don't quite come together (Illus. 7–12). Hold the bit on the top and bottom only, to avoid getting your fingers between the cutting edge and the tool rest or grinding wheel, and use a sweeping motion on the curved parts of the cutter.

Grinding is usually used only to make the curved parts of the cuts fit each other better. By grinding back the straight cutters, you can sometimes improve the relationship between the bead cut and the slot cut, but this can usually also be accomplished by moving the fence in or out on the cope cut.

High-speed steel blanks that lock into a head that fits on the shaper spindle can be purchased and ground to fit your own special needs (Illus. 7–13). These are especially good for making high-profile bolection mouldings. These loose-knife cutterheads have a reputation for being unsafe, but recent OSHA (Occupational Safety and Health Act) regulations have forced modifications of the design to make them safer. When grinding these knifes, it is important to get them balanced and cutting smoothly. Grind one knife to shape; then use it as a pattern to carefully mark out and grind the others.

Cope-and-Stick Cutters

Getting a cope-and-stick profile to match nicely depends on the straight cutters that cut out the slot, as well as the beading cutters. Stick cutters are usually stacked on the spindle in the following order: a beading cutter on the bottom, and then one or more straight cutters to cut the slot for the panels or the rabbet for the glass, and sometimes another beading cutter on the top. The top cutter is optional, as the same result can be achieved by flipping the workpiece over, end for end, and repeating the cut. Some types of cutters, such as reversible cutter sets (where the same cutter cuts both the cope bead and the stick bead) are stacked the opposite way for the stick cut, with the single bead cutter on top (Illus. 7–15).

On the other hand, you do not have to use straight cutters to make the cope or end cut for panel doors. Spacing collars are stacked in place of the straight cutters, and bead cutters that are the negative of the stick cutters undercut the ends of the rails or mullions so that the bead can fit into them. This cut leaves a stub tenon of a variable depth that will fit into the slot cut by the stick cutters. The cope cut, therefore, depends on the placement of the guide fence for the relationship between the bead and the stub tenon.

Shaper Fences

Standard shaper fences usually consist of two "tables" that are independently adjustable, much like the in-feed and out-feed tables of a jointer. Since many shapers are equipped with a special switch that will reverse the rotation of the cutters, either table of the fence can be either in-feed or out-feed, depending on the direction of the cut. Different cutting directions can be useful for template cutting, difficult grain, reversible cutters, or other special needs.

This type of fence (two independent tables) is useful

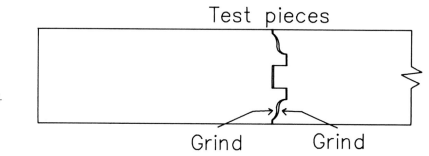

Illus. 7-12. To improve the match of cope-and-stick cutters, make a pair of test cuts and then grind only in the areas where the pieces don't come together.

Illus. 7-13. Cutterheads that hold removable knives that can be ground to individual specifications are available for most shapers.

VARYING CUTTER—DEPTH RELATIONSHIPS

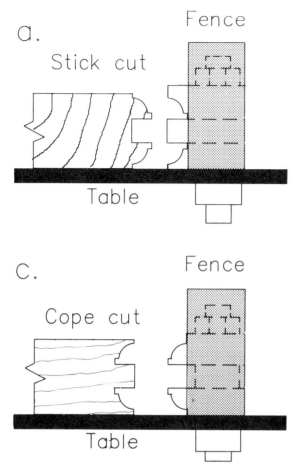

a.

Stick cut

Fence

Table

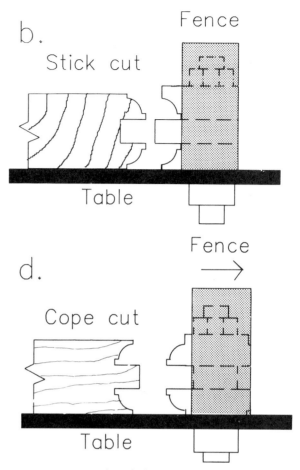

b.

Stick cut

Fence

Table

c.

Cope cut

Fence

Table

d.

Fence →

Cope cut

Table

Illus. 7-14. As shown in a and b, you cannot vary the depth of the groove on the stick cut by moving the fence. A longer straight cutter is used in b to cut a deeper groove. When you are cope-cutting though (c and d), you can vary the length of the stub tenon somewhat by moving the fence in or out.

Illus. 7-15. Some cutters, such as this reversible set, use the same bit for both cope and stick beading. The bit cuts near the bottom of the workpiece for the cope, and at the top edge (as shown) for the stick. Only one bead is cut per pass, so you must flip the workpiece over and make a second pass to complete both the cope and stick.

for some types of moulding cutting, but can also cause problems when you are setting up for cope-and-stick cutting or panel cutting. Here, it is more important that the fence be absolutely straight, and square to the table of the shaper.

You can modify a two-table fence to work better for stick cutting or panel cutting by attaching a wide, carefully jointed board, with holes cut out for the cutters, to the existing fence mechanism. This will help keep the in-feed and out-feed sides better aligned. You will almost never be removing the entire edge from the workpiece when stick-cutting, so there will be no need to offset the two parts of the fence.

For cope cutting you will want to make another special fence like the one shown in Illus. 7–16. With this fence you can greatly improve the accuracy of the cope, especially on small pieces. This fence has a thin piece of wood let into its face at the right height so that the stub tenon of the workpiece is constantly in contact with it as it passes the cutters. This prevents the workpiece from accidentally falling too far into the cutters as it passes the cutout where the cutters project through the fence. A mitre guide or special holding jig (Illus. 7–17) for small pieces helps keep the workpiece square as it is fed past the cutters, and a backer block is necessary when cutting across the grain to prevent chipout as the cutter comes through the back of the workpiece.

Preparing Stock for a Cope-and-Stick Door

Remember the following when preparing stock for a cope-and-stick door:

1. The cope-and-stick joint interlocks in such a way that you will have to add a certain amount to the length of the rails to compensate for the undercut on the ends of the rails. So, if you are making a 3-foot-door, and the stiles are 5½ inches wide, leaving 25 inches between them, you will have to add twice the depth of the cope cut to get the actual length to which you should cut the rails. If the cope cut is 7⁄16 inch deep, the rails should be cut to 25⅞ inches.

2. If you are going to use a true mortise-and-tenon joint, a special type of cope-cutting bit, with an auxiliary table and fence, will be necessary (Illus. 7–18). Because the tenon will be projecting out from the ends of the rails, and will usually take up the same width as the stub tenon that is formed between the cope cuts, use a cope-cutting bit that is hollow inside to accept a lock nut. This lock nut shouldn't project above the top of the bit, and the bit must fit on the very top of the spindle. This allows the tenon to pass over the bit. The end of the tenon rides against a fence that is offset the proper amount. Often, a raised auxiliary table must be clamped

Illus. 7-16. By making a special fence for cope cutting, like the one shown here, you can greatly improve the accuracy of your cuts. The thin strip of wood let into the face of the fence supports the end of the workpiece at all times so that it won't drop too deeply into the cutters.

Illus. 7-17. You can make a special holding jig that will prove useful when stick-cutting muntins and mullions by cutting the cope profile on a wide piece of stock. Screw a thin backer piece into the end of it; this piece projects out and pushes the workpiece.

to the shaper to raise the work high enough for this kind of cutting with the bit on the very top of the spindle.

A simpler solution to this problem is to use the spline–tenon method described on pages 68 and 70 for your stile and rail joints. With this method, the mortises are all cut before the shaper work is done, and a normal setup of the cope cutters can be used for all rail and mullion ends.

Cope-and-Stick Cut with One Shaper

Begin making a cope-and-stick run by making a sample of the stick cut on a scrap piece that's exactly the same thickness as the stock you will be using. The depth of the cut will depend on the design of the cutters you are using, but should usually be just enough to cut the full profile of the bead. If you cut any deeper, you will be removing wood from the edge of the piece, and will have to offset the out-feed fence to support the work as it leaves the cutters. When the depth is just right, the full profile of the bead will be cut, but no width will be removed from the edge of the board.

Once you have a good sample of the stick cut, break down the machine and set up the cope cutters and cope fence. Use another piece of scrap to get a cut that matches the stick cut so that the joint closes perfectly. Now you are ready to begin making the cope cut on the workpieces.

It is usually best to make the cope cut first, using a square backer piece to prevent breakout as the cutter comes through the end of the piece (Illus. 7–19); however, if necessary, you can make a backer with the cope cut on it to back a piece that already has the stick cut on it. Also, if you have lots of muntins or mullions of the same length, you can cut them to length as wide pieces and put the cope cut on the ends first before ripping them and shaping the stick cut on each (Illus. 7–20 and 7–21). Make sure that you don't miss any. If you have muntins for multiple lights, make some extra pieces in case you miscut any when making the stick cut.

When all the cope cuts have been made, break down the setup again and put the stick cutters and the stick-cutting fence in place. Make test cuts on scrap pieces until they match the cope cuts perfectly. Be sure to use some type of protective cover over the top of the cutters when making the stick cuts. This cut removes more wood, and often the cutters project up past the top of the workpiece. A piece of 2-inch material clamped to

Illus. 7-18. If you are using a true mortise-and-tenon joint, a special cope-cutting setup will be necessary. A nut that fits down inside the cutter holds the cutter on the spindle; this allows the cutter to cut right to the bottom of the tenon as it passes over it.

Illus. 7-19. It is usually best to make the cope cut first. Use a piece of scrap stock to back the workpiece and prevent chip-out as the cutters go through it.

Illus. 7–20 and 7–21 (below). Cope muntin and mullion ends before ripping the stock to its final width to both ensure safety and uniform length in matching pieces.

Illus. 7-21.

Illus. 7-22. When stick-cutting with a fence, clamp a cover piece to the fence to both hold the workpiece flat on the table and to keep fingers away from exposed cutters.

the fence just above the work will help keep the workpieces flat against the table, and will help keep your fingers out of harm's way (Illus. 7–22).

It will be very helpful to set up an auxiliary roller for both in-feed and out-feed, if possible, when you are making the stick cuts on the stiles. It is critical that the stiles be fed smoothly and flatly all the way along their lengths, and it's a real struggle to do so without something to support their lengths at the beginning and end of the cut. Be especially careful not to drop the beginning or the end of the stile into the hole in the fence as you make the cut. Keep the workpieces tight against the in-feed as you start the cut, and transfer the pressure to the out-feed fence as you near the end of the cut. If you do end up cutting too deep on a stile or rail, you can usually remove ⅟₁₆ or ⅛ inch on a jointer, and then make the cut again; however, with thinner pieces, such as the muntins between panes of glass, this will be impossible. That's why it's a good idea to cut a few extra pieces.

When stick-cutting muntins and other small pieces, make a special push stick or holding jig that will steady the pieces and keep your fingers away from the cutters (Illus. 7–16). Take a piece of scrap 6 inches wide by 12

inches long, and make the cope cut along one edge. Round the corners on the other edge, and plane down the coped side so that it's slightly thinner than the workpieces and won't bind on the cover piece you clamped to the fence. Now, screw a backer piece to the back end of the piece so that it projects out about ¼ inch. The workpieces can now be pushed past the cutters with this block. The first edge of the workpiece is relatively easy to keep straight because it still has a wide bottom edge on the table, but for the second cut there would be more chance of it tipping one way or the other if it were not for the coped edge on your pusher, which will interlock with the already cut edge and keep the piece straight.

Cope-and-Stick Cut with Two Shapers

If you have two shapers, one set up with cope cutters and one set up with stick cutters, the cutting procedure is basically the same, except that you can go back to either machine at any time and remake a piece or a cut. This is especially helpful when you are making multi-light doors or windows, as it can be very difficult to accurately figure the lengths of the upright mullions without first making the stick cuts on the rails and horizontal mullions. Even a small error here can become a large one when it is repeated several times.

If only two shapers are being used, be sure to make all the frame pieces and dry-assemble the entire framework before taking the bits off the stick-cutting machine to set up for panel shaping. Usually, the same fence that is used for stick cutting can be used for making the panels.

Panel Cutting

Flat panels of a uniform thickness are the first prerequisite for successful panel cutting. It will be impossible to get a uniformly thick edge on a twisted or bowed panel, though small inconsistencies can be planed or sanded out by hand.

Panels can be made in either of two ways on the shaper (Illus. 7–23). Either lay the board flat on the table and use a large diameter, low-profile cutter, or stand up the board perpendicular to the table and guide it along a high fence. This type of panel cutter has a high-profile and a much smaller diameter, which is bet-

ter for smaller, less powerful shapers, but cannot be used to follow the edge of a curved or irregular-shaped panel, like the low-profile panel cutter can. With the high-profile cutter, it is also much easier to make the mistake of dropping the end of the panel into the cutter hole, and, for this reason you may find it necessary to make a special high fence for panel cutting that allows you more control of the workpiece.

Always make the cuts across the end grain of the panels before doing the edges. This way, any wood that is chipped out at the ends of the cross-grain cuts will be removed by the edge-grain cuts.

Because panel cutting removes a lot of wood and puts a considerable strain on the shaper and cutters, it is best with smaller machines to start with a partial cut, and allow yourself two passes all around to complete the panel raising. This will also decrease the risk of chipping out large hunks of wood where the grain is contrary to the rotation of the bits, and generally makes for a smoother cut and less need of finish sanding.

Even the sharpest cutters will leave a surface that needs some finish sanding, especially where you have cut across the end grain. The low-profile cutters, when they are sharp, will cut almost perfectly on the sides of the panels. The high-profile cutters leave a scalloped machine mark like that left by a planer or jointer. This mark should be sanded out.

SHAPER RAISED PANELS

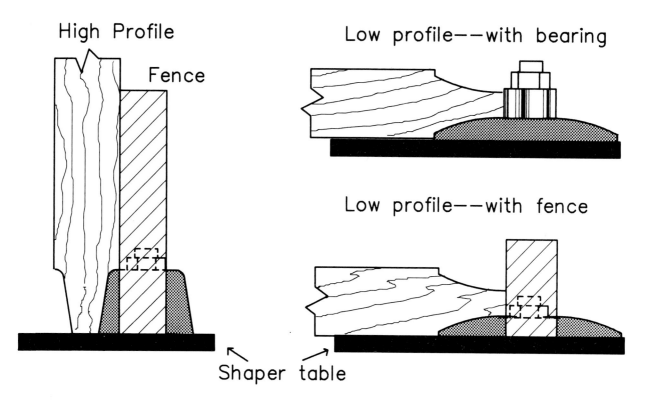

Illus. 7-23. Panels can be shaped either in a vertical position against a tall fence, or flat on the table with a fence or bearing to guide them.

80 × 34″ Shaper-Made Four-Panel Door

Level Two

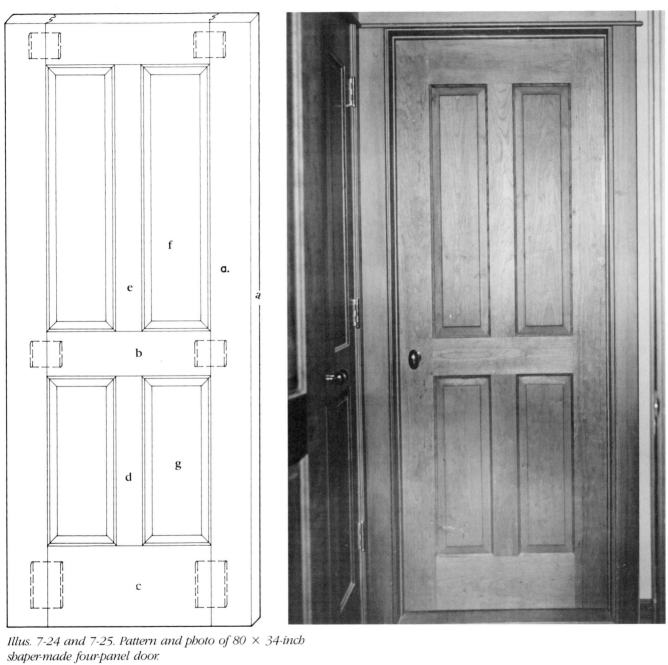

Illus. 7-24 and 7-25. Pattern and photo of 80 × 34-inch shaper-made four-panel door.

80 × 34″ Four-Panel Door

description	no. of pieces	dimensions
a. stiles	2	80 × 5½ × 1½″
b. top and lock rails	2	*23¾ × 5½ × 1½″
c. kick rail	1	*23¾ × 11 × 1½″
d. lower mullion	1	*22½ × 4½ × 1½″
e. upper mullion	1	*35½ × 4½ × 1½″
f. upper panels	2	35⅜ × 9⅜ × ¾″
g. lower panels	2	22½ × 9⅜ × ¾″

*Lengths based on cope cut depth of ⅜″

The door shown in Illus. 7–24 and 7–25, though not the simplest one to make, is a very popular interior-passage door. An order for 20 or 30 four-panel doors for the interior of a home or building is not uncommon.

The proportions of this door are determined by the position of the lock rail, usually centered on 36 inches from the floor, the height of the kick rail (about 11 inches), and the width of the door itself (Illus. 7–26). A 3-foot-wide door with 5½-inch stiles and a 5-inch center mullion will need panels 11 inches wide, which is about the widest that a solid wood panel should be built. For slightly narrower doors, the stiles and mullions can be left a little wider, but should be reduced proportionately for doors under 30 inches wide.

To build this door, prepare the stock and cut the rails to the exact length that is needed. Leave the two pieces for the center mullions long until you have made the cope-and-stick cut on all the other pieces. Assemble the stiles and rails, with the lock rail at the correct distance from the bottom of the door; then measure the length for the mullions from the bottoms of the grooves in the rails. Cut them to length and make the cope-and-stick cut on them. No mortise-and-tenon or dowel joint is necessary where the mullions meet the rails; the cope-and-stick joint itself will be strong enough.

Mark the center of each rail, and also the center of the ends of the mullions. Line these marks up as you dry-assemble the door, and check with a long straight edge to be sure that the center mullion is perfectly straight and centered.

Now, cut the panels to size and shape them to fit the groove in the frame. Use a scrap piece or one of the rails to check the thickness of the panel edges, and sand or plane the panels where necessary. Be sure to finish the panels entirely before assembling the door.

For more information on assembly techniques for this door, see page 72.

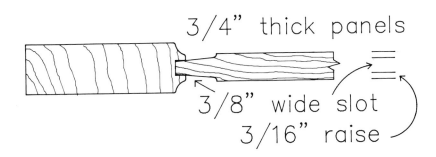

3/4" thick panels

3/8" wide slot

3/16" raise

Illus. 7-26. Cross-section of door.

8
FINISHES, MAINTENANCE, AND REPAIR

Choosing a Finish

The wooden surfaces of doors, whether they are subjected to the extremes in weather or not, are bound to be handled, scratched, exposed to cleaning solutions, and bleached by sunlight, as well as suffer other abuses too atrocious to mention. This harsh treatment rules out altogether some finishes such as lacquers and polishes, and forces the craftsman and homeowner to choose between the advantages and disadvantages of the remainder.

A door's surface should be durable, easy to clean, and as easy to maintain as possible. Old favorites such as enamel paints and spar varnishes still work well and produce the smoothest surfaces, but do not necessarily give the longest-lasting protection. Synthetic varnishes are more durable, but, like all varnishes, won't hold up in direct sunlight. Properly applied acrylic-latex paints or exterior-grade stains are the longest lasting, but don't produce the kind of hard, glossy finish that many people want.

Enamel paints have always been a favorite for finishing doors. They dry smooth and hard, are nearly impervious to moisture and to other chemical solutions, and protect the wood from ultraviolet damage. High-quality enamels come in a wide range of colors, and different colors can be applied to parts of the door to accentuate certain features. The way a door is painted can as easily be a work of art as the way it is built, and should not be overlooked as a means of expression.

If you want to feature the natural beauty of the woods that you have used to create the doors, you will have to rely on stains, varnishes or oils to protect and maintain that beauty. Varnishes will do well in the interior of a home or in exterior areas that are not exposed to direct sunlight, but should not even be considered for work that will be directly exposed to sun and rain. Some varnishes are elastic and expand enough to withstand the normal swelling and shrinking of an exterior door, but their biggest failing is their inability to shield the wood from ultraviolet radiation. Ultraviolet radiation rapidly breaks down the lignin that binds the wood

fibres together, thus destroying the foundation of the varnish and causing it to easily chip and peel; it also bleaches or discolors wood rapidly, destroying that beautiful wood color in as little as one year's time. If you simply must varnish the exterior of a door that is exposed to direct sunlight, it would be worthwhile to consider building a roof over it to protect it.

Drying oils, such as linseed or synthetic oil, soak into the wood and harden, giving a look and feel that is much like a carefully applied varnish or French polish. These oils should not be used in exposed areas either. Instead, use them for work in sheltered areas. The advantage of this type of preparation is that the oils can be poured on and rubbed with wet and dry sandpaper or steel wool to produce a polish that is more in the wood than on it.

You can reapply drying oils periodically without removing the previous coats of finish, and thus reduce maintenance time considerably (Illus. 8–1). But an oil does not even protect as long as a varnish, so you have to maintain it more carefully to avoid damage to your work.

Exterior-grade, semitransparent stains offer a compromise between opaque paints and short-lived varnishes, and are long lasting and easy to maintain. These stains, which soak into the wood and harden like an oil, protect the wood by repelling moisture, preventing mildew and other fungal growths, and by blocking the majority of the sun's ultraviolet rays. Though they do leave the grain and structure of the wood clearly visible, they also color it. The pigments, which are necessary to protect the wood from sun damage, are often formulated to enhance and deepen the natural colors of various common woods such as redwood, cedar, teak, mahogany, pine, spruce, and fir. Generally, the darker the stain, the better the protection.

These stains are easy to apply, even on rough wood surfaces, and since they do not build up a surface film, they can be easily reapplied after a few years when the finish begins to dull. Many companies also offer prod-

Illus. 8-1. Drying oils, poured on and scrubbed with an abrasive, can give the look of hand-rubbed polish, repel moisture, and are very easy to maintain.

ucts that will rejuvenate old weathered wood before the application of the semitransparent stains.

You can make your own stain by following this recipe developed by the Forest Products Laboratory; the ingredients for the stain are shown below. The tints shown will produce a cedar-brown color, but you can vary this color by using universal tints available from most large paint dealers. Most of the other ingredients can be found at any hardware or paint dealer. The amounts shown in the table will produce five gallons of stain at a cost considerably less than that of most commercially available exterior stains.

Boiled linseed oil—3 gallons
paraffin (melted)—1 pound
burnt sienna tinting color—1 pint
raw umber tinting color—1 pint
mineral spirits—1 gallon

Melt the paraffin in a double boiler, being careful not to get it too hot. Add the linseed oil/mineral-spirits solution. To ensure that you don't breathe the fumes from any of these materials, work outside and wear gloves, goggles, and an organic-vapor respirator. If you live in a moist area where mildew is likely to be a problem, use half as much linseed oil and make up the difference with mineral spirits.

Surface Preparation

Whether you plan to paint, varnish, or stain your work, the surfaces should be clean, smooth, and free of major cracks or imperfections. Paint will stick better to vertical, tight-grained wood. Many people mistakenly think that paint will cover unevenness or coarse woodwork. Saw-kerf, scratches or rough, unsanded grain can show through even after several coats of primer and paint.

To get the best results on painted work, fill cracks or dents with a plastic or epoxy filler paste, sand them flush, and apply several coats of primer, sanding in between coats to create a smooth, defect-free surface on which to apply the paint.

When working on hard woods, you may only have to sand lightly with 120 or finer-grit sandpaper after you have planed the entire door or window to remove any unevenness at the joints or other imperfections, and have removed planing marks with a sharp cabinet scraper.

If the sanding reveals more imperfections, you may have to repeat the scraping, and then sand some more. Be careful not to work a hollow into a flat surface. Work as much on the high areas around a defect as on the defect itself.

For softer woods such as redwood, fir, pine, and others, the procedure is somewhat different. These woods will plane nicely, but they do not look good when scraped. So start sanding with a coarser-grit sandpaper—100 grit is usually coarse enough—dampen the surface of the wood with a damp rag to raise the loose grain, let the wood dry for a few minutes, and sand evenly and in the direction of the grain (Illus. 8–2).

Illus. 8-2. Plane soft woods and then wet them to raise the grain, as shown, before sanding.

Orbital sanders do this type of sanding nicely, but belt sanders should be avoided because they dig in very easily and damage more of an area than they remove.

After the coarse sanding, use a finer grit; usually 150- or 220-grit sandpaper is sufficient. You may have to

Exterior wood finishes: types, treatment, and maintenance

Finish	Initial treatment	Appearance of wood	Cost of initial treatment	Maintenance procedure	Maintenance period of surface finish	Maintenance cost
Preservative oils (creosotes)	Pressure, hot and cold tank steeping	Grain visible; brown to black in color, fading slightly with age	Medium	Brush down to remove surface dirt	5–10 years only if original color is to be renewed; otherwise no maintenance is required	Nil to low
Waterborne preservatives	Brushing	Grain visible; brown to black in color, fading slightly with age	Low	Brush down to remove surface dirt	3–5 years	Low
	Pressure	Grain visible; greenish or brownish in color, fading with age	Medium	Brush down to remove surface dirt	None, unless stained, painted, or varnished as below	Nil, unless stains, varnishes, or paints are used as below
	Diffusion plus paint	Grain and natural color obscured	Low to medium	Clean and repaint	7–10 years	Medium
Organic solvent preservatives	Pressure, steeping, dipping, brushing	Grain visible; colored as desired	Low to medium	Brush down and reapply	2–3 years or when preferred	Medium
Water repellent	One or two brush coats of clear material or, preferably, dip applied	Grain and natural color visible, becoming darker and rougher textured	Low	Clean and apply sufficient finish	1–3 years or when preferred	Low to medium
Semitransparent stains	One or two brush coats	Grain visible; color as desired	Low to medium	Clean and apply sufficient finish	3–6 years or when preferred	Low to medium
Clear varnish	Three coats (minimum)	Grain and natural color unchanged if adequately maintained	High	Clean and stain bleach areas; apply two more coats	2 years or when breakdown begins	High
Paint	Water repellent, prime, and two topcoats	Grain and natural color obscured	Medium to high	Clean and apply topcoat, or remove and repeat initial treatment if damaged	7–10 years	Medium

Table 1. Exterior wood finishes.

Table 2. *Finishing methods for exterior wood surfaces, and their suitability.*

Type of exterior wood surfaces	Water-repellent preservative		Semitransparent stains		Paints	
	Suitability	Expected life (yrs)	Suitability	Expected life (yrs)	Suitability	Expected life (yrs)
Siding:						
Cedar and redwood						
Smooth (vertical grain)	High	1–2	Moderate	2–4	High	4–6
Roughsawn or weathered	High	2–3	Excellent	5–8	Moderate	3–5
Pine, fir, spruce, etc.						
Smooth (flat-grained)	High	1–2	Low	2–3	Moderate	3–5
Rough (flat-grained)	High	2–3	High	4–7	Moderate	3–5
Shingles						
Sawn	High	2–3	Excellent	4–8	Moderate	3–5
Split	High	1–2	Excellent	4–8		
Plywood (Douglas-fir and southern pine)						
Sanded	Low	1–2	Moderate	2–4	Moderate	3–5
Textured (smooth)	Low	1–2	Moderate	2–4	Moderate	3–5
Textured (rough sawn)	Low	2–3	High	4–8	Moderate	4–6
Medium-density overlay					Excellent	6–8
Plywood (cedar and redwood)						
Sanded	Low	1–2	Moderate	2–4	Moderate	3–5
Textured (smooth)	Low	1–2	Moderate	2–4	Moderate	3–5
Textured (rough sawn)	Low	2–3	Excellent	5–8	Moderate	4–6
Hardboard, medium density						
Smooth						
Unfinished	—	—	—	—	High	4–6
Preprimed	—	—	—	—	High	4–6
Textured						
Unfinished	—	—	—	—	High	4–6
Preprimed	—	—	—	—	High	4–6
Millwork (usually pine)						
Windows, shutters, doors, exterior trim	High		Moderate	2–3	High	3–6
Decking						
New (smooth)	High	1–2	Moderate	2–3	Low	2–3
Weathered (rough)	High	2–3	High	3–6	Low	2–3
Glued-laminated members						
Smooth	High	1–2	Moderate	3–4	Moderate	3–4
Rough	High	2–3	High	6–8	Moderate	3–4
Waterboard			Low	1–3	Moderate	2–4

Wood	Weight (lbs/ft) at 8 percent moisture content	Ease of keeping well painted (I = easiest, V = most exacting)	Resistance to cupping (1 = best, 4 = worst)	Conspicuousness of checking (1 = least, 2 = most)	Color of heartwood (sapwood is always light)	Degree of figure on flat-grained surface
Softwoods						
Cedar						
Alaska	30.4	I	1	1	Yellow	Faint
California incense	24.2	I	—	—	Brown	Faint
Port-Orford	28.9	I	—	1	Cream	Faint
Western redcedar	22.4	I	1	1	Brown	Distinct
White	20.8	I	—	—	Light brown	Distinct
Cypress	31.4	I	1	1	Light brown	Strong
Redwood	27.4	I	1	1	Dark brown	Distinct
Products overlaid with resin-treated paper		I	—	1	—	—
Pine						
Eastern white	24.2	II	2	2	Cream	Faint
Sugar	24.9	II	2	2	Cream	Faint
Western white	27.1	II	2	2	Cream	Faint
Ponderosa	27.5	III	2	2	Cream	Distinct
Fir, White	25.8	III	2	2	White	Faint
Hemlock, Western	28.7	III	2	2	Pale brown	Faint
Spruce	26.8	III	2	2	White	Faint
Douglas-fir (lumber and plywood)	31.0	IV	2	2	Pale red	Strong
Larch, Western	38.2	IV	2	2	Brown	Strong
Lauan (plywood)		IV	2	2	Brown	Faint
Pine						
Norway (red)	30.4	IV	2	2	Light brown	Distinct
Southern (lumber and plywood)	38.2	IV	2	2	Light brown	Strong
Tamarack	36.3	IV	2	2	Brown	Strong
Hardwoods						
Alder	28.0	III	—	—	Pale brown	Faint
Aspen	26.3	III	2	1	Pale brown	Faint
Basswood	25.5	III	2	2	Cream	Faint
Cottonwood, Eastern	28.0	III	4	2	White	Faint
Magnolia	34.4	III	2	—	Pale brown	Faint
Yellow-poplar	29.2	III	2	1	Pale brown	Faint
Beech	43.2	IV	4	2	Pale brown	Faint
Birch, Yellow	42.4	IV	4	2	Light brown	Faint
Cherry	34.8	IV	—	—	Brown	Faint
Gum	35.5	IV	4	2	Brown	Faint
Maple, Sugar	43.4	IV	4	2	Light brown	Faint
Sycamore	34.7	IV	—	—	Pale brown	Faint
Ash, White	41.5	V or III	4	2	Light brown	Distinct
Butternut	26.4	V or III	—	—	Light brown	Faint
Chestnut	29.5	V or III	3	2	Light brown	Distinct
Elm, American	35.5	V or III	4	2	Brown	Distinct
Walnut	37.0	V or III	3	2	Dark brown	Distinct
Hickory, Shagbark	50.3	V or IV	4	2	Light brown	Distinct
Oak, White	45.6	V or IV	4	2	Brown	Distinct
Oak, Northern Red	42.5	V or IV	4	2	Brown	Distinct

Table 3. Characteristics of woods for painting and finishing (omissions in table indicate inadequate data for classification).

make sanding blocks to get into some areas like corners or to sand large surfaces if you are working by hand; fold a heavy cloth like felt or velour around your sanding blocks to soften them and prevent scratching.

You can sand mouldings by hand. Fold a small piece of sandpaper into thirds. This will keep it from unfolding, and also prevent it from getting under slivers and causing more damage. Sand the edges of all doors to a slight roundness to make them more comfortable to handle.

Set all nails, and use a sandable wood putty or other filler to fill the holes; sand the hole until there is no trace of the putty left on the surface around the hole. Clear finishes will often accentuate the difference in color between the wood and a filler; so if you must use a filler, use it sparingly.

Another method of filling cracks, especially where joints have not come together completely, is to cut a thin, wedge-shaped piece of wood off a large piece with the table saw, apply glue to both sides of it, and then drive it into the crack (Illus. 8–3). Allow the glue to dry, and then carefully pare the piece down flush to the surface with a sharp chisel. Smooth it with the plane or sander to make it perfectly flush and nearly invisible.

Illus. 8-3. Thin wedges of wood, which taper to nothing, can be used to fill cracks where clear finishes will be used.

Dents in woods can often be removed by the application of heat and moisture. Use an iron over a wet cloth to force moist heat into the area, and then sand the grain after it has dried.

Before applying primers, varnishes, or oils, apply at least one coat of a water-repellant sealer to the surface. These sealers, which contain petroleum oils, and often a mildewcide, soak into the grain of the wood, protecting it for years from rot and mildew, and greatly prolong the life of a paint or varnish coating. Soak especially well the end grain and joints where moisture can more easily enter the wood. If you plan to use a clear finish, purchase a clear sealer.

Stripping Old Paint and Varnish

If you are renovating or repairing an older door, rather than building a new one, it is best to remove the many layers of cracked and chipped paint before starting anew. Paint applied over too many layers of old paint will crack and peel easily. Also, many layers of paint tend to build up on trim- and jambwork over the years; this trim and jambwork often reveal fine high-grade hard woods when stripped.

There are many methods available for stripping paints from wood, including heat, abrasion, and chemical strippers. If you're not really interested in removing the paint to get to the bare wood, but simply want to remove loose chips and prepare the surface for repainting, then abrasion may be the best method.

Many varieties of paint scrapers are available in hardware and paint dealers. Get one that suits your job, big or small, and maintain its sharpness as you work by filing the edge so that it is flat and has very sharp corners. The paint scraper will remove the bulk of the cracked and peeled paint. Then smooth the surface further by sanding with an orbital sander, which will remove the high spots and flatten the surface. Remember that older paints contain lead, and the dust from them can be toxic. Always wear an organic vapor mask when stripping old paint, and work outdoors if possible.

Go over the surface with a wire brush at this point; the wire brush will rough up even the low spots so that they will accept putty or paint better. You can apply body fillers or vinyl puttys with a putty knife to help fill in the low spots and further flatten the surface; several filling and sanding cycles may be necessary to totally flatten the surface before priming. The main purpose for priming over old paint is to even the color so that fewer coats of paint are needed, but primers are also chalky when dry and, therefore, can be easily sanded.

If you want to remove the old paint entirely, a combination of heat and chemicals may be the best approach (Illus. 8–4). Complete stripping is sometimes a good idea, even if you plan to repaint. Heat guns and heat plates can often be rented from rental centers. The plates will do a good job on large, flat expanses, and the guns, which blow hot air like a large hair dryer, are good for getting into corners and convoluted spots, but both can scorch the wood or surrounding materials, and the intense heat can also cause window glass to crack.

Illus. 8-4. If you plan to strip all the old paint, begin by using a propane torch or heat gun to bubble the paint off. In some areas, such as around glass, chemical strippers will be safer.

Caustic strippers are the cheapest of chemical strippers, but if they are not properly neutralized after the paint is removed, they can bleed out of the wood and destroy the new finish. Methylene-chloride-based, solvent-type strippers are preferred by professionals for on-the-job use because they do a quick and thorough job without harming the wood.

If possible, move the pieces that you intend to work on from the building to a well-ventilated shop area that is as warm as possible. You may even want to consider removing the interior trim and mouldings if the situation warrants it.

If you have to work in the building, protect the walls and floors, as well as yourself. Wear goggles and an organic vapor mask, as well as gloves and old clothes. Cover the walls and the floors. Test your stripper on the areas you intend to strip, and on materials that you don't want damaged.

Brush the solvent on, wait the recommended time, and check a piece to see how deeply it has penetrated. If you are removing many layers, you may have to do it in stages, because the stripper shouldn't be left on the wood so long that it dries out. A large paint scraper will work well on flat areas, but a knife, ice pick, three-cornered scraper, or other tool may be necessary to get into tight corners and ornate work.

Anything can be stripped, but if the woodwork is too ornate or too many coats of paint have been applied over the years, it may be a difficult and timeconsuming job. No-rinse strippers are quite weak (30–50% methylene chloride) compared to the stronger (50–85%) brands that must be rinsed afterwards. If your job is extremely tough, try the latter. Rinsing can be done with either water or lacquer thinner. When all the paint has been removed, and the wood rinsed, let it dry overnight, sand it lightly, and it is ready for refinishing.

Priming and Painting

An alkyd (synthetic oil)-based primer is considered the best for either oil or latex paint. The best thickness for the primer coat is between .004 and .006 inch. If it is applied any thicker than this, it will be more prone to cracking and peeling prematurely.

You can continue the process of sanding down the high spots and filling in the lower spots by working the primer with medium sandpaper after it has thoroughly dried, but try to do as much of your puttying or filling as possible before priming. If you have to sand or putty after the first primer coat (the first coat will often show you defects that you couldn't see before), reprime the area and allow it plenty of time to dry before applying the finish coats.

Painting is best done on warm, dry days in a well-ventilated but dust-free area. Perhaps the biggest mistake that inexperienced painters can make is to recoat before the previous coat has dried thoroughly. If you paint, especially with enamel, over a coat of sealer or primer that is not yet dry, you will trap volatile oils under the coat and make it impossible to get the top coat to dry properly. In extreme cases, the paint will have to be removed completely because it will not dry.

If you are unsure whether a coat of paint is completely dry, scratch it with a fingernail or press a piece of tape against it and see if a chip is lifted off. If it is, the paint is not yet dry.

Do not wait too long between coats of paint. For best adhesion between coats, repaint in less than one week's time. When you paint, apply the paint to the work with one or two horizontal brush strokes, and then use long, even vertical strokes to spread that paint over as wide an area as it will cover (Illus. 8–5). Two thin, even coats are

Illus. 8-5. First apply a heavy stroke of paint across the grain, and then brush along the grain with long strokes until the coat of paint is thin and even.

usually all that's needed if you did a proper job of sealing and priming.

Whenever possible, lay doors out flat for painting, doing first one side and then the other. If this is not possible, watch carefully for runs and drips. Wait a few minutes after you've finished a piece, and wipe out any drips with long, even brush strokes. Avoid heavy build-ups of paint around mouldings, panels, and other raised edges.

The most crucial and most often overlooked areas of doors are the top and bottom. Exposed end grain or open joints will rapidly soak up moisture and ruin the door if it is not completely sealed and painted.

Latex paints often won't stick as well to a weathered surface or to old oil paint. If you are repainting with latex, it may be necessary to apply a coat of primer first for best adhesion. If you are in doubt about whether the paint will stick to the area, paint a small section and allow it to dry thoroughly. Then apply a piece of tape to the area; if it lifts the new paint off, sand and prime before painting with latex.

Applying Varnish or Oil

Varnished or oiled natural-wood surfaces are always admired, and are easy to maintain on the inside of a home. Varnished interior doors will last for years without having to be recoated. Often, doors are painted on the outside and given a clear finish inside. But getting a smooth, defect-free finish to begin with can be tricky.

The term varnish generally refers to clear (or nearly clear) finishes that build up a protective film of solids on the surface of the wood. Early 18th- and 19th-century craftsmen often made their own varnishes from recipes that were handed down from master to apprentice. These recipes were guarded and kept secret. They generally contained either alcohol or various types of oils as a solvent for resins and gums that were derived from natural sources such as trees, plants, insects, and fossil deposits.

Making these varnishes can be dangerous because the materials must often be heated, and it is very difficult to get good results with small batches. Varnishes based on the old formulas, such as sandarac, elemi, mastic, and copal varnishes, are often available through art-supply dealers today.

For our purposes, varnishes can be classified as natural and synthetic. The old favorite in the natural varnish category is spar varnish, which is made up of tung oil, linseed oil, and driers. Spar varnish has a very soft, elastic finish that can be applied undiluted with good results if the surface is completely free of dust, and if great care is taken to spread the varnish very thinly and evenly. Because of its softness, spar varnish doesn't sand well. For best results, allow as much drying time as

possible, use wet and dry sandpaper, and dampen the surface when sanding.

Synthetic varnishes include phenolic-based liquids and polyurethanes which dry to form a thin plastic coating over the work. These varnishes work and feel much the same as natural varnish, but the surface is harder, more resistant to staining and moisture, and easier to sand.

Both natural and synthetic varnishes may take a long time to dry if the atmospheric conditions are damp or cold. The drying time can be improved considerably if you mix in small amounts of liquid driers that are available from most paint dealers. Synthetic varnishes will often be dry to the touch in a couple of hours if driers are used.

For the best result when applying any type of varnish, seal the wood first with a sanding sealer. This is a shellaclike sealer that dries quickly, and can be easily sanded to a perfectly smooth finish. After sanding with 220-grit paper, wipe everything down very carefully with a clean tack cloth, and make sure that the air in the workplace is as free of dust as possible. Several thin coats will always give you better results than fewer thick coats.

I like to thin the varnish about 40% with mineral spirits, add about 10% drier, and brush it on very carefully with a disposable foam-rubber brush, which will actually lay it on flatter than a bristle brush and won't cause any problem with loose bristles. Once again, the evenness of the coat is crucial. Varnish runs even easier than paint. Apply the varnish with one or two vertical strokes, and then use horizontal strokes to spread it. Soak up any extra varnish that builds up around mouldings, etc. Make each coat as thin as possible.

You can obtain a hand-rubbed varnishlike finish by thinning spar varnish with ⅓ turpentine and ⅓ linseed oil, and applying the mixture as if it were an oil. Pour it on, rub it with fine wet and dry sandpaper or a plastic steel-wool substitute (steel wool is not recommended because the metal can react with tannin in the wood to cause dark stains), and finally wipe each coat off with a clean rag. You can repeat this process any number of times to create a very polished surface that doesn't have a thick build-up of finish. The same application process can also be used with tung oil or synthetic oils; all these varnishes will give much the same result.

Maintenance of Doors

When you use the proper finish at the beginning, the maintenance of doors will be minimal. Painted or stained doors, especially those that are protected from direct sunlight, can be expected to last for ten years without having to be repainted. The proper finish will also prevent doors from swelling to the point where they will stick or not close, stressing the hinges and jambs, and compounding what may have been a small problem.

If you notice that a door is sticking or not closing properly, first check the hinges. If the screws have loosened a bit, allowing the hinge or hinges to flop around, the door will sag away from the hinge jamb and bind on the lock jamb when it is closed. Often, the screws can simply be tightened to solve the problem, but if they are stripped, or the wood is cracked, you may have to fill the screw hole or crack with epoxy glue and allow the glue to dry before redrilling and resetting the screws.

If the hinges seem to be tight, then the problem is most likely the expansion of either the door or the surrounding woodwork, which is caused by moisture entering the wood. This is a danger signal, indicating either that the finish has not worked or that important areas such as the end grain were not finished properly, and should be dealt with immediately. Plane down the edge of the door, checking frequently to see how it is fitting; you can usually do this with a block plane with the door in place. When the door is closing freely again, refinish any areas that are not properly sealed.

You can sometimes use shims of cardboard under one of the hinges to straighten the hang of a door relative to the jamb, thus solving problems caused by the settling of the building. If the door binds at the top, and has a larger than necessary clearance at the bottom on the lock jamb, try to tighten the top hinge, and place a cardboard shim under the bottom hinge to straighten it out. Sometimes a 10d nail driven through the jamb in an area where the door is binding will pull the jamb back enough to solve the problem so that you will not have to plane and refinish.

As soon as signs of cracking or chipping show in the finish of an exterior door or window, it is time for you to refinish it. If you refinish as soon as possible, the dam-age will be minimal, and the refinishing will be easier to do; however, if possible, wait for the warmest and driest part of the year to do the work.

Old paint does not have to be removed entirely, but any loose paint should be scraped off. Putty dents, low spots where paint has been chipped off, and prime areas where bare wood shows, especially if the edge has been planed down. A few hours of maintenance can add years to the lifespan of your doors and windows.

Repairing Doors

Doors that have sustained heavy damage can, in many cases, still be repaired. The most common form of damage to doors is rot, usually in the area of the joints between the stiles and rails, near the bottom (Illus. 8–6).

If the repair is called for before the rot has gone too far, chisel or rout the rot out until you reach solid wood; then cut a piece of wood and glue it in to fill the hole (Illus. 8–7). Epoxy glues are the best glues to use for this type of work because they retain their strength even if there is a crack between the pieces of wood. Use epoxy filler paste to fill any cracks around the patch after it has been glued in place (Illus. 8–8). Once the surface has been rebuilt, plane it down flush to the rest of the door, treat it with a sealer that contains a fungicide, and prime and paint it. Rot will often run rapidly up the grain of a stile, but it won't do any serious damage as long as the wood is protected from moisture.

Broken muntins in doors with multiple panes of glass can usually be reconstructed from the broken parts. Remove all surrounding glass and putty, and clean any surfaces that were previously glued. Wood that has been broken cleanly can easily be reglued. If splinters are missing, they can be patched in with wood or putty. If you must patch in a piece of wood where it will show,

Illus. 8-6. Test for rot by sticking the tip of a pocket knife into the wood. If it sinks in easily, the wood is rotten.

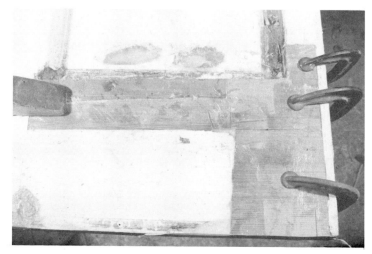

Illus. 8–7 and 8–8. You can remove rotted sections of doors with a chisel and/or router and fill the area with new wood or plastic fillers. When damage is as severe as shown at top left, apply the new wood across the joints to strengthen them (top right).

Illus. 8–8.

Illus. 8-9 and 8-10. You can repair doors that have simply developed wide cracks at the joints by filling the cracks with epoxy paste and reclamping. The paste is made from epoxy glue and fillers such as Q-cell or microfibres.

use a sharp chisel to flatten the surface you will be gluing it to, and then cut a piece of wood that matches as well as possible the color and grain of the piece you are fixing. Glue the patch in place first, and then shape it with chisels, files, or planes after the glue has dried.

Another common problem is leaking, or split panels. You can sometimes remove panels by prying out the moulding on one side or the other, but on a well-made door the panel will be housed in a slot that is cut into the frame pieces. If it is necessary to remove a panel from this type of door, use a router with a flush-cutting bit with an inboard mounted bearing to cut out the moulding around the panel. If the door will be exposed to driven rain, it is probably best to cut the rabbet from the outside to allow for better drainage.

Now, to complete the reconstruction, remove the old panel and insert and mould a new panel. Bed the new panel in a heavy bead of a flexible caulk to prevent leakage and, for best results, use a bolection-type moulding securely glued to the frame members. Fill any cracks between the panel and the moulding with flexible caulk, and paint carefully with enamel or latex paint.

INDEX

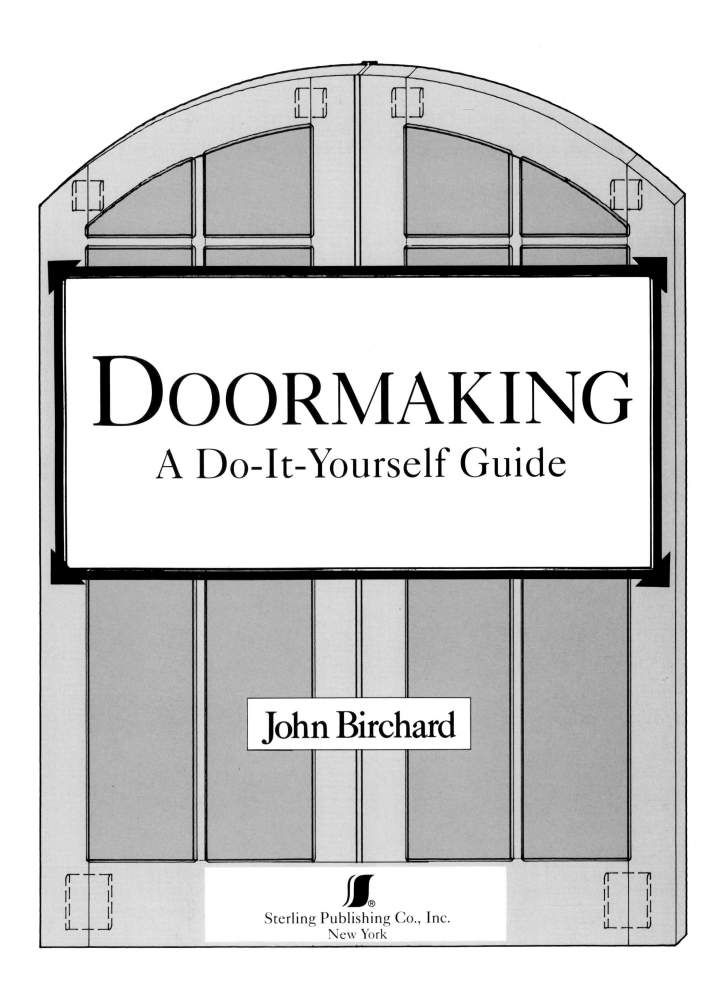

DOORMAKING
A Do-It-Yourself Guide

John Birchard

Sterling Publishing Co., Inc.
New York

This book is dedicated to Barbara, Brook, and Ryan.

Acknowledgments

Thanks to Bill Spencer, Terry Klingman, Larry Martin, Jody Evans, Lee Josephs, Tim Scully, Doug Christie, Al Garvey, Peter Good, and the many other unknown craftspeople who made this book possible.

JOHN BIRCHARD is a custom doormaker, photographer, and writer living in Mendocino, California. If you wish to consult with him, please write ℅ Sterling Publishing, 387 Park Ave. South, New York, NY 10016.

Edited by Michael Cea

10   9   8   7   6   5   4   3   2   1

Published by Sterling Publishing Company, Inc.
387 Park Avenue South, New York, New York 10016
The original edition of this book was published
under the title *Doormaking Patterns and Ideas*
© 1999 by John Birchard
Distributed in Canada by Sterling Publishing
℅ Canadian Manda Group, One Atlantic Avenue, Suite 105
Toronto, Ontario, Canada M6K 3E7
Distributed in Great Britain and Europe by Cassell PLC
Wellington House, 125 Strand, London WC2R 0BB,
England
Distributed in Australia by Capricorn Link (Australia)
Pty Ltd.
P.O. Box 6651, Baulkham Hills, Business Centre,
NSW 2153, Australia
Manufactured in the United States of America
All rights reserved

Sterling ISBN 0-8069-4340-X